CLOSER

MAJOR LEAGUE PLAYERS REVEAL THE INSIDE PITCH ON SAVING THE GAME

KEVIN NEARY

with **LEIGH A. TOBIN**

foreword by **BRAD LIDGE**

2008 WORLD SERIES CLOSER

RUNNING PRESS
PHILADELPHIA · LONDON

APR 2013

© 2013 by Kevin Neary and Leigh A. Tobin

Published by Running Press,
A Member of the Perseus Books Group
All rights reserved under the Pan-American
and International Copyright Conventions

Printed in the United States of America

Books published by Running Press are available at special discounts for bulk
purchases in the United States by corporations, institutions, and other
organizations. For more information, please contact the Special Markets
Department at the Perseus Books Group, 2300 Chestnut Street, Suite 200,
Philadelphia, PA 19103, or call (800) 810-4145, ext. 5000, or e-mail special.
markets@perseusbooks.com.

Topps baseball cards used courtesy of The Topps Company, Inc.

ISBN 978-0-7624-4679-7
Library of Congress Control Number: 2012953911

E-book ISBN 978-0-7624-4716-9

9   8   7   6   5   4   3   2   1
Digit on the right indicates the number of this printing

Cover & Interior design by Matt Goodman
Edited by Geoffrey Stone
Typography: Times and Trade Gothic

Running Press Book Publishers
2300 Chestnut Street
Philadelphia, PA 19103-4371
Visit us on the web!
www.runningpress.com

For my three wonderful children, Matthew, Emma, and Grace; and especially for my wife, Sue, who continues to amaze me each and every day.
—*Kevin Neary*

For my wonderful family, and especially for my husband, Eric, my rock, who supports me through all the good and the bad.
—*Leigh Tobin*

ACKNOWLEDGEMENTS

Cindi Adler (Los Angeles Dodgers), Robert Astle, Steve Barr (Little League International), Louis Barricelli (MLB Network), Brian Bartow (St. Louis Cardinals), Tyler Beckstrom (Boras Corporation), Court Berry-Tripp (Cleveland Indians), Matthew Birch (California Angels of Anaheim), John Blake (Texas Rangers), Frank Blum (Walt Disney World Company), John Boggs, Larry Bowa (MLB Network), Brian Britten (Detroit Tigers), Rob Butcher (Cincinnati Reds), Ryan Cavinder (California Angels of Anaheim), Matt Chisholm (San Francisco Giants), Adam Chodzko (California Angels of Anaheim), Bonnie Clark (Philadelphia Phillies), Jerry Coleman (San Diego Padres), Chris Costello, Colby Curry (Kansas City Royals), Fernando Cuza, Gene Dias (Houston Astros), Joe Dier (Mississippi State University), Chris Eckes (Cincinnati Reds), Dan Farrell (St. Louis Cardinals), Lorraine Fisher (MLB Network), Pam Ganley (Boston Red Sox), Darrin Gebers, Heather Greenberg (Topps, Inc.), Matthew Gould (Major League Baseball), Brad Hainje (Atlanta Braves), Dave Haller (Tampa Bay Rays), Andrew Heydt (Tampa Bay Rays), Dani Holmes-Kirk (Chicago Cubs), David Holtzman (Kansas City Royals), Brad Horn (National Baseball Hall of Fame & Museum), John Horne (National Baseball Hall of Fame & Museum), Jay Horwitz (New York Mets), Jeff Idelson (National Baseball Hall of Fame & Museum), Josh Ishoo (San Diego Padres), Nate Janoso (Cleveland Indians), Greg Jones, Dave Kaczmarczyk, Doug Kemp (Philadelphia Phillies), Mike Kennedy (Colorado Rockies), Amanda Koch (Philadelphia Phillies), Paul Kuo (Beverly Hills Sports Council), Patrick Kurish (Tampa Bay Rays), Art Kusnyer (Chicago White Sox), Andrew Levy, Jerry Lewis (Detroit Tigers), Stephen Light (National Baseball Hall of Fame & Museum), Scott Littlefield (Walt Disney

World Company), Gloria Liu (Topps, Inc.), Donny Lowe (National Baseball Hall of Fame & Museum), Kendall Loyd, Dr. Michael Marfori, Michelle Marks, Pete Mayta, Adrienne Midgley (Atlanta Braves), Warren Miller (San Diego Padres), Jim Misudek (Atlanta Braves), Hal Morningstar, Craig Muder (National Baseball Hall of Fame & Museum), Patrick O'Connell (Arizona Diamondbacks), Tom O'Reilly (Walt Disney World Company), Veronica Owens, Paul Perrello, Bret Picciolo (San Diego Padres), Richard "Babe" Plant, Rich Rice (Texas Rangers), Carmen Rios-Molina, Tom Rodowsky (Walt Disney Imagineering), Joe Ruti (Chicago White Sox), Dave Schofield, Marty Sewell (Miami Marlins), Larry Shenk (Philadelphia Phillies), Jay Stenhouse (Toronto Blue Jays), Dr. Frank Stone, Geoffrey Stone, Bean Stringfellow, Amy Summers (Los Angeles Dodgers), Bart Swain (Cleveland Indians), Peggy Thompson (Detroit Tigers), Rick Thompson (Detroit Tigers), John Timberlake (Philadelphia Phillies), M.J. Trahan (Houston Astros), Jim Trdinich (Pittsburgh Pirates), Alexandra Trochanowski (New York Yankees), Mike Vassallo (Milwaukee Brewers), Rick Vaughn (Tampa Bay Rays), John Wathan (Kansas City Royals), Mike West, Joe White, Casey Wilcox (Arizona Diamondbacks), Shana Wilson (San Diego Padres), Joe Yodice, Melody Yount (St. Louis Cardinals), Ed Zausch, Kim Zayotti, Jason Zillo (New York Yankees), Seta Zink, Grace Zwit (Chicago White Sox)

CONTENTS

THE EARLY YEARS

THE TRANSITION YEARS

THE MODERN DAY CLOSER

FOREWORD

People often ask me, "What did it feel like to throw the final pitch of the 2008 World Series?" Amazingly, every time I think back to that moment I still remember it like it just happened. Adrenaline. Crowd screaming. Everyone anticipating. Zone it out. Focus. Throw your best slider. Pick up target. Breathe, or at least try to breathe, and let it go. A swing. He missed it! WE WON THE WORLD SERIES! Under a pile of teammates, I was still screaming for joy. I was able to be the last one on the mound because I was the closer.

Trying to put that moment into words is a lot harder than it sounds. In fact, it is hard to find any words to describe each outing a closer has. The adrenaline builds all game; when they call you in, you know the game will be on the line. You pace back and forth, stretching, waiting, and anticipating. Your routine is crucial; it allows you to focus, it allows you stay calm, and to stay collected. You go out for your warm-up, and if you're not at your home stadium, you know the fans will be all over you. You better have a thick skin, and you better be able to lock it in. The gate opens. You run out and feel like you could run through a brick wall. When you pitch at home, you come out to your favorite song. On the road, it's entirely different, the other team's highlight reel starts. The fans start screaming and are on their feet. It's you, the closer, who is standing in their way of victory. You've got two choices: either get the job done or go home the goat of the game. There is no average outing for a closer.

The fear of failure you hear people talk about is a driving force, and it is overshadowed only by the joy of nailing down the victory. It is intense, as intense as it gets. When that final out is recorded by you, everyone on your team is happy; everyone is a winner on that night. Everything is right in the world. Your job is done, at least for that night.

However, it doesn't always turn out the way you envision it. I have seen the other side, too, the blown save, which is what happens when you are not lucky enough to be in the zone. It is a crushing defeat, and you feel horrible. Any closer worth his weight hates letting his team down more than letting himself down. We are our worst critics, our toughest judges. But the great news is, it's baseball, and we play *a lot* of baseball. You may get another chance and you may not, but either way it is important to get over a blown save quickly, to forget about it, and remember what doesn't kill you makes you stronger!

Closers are a rare breed. They come in all shapes and sizes. There are the guys with the obvious talent, the 100 mph fastball, but who don't have the head to go with it. Then there are those players who don't have the "stuff" but have the head to get the job done. These guys aren't as easy to pick out, but they can be just as talented. I have seen guys who can absolutely dominate in the closer position with a 90 mph fastball, and I have seen some who make everyone wonder why they can't get it done with their 100 mph cheese. What it takes to be the best is a combination of both the stuff and the head. Not many guys have both, but when you see someone like Mariano Rivera take the ball, remember that even closers have tremendous admiration for his ability. We admire his nasty cut-fastball, his cool demeanor, and the confidence that lets everyone in the stadium know the game is over, so just sit back and enjoy.

People sometimes ask me if there is some sort of fraternity between closers, a special bond we all share. I was lucky enough to have Billy Wagner as my mentor in Houston. Billy knew instinctively that I would be a closer someday, much in the same way that today I can tell who will be the next superstar closer. We end up talking to each other because we can all relate to big pressure and important situations, and, yes, we all do share a special bond. We sympathize with each other regarding the stress of the unique position. We are all on the same team in a way, encouraging each other, pumping each other up, telling each other how "nasty" we are. The truth is, we all cringe when we watch another closer blow a game. We know what it's like, and we know it's not fun. We also know there is no better job in the world. What other occupation on earth lets you sit in a major league clubhouse for a few innings and watch a game while you stretch and heat yourself up for your big stage entrance? If there is a better job, I certainly want it!

It may seem like a roller-coaster ride to some, but there is nothing like it in sports. It's a dream job. I feel so blessed to be able to have my baseball experiences, to be able to know the highs and the lows. When I look back at all the big games I pitched, I try to remember what went right or what went wrong. It encourages and drives me to better myself and to use my experience to help the younger players. They will have tough games, and they will ask me what it was like to throw that last pitch of the 2008 World Series. I tell them that I hope one day they, too, will be lucky enough to be in a similar situation, to close a big game and know that they have the best job in the world.

Generations of pitchers have grown up viewing the closer role in varying ways. For the older generation, it simply did not exist. There were relief pitchers, and generally they were pitchers who just couldn't handle the prestigious starting roles. The current generation believes a baseball team cannot win without the treasured closer. The generation between the two showcases the evolution of the closer role.

—Brad Lidge, 2008 World Series closer

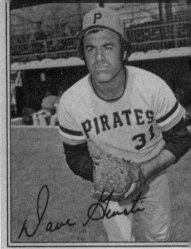

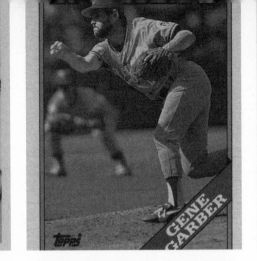

THE EARLY YEARS

It is amazing; you play three hours and nine innings, and most of the time it all comes down to the performance of one guy—the closer.
—*Roger McDowell*

RICH
GOSSAGE

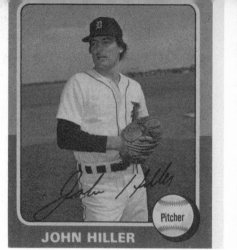

JOHN HILLER

Pitcher

AL
HRABOSKY
ST. LOUIS CARDINALS

PITCHER

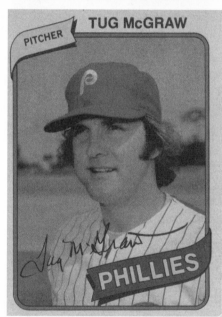

TUG McGRAW

PITCHER

PHILLIES

KENT
TEKULVE
PITCHER
PIRATE

KENT

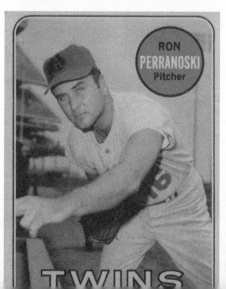

RON
PERRANOSKI
Pitcher

TWINS

ELROY FACE
1953–1969

ROY FACE
pitcher PITTSBURGH PIRATES

E lroy Face is proof that you do not have to be a giant to succeed in not only baseball, but as a major league pitcher. The five-foot-eight, 155-pound right-hander is arguably considered the pioneer of the modern day closer. In his sixteen years in the majors, he went 104-95, with a 2.48 ERA and 193 saves in 848 games.

Against all odds, Face succeeded even though he did not even start playing baseball until he went to Averill Park High School in 1944. "I didn't start playing baseball until I was sixteen years old in high school," said Face. "We didn't have a Little League from the small town I came from. By the second year I played in high school we won the championship. In 1946, I joined the army. Shortly after that, I was drafted by Branch Rickey, not once, but eventually twice. I was drafted first by the Dodgers from the Phillies, and then again from the Dodgers, I went on to the Pirates."

A Stephentown, New York native, Face was signed by the

Philadelphia Phillies as an amateur free agent in 1949 and assigned to Class D. After two seasons with the Phillies and no promotion, he was drafted by the Brooklyn Dodgers on December 4, 1950, in the minor league draft. Two years later, he was drafted again, on December 1, 1952, by the Pittsburgh Pirates in the Rule 5 draft.

Like most pitchers from his generation, he began his career as a starter. "I remember in 1949 I was a starter in the minors at Bradford and I went 14-2, and then I went 18-5 the following year, and then the Phillies let me go!" Face recalled. "So, again, that is when Branch Rickey was able to grab me for the Dodgers. At Pueblo, Colorado, for the Dodgers minor league affiliate, I went 23-9 for a sixth-place team. Overall that year, I started thirty-two games and completed twenty-five of those and I led the league in ERA [2.78]."

After being drafted by the Pirates, Face stayed on the major league roster for the 1953 season, making his major league debut on April 16 versus the Phillies in a 14-12 win at Forbes Field. He entered the game in the fifth inning, allowing three runs on four hits and a walk, and managed just one out. Overall he had a very mediocre season, starting thirteen of his forty-one games, going 6-8, with a 6.58 ERA. It was then he knew he needed another pitch in order to have success.

Veteran and former Yankee reliever Joe Page was in camp with the Pirates in 1954, working on a comeback. "I would watch Joe Page and how he threw his forkball, and I knew I needed an off-speed pitch," Face remembered. "I saw what it was doing for him, so I went down to New Orleans to work on a new pitch. It probably took me a half season to get it working for me. Prior to throwing the forkball I was strictly throwing the fastball and curveball and that was my complete repertoire."

Face spent the 1954 season pitching for the New Orleans Pelicans under Manager Danny Murtaugh—and perfecting his forkball, the pitch that would make his career. Contrary to the belief of some, Page did not teach the pitch to the young pitcher. "I didn't even ask him to compare it to his until I learned to pitch it on my own first," Face said. "We actually didn't even get together until he retired. I worked on the pitch, and he and I compared it to the one he threw then."

So, it wasn't Page, but Danny Murtaugh who probably had the greatest impact on his career, "because he was the one who took me out of the starting rotation and made me strictly a closer," Face said.

In 1955, Face returned to the majors and his stellar career—mainly in relief—began.

That first year with his new pitch, he split his time between starting and relieving (3.58 ERA, ten starts in forty-two games, with five saves). In 1956, he led the National League with sixty-eight appearances as his start total dropped to three games. It was in 1956 that he pitched in nine straight games (September 3–13, sixteen and one-third innings), a feat unheard of these days.

"If I didn't pitch for four or five straight games, I felt as though I wasn't as sharp," Face recalled. "In 1952, when I was in the minors in Fort Worth, Bobby Bragan was the manager; he eventually became the manager of the Pirates (1956–57). During those days he was my manager in the minors, and I was one of his starters, but during my off days and in between starts, he put me in the bullpen because my arm could bounce back and responded so well. So, that is why when he came to the Pirates as the manager, he knew what I could do, and that is why he let me pitch nine straight games in a row and he wasn't afraid to use me."

He made one last career start in 1957, appearing in fifty-nine games (second-highest total in the NL) and picking up ten saves. In 1958, Face went 5-2 with a 2.89 ERA. He led the NL with twenty saves and forty games finished, and his seventy-seven games were the second highest in the NL. But all that faded in comparison to his 1959 season.

His sensational 1959 season marked his first selection to the all-star teams (there were two All-Star Games each season from

1959–62). His legendary 18-1 record (.947 winning percentage), still stands as a major league record; he earned seventeen straight wins before his first and only loss on September 11 at Los Angeles. His win streak actually reached twenty-two games, including five from the previous season. The loss was also his first in ninety-nine appearances, also dating back to 1958. Not only did he win eighteen games, he added ten saves to account for twenty-eight of the club's seventy-eight wins for the season and compiled a 2.70 ERA.

"A blown save happens," Face stated. "I remember a blown save I had in 1959, the same year I went 18-1, and it was on a broken-bat single. I remember Charley Neal hit it and I still remember that blown save to this day." (That blown save against the Dodgers resulted in his lone loss of the season.)

Face's durability and consistency over the next several years put him in the All-Star Games in 1960 and 1961. He led the league in: saves, with seventeen in 1961 and twenty-eight in 1962; games finished, with sixty-one, forty-seven, and fifty-seven from 1960 to 1962 respectively; and appearances in 1960 (sixty-eight). With two exceptions, his ERA stayed below 3.50 in each of his seasons with the Pirates through 1968.

His greatest moment came in his lone postseason series—the Pirates' 1960 World Series triumph over the New York Yankees in seven games. "I closed them down in three games," Face recalled. "I'm not certain, but I think I was the first closer to record three saves in a World Series. I almost had a fourth save, if the situation was right in game seven." Face did join an elite club of closers who have three or more saves during a World Series.

In his sixteen years of Major League Baseball, there were sure to be a few funny moments as well. "I remember I was pitching in this game in Chicago," began Face. "I came in to close. I had a runner on first and one out. I got the next out and then Billy Williams stepped up to bat. I eventually got a 1-1 count on Williams, and then I throw the next pitch right down the plate and he took it for strike two. The next thing I know, the catcher came out to visit me on the mound and he said, 'Do you know the runner on first is now standing on second?' I said, 'How did that happen?' And he said, 'Because you wound up, and as soon as you did, he took off, and that is why Williams took the pitch.' Williams, you see, took the pitch—this way, the runner would be in scoring position and he could knock in the tying run. Eventually, I got Williams to pop up and end the inning and the game. When I got to the dugout, the manager, Danny Murtaugh, was standing at the top step and said, 'What are doing out there?' The best answer back I could muster up was, 'I knew what I was doing, and it was the only way I could get Williams to take a strike!'" he concluded with a big laugh.

The eighty-four-year-old rarely entered the game in the ninth inning, with no one on and no outs. In his day, most relievers/closers pitched multiple innings. "Every team had a closer back then," Face said, "but a closer had to be ready by the sixth or seventh inning. It wasn't just a one-inning save back then, with no one on and your team has the lead. We normally faced batters with runners on base and many times the game was tied.

"I remember I came as a closer into a game in the ninth inning against Chicago and we were tied," he recalled, "and I eventually got the victory in the fourteenth inning. In 1956, I pitched in nine straight games. The bullpen was always considered the workhorse on the team and it didn't matter if there was a lefty or a righty up to bat. It didn't make a difference. When I finished my career I pitched in a total of 848 games and worked 1,375 total innings, which is almost an average of two innings per appearance."

Like closers of today, Face usually had an idea if he was coming into a game, although he had to be prepared earlier in the game. "I knew whenever that call came down to the bullpen from the seventh inning on that it was for me to come in," said Face. "I remember on the days that I didn't feel 100 percent or when I was tired, I would go to the clubhouse and take a nap, and when the seventh inning came around, someone would come into the clubhouse and say, 'Elroy, it's the seventh inning, time to get up!'

Then my nap would be over, but once in a while I got to sleep a little longer if we were up five or six runs or down five or six runs. But if the situation called for me to win or save the game, that call would be for me."

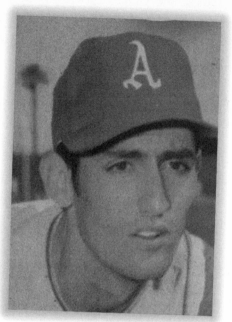

ROLAND "ROLLIE" FINGERS
1968–1985

Roland "Rollie" Fingers was born on August 25, 1946. The right-hander, widely considered the pioneer of modern relief pitching, is probably more known for his famous handlebar mustache than his hall-of-fame career.

Fingers' career began in 1964 when he received the early Christmas present of being signed by the Kansas City Athletics as an amateur free agent on December 24. But his signing was not his first taste of baseball.

"I grew up with baseball," Fingers stated. "When I was little my dad played in the minor leagues in the St. Louis organization. He and Stan Musial were roommates. This is when Stan Musial was a pitcher. They roomed together, and then suddenly one day Stan played in a game in the outfield and went four for four and never went back to pitching another baseball game. I guess that is how Stan became 'the Man.' I grew up in the middle of baseball all of my life. My father taught me everything about the game. Most of all, he taught me the proper mechanics of how to throw a baseball correctly. That is the biggest thing when you are a kid is to find someone who knows the proper way of throwing a baseball so you are not hurting your arm. There is a certain way of throwing a baseball and he taught me the right way. So, I've been around this game all of my life, playing when I was nine when I first got to Little League and then all of the way up through Pony League, high school, American Legion, and then in the professional ranks. I have been around it forever."

In 1968, the same year the Athletics moved from Kansas City to Oakland, Fingers made his major league debut. In the early years, he made a few starts, but his niche was relief. Over the course of his career, of the 944 games he pitched, 907 came in relief. He earned 341 career saves, with a career-best of thirty-seven in 1978 (in $107^{1}/_{3}$ innings).

Something like 10 percent of his saves were three innings or more—unheard of these days. "I don't know the exact number," Fingers laughed, "but I know there were a lot of them. I do know that I had fourteen or fifteen saves that were four innings. The starter went five innings and I went the sixth, seventh, eighth, and ninth. I also know that I had two hundred saves that were one and two-thirds of an inning to two innings. I'm not too much into the statistics of how long or how many innings I went. Your closer role of today is totally different than the game we played, coming in for just one inning with the lead and with no guys on base. When I played the game, the starter would go out there and finish unless they were really in trouble, and then the relief pitcher would come in. I don't know how many games I came into with the bases loaded and nobody out. They don't do this nowadays. These guys of today come in with nobody on and nobody out."

If he were pitching today, his approach would vary greatly. "It would be different because when I was playing I had to be ready to go in at the sixth inning," said Fingers. "If the pitcher would get into trouble, I'd be warming up. If he then got out of it, then I'd sit down. In a game I might be up three to four times in the bullpen. These guys today, they are only going to go in at the ninth inning, so in the eighth inning they can get up and start getting loose and they know they are only going to pitch one inning. They only have to get up and throw once! I was constantly getting up and sitting down. When I was playing, you had to learn how to warm up. You had to watch the game while you were standing on the mound in the bullpen. You had to see the whole game from down there."

He shared that the biggest asset a relief pitcher can have is control. "You have to be able to throw the ball where you want," explained Fingers. "You have to be able to get a first-pitch strike. You have to be ahead of the hitters. If you stay ahead of the hitters and throw the ball where you want to then you can be a successful relief pitcher. What good is a 96 mph fastball if you can't throw it through an open garage? You have to be able to hit the glove, and if you hit the glove, the tenth man who is on the field will be your friend, and he is the umpire. If you show the umpire that you've got great control, then he is probably going to give you a lot of pitches that are slightly off the plate. You'll be getting more third strikes when you show great control and that you know what you're doing on the mound. It's all about throwing strikes and not wasting pitches, that is why pitchers like Greg Maddux and Mariano Rivera have been so successful. They can both hit spots. They are not overpowering, but their ball is always moving. I don't think the two of them ever threw a straight ball. In Mariano Rivera's case, he is such a great pitcher. You know that the cut-fastball is coming every time, and he doesn't make mistakes. That is the key to being a great relief pitcher—not making mistakes and knowing where to throw the ball."

Relievers were a different breed in the seventies. They had to be prepared for any situation. "That is how it was back then. If something happened in the sixth inning with the starter and he was getting racked up, I would have to go in. There was no such thing as a long reliever or a setup man and a closer. I was everything, and we had to do it all back then. The difference today, teams carry sometimes up to thirteen pitchers. In my day, when I was playing, we had nine or ten pitchers at the most. When you looked down at the bullpen you usually saw only three or four guys down there. Today, you look down, there could be seven, eight, or nine guys down in the bullpen. When I played, I had to be the long reliever, the setup man, and the closer all in the same game. And when you did come in, it wasn't like it was like bases empty and there was no jam to get out of."

Despite the physical demands, most relievers in the early days believe the job then was more mentally challenging and Fingers is no exception. "By the end of the year you were more mentally and emotionally tired than physically tired. If you pitched in seventy some games in a year, you probably came into sixty of those games with the game on the line. It could wear on you more mentally, I believe, than physically because of all the pressure situations. After a while it was just another job. I mean you come in and just do what you have to do. You don't even think about it really. That is why if you do it enough times in a season, it will just wear on you."

In Fingers' experience, coaches would only visit the mound to give him a breather. "Usually when I came in, I wasn't going to see a coach again unless I got completely rocked. I do remember one game when A's manager, Dick Williams, came out to the mound," Fingers recalled with a slight smile. "He was there 'cause I just gave up three consecutive hits in a row in a game against Chicago. The lead went from 4-1 to 4-3. Dick Williams came out to the mound, and he was pissed off. He looked to [catcher] Gene Tenace because he didn't want to talk to me because he said I wasn't going to give him the truth anyway. He said to Gene Tenace, 'How's he throwing?' And Gene said, 'I don't know, I haven't caught anything yet.'"

The six-foot-four reliever has a signature mustache that makes him look like a throwback to the early 1900s. "I have the handlebar moustache and it's always worked for me," explained Fingers. "The owner of the A's, Charlie Finley, offered any of us $300 if we could grow a moustache by opening day in 1972. That was a lot of money back then. He did it because there wasn't any facial hair in baseball back then. We started it as a team in 1972 with the Oakland A's, and the only reason why we did it was to get $300 out of Charlie Finley. And then we started winning, beginning in 1972. And then we won the series in '73 and '74, and after three World Series Championships it was tough to think about cutting the moustache off."

Needless to say, those World Series Championships were very meaningful to Fingers. "You grow up as a kid and dream of being in the World Series and getting that last out in the game and standing on the mound. I got the opportunity to do that twice. It doesn't get any better than that. Getting that last out in the World Series and winning it. I got Pete Rose to fly out to left field in 1972, and then got a ground ball back to me in game five in 1974 to win my second World Series. They are the two moments in my life that I will keep with me forever!"

Fingers retired following the 1985 season. It took seven years, but in 1992 Fingers became just the second reliever to be elected to the National Baseball Hall of Fame (Hoyt Wilhelm preceded him).

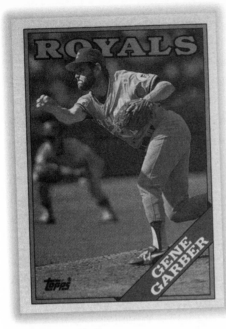

GENE GARBER
1969–1988

Gene Garber was a reliever who pitched during the early formation of the closer role. He was selected by the Pittsburgh Pirates in the twentieth round of the 1965 draft and ended up pitching in the majors for nineteen years with the Pirates (1969–70; 1972), Kansas City Royals (1973–74; 1987–88), Philadelphia Phillies (1974–78), and Atlanta Braves (1978–87).

The sidewinding right-hander, like many other closers, began his career as a starter. He made his major league debut on June 17, 1969, in a start against the Chicago Cubs, earning a no-decision in the Pirates' 4-3 win.

For the next couple of seasons he bounced between the majors and minors, and pitched mainly as a starter, but had a few relief appearances sprinkled in. It wasn't until he was in his second season with the Royals, in 1974, that he pitched solely in relief.

Garber pitched for nineteen seasons and feels he had two defining moments in his career. "I will always be remembered for stopping Pete Rose's forty-four game hit streak when I was on the Braves."

It happened on August 1, 1978, when Rose's Cincinnati Reds were facing the Braves. Garber entered the game in the seventh inning and got Rose to line into a double play. He insisted on remaining in the game to face him again in the ninth inning, despite a 16-4 lead. Rose was due to bat third, and Garber ended up striking him out on a change-up.

After the game, an irritated Rose said, "Those guys were pitching like it was the seventh game of the World Series." To which members of the Braves replied, "He was hitting like it was the seventh game of the World Series."

His other defining moment came with the Phillies in 1977. "Over the years it has been referred to as Black Friday. It was a playoff game against the Dodgers in 1977," Garber explained. "It was the seventh inning and I was called in. We had a one-run lead. I got three outs in the seventh and three outs in the eighth inning. I then got the first two outs in the ninth. I even had a two-strike count on the pinch hitter, Vic Davalillo, but he was shocked to notice Ted Sizemore, our second baseman, playing unusually deep, so he laid down a drag bunt for a single. We never had a play on the ball. From then on it just kept mushrooming, and worst of all we went on to lose that game and the Dodgers went up 2-1 in games.

"I remember the ball that Manny Mota hit to left and how it went off Greg Luzinski's glove," said Garber, thinking back to the Black Friday loss. "It was so windy that day and honestly that was the first time I ever remember a ball hitting his glove that he didn't catch. I thought the game was over then, but things just continued to go bad for us. There were five things that happened in that inning that never happened before. But that's how funny things are—we always seem to remember the negative.

"That loss set the table for the next game, taking all of the wind out of our sails, when Tommy John for the Dodgers faced off against our Steve Carlton. It poured all night long, but we continued to play and again we went on to lose that game by the score of 4-1, and we were out of the playoffs."

Garber compiled 218 career saves, only eighty-eight of which were one inning or less. In his day, the word *closer* was not used. "Back then you were either a long reliever or a short reliever. If you were a short reliever, you could go in anytime from the sixth inning on. The long reliever could go in for the first five innings," explained Garber.

"You never thought about the save back then; rather it was about closing out the game and getting the victory," he continued. "Today it is the opposite. You play the game in order for you to give the closer the opportunity to get the save. It's all a part of the show."

Garber is not particularly fond of some of the new "rules" of the game. "One of my pet peeves is charging the closer with a blown save if he doesn't preserve the victory, regardless of what the circumstances were along the way, like a passed ball or an error," he said. "It is still a blown save and it rests all on the closer.

"I remember in 1979, I broke the record for most losses by a relief pitcher in a season and I picked up three of those losses in one week, and the ball never made it out of the infield in any of those games. I ended the season 6-16 that year. It's ironic how the closer of today is supposed to be perfect."

Garber went on, "Another one of my pet peeves is pitch count. It is the worst thing that ever happened. Today's mind-set for starting pitchers is just to get in six or so innings, and then at that point they are only looking to come out. You tell them they should be tired now. I remember Jim Kaat had this expression he'd like to use: 'You gotta use it, but don't abuse it, so you don't lose it!' I remember in our day if you didn't complete games, you were not perceived to be a complete pitcher. I remember I pitched one thousand innings in the minor leagues before being called up for good. Yet, I don't think it took years off my career because I was still pitching until I was forty years old.

"My philosophy is if you don't expect much out of someone

then you aren't going to get it. If the expectation is low, then everyone is satisfied with just the minimum. I'm not sure why these pitchers, who are making the money that they do, can't consistently pitch every four days if they are only going six innings anyway. You even hear some managers today complain that they don't have enough pitching and yet they might have thirteen pitchers on their staff. In our day, we had eight pitchers normally on staff.

"I remember when I got traded from the Phillies to the Braves I got Bobby Cox in trouble. The reason was I had pitched for eight straight days and we were headed into Dodger Stadium. The first night Bobby turned to me and said, 'I'm giving you the night off.' And it looked that way when the Dodgers went up 8-0. But, wouldn't you know it, we struggled back and went ahead 9-8. Bobby called down to the bullpen in the eighth inning and asked me, 'Could I pitch?' I said, 'Yeah, I can pitch.' I went in and saved the game and got the victory for the team. Then the next day someone came up to me when I got to the clubhouse and said, 'Did you look at the lineup today?' Then I looked at it and it had Gene Garber batting second and playing centerfield. So, I went up to Bobby and asked, 'Do you want me to take batting practice?' Bobby said, 'Yep, you're taking batting practice.' So, I went ahead and took batting practice with the regulars. I remember being on deck after the first guy got out and before I walked to the plate Bobby called time and put a pinch hitter in. He turned to me and said, 'Good game! I'm pinch-hitting for you.' After the game he got a call from the league president, who said, 'What are you doing? You're making a farce out of this game!' Bobby said, 'I'm not making a farce out of the game. This was the only way I could assure Garber was getting the day off!' It was a pretty funny story for us all."

The pitcher, who grew up on a dairy farm, is now a farmer himself in Pennsylvania. He was hardworking as a pitcher and continues with that work ethic in his current position. "I've had two jobs in my life," said Garber, "and I've loved them both."

Each job is physically demanding, but "there is a mental part to baseball, too, meaning you have to want the ball," Garber explained. "You have to be able to say to yourself, 'If my club has the lead, then I am the best pitcher out there for our team to secure the win.' You had to have this mental toughness to be able to do that. Of course, that was tough to say when you pitched after Hall of Famers Steve Carlton and Phil Niekro," he said with a grin. "But once you got the ball, that was the mind-set you had to take going in and before you were ready to pitch."

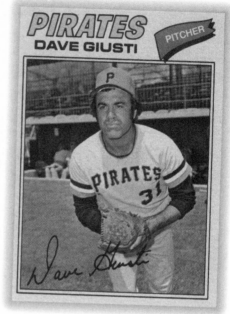

DAVE GIUSTI
1962–1977

D ave Giusti played for fifteen years in the major leagues for the Houston Colt 45s/Astros (1962; 1964–68), St. Louis Cardinals (1969), Pittsburgh Pirates (1970–76), Oakland Athletics (1977), and Chicago Cubs (1977). The right-hander was an excellent starter for the first half of his career. It wasn't until 1970, after being traded to the Pirates, that he had his first real taste of relieving.

Born on November 27, 1939, in Seneca, New York, Giusti attended North High School, followed by Syracuse University. He played both baseball and basketball for the Orangemen, pitching the team to the College World Series in 1961. And it was with Syracuse that he learned the palm ball, the pitch that would bring him so much success.

"All of my pitches seemed to complement each other," said Giusti. "If I didn't have a good fastball, then my palm ball or change-up wouldn't have been so successful, and so on. I actually learned the palm ball from Ted Kleinhans, who was my college coach at Syracuse. Kleinhans also taught Jim Konstanty the palm ball. I remember when I was pitching in college I knew I needed to come up with something and Kleinhans was there to teach it to me, and I thought it was a good pitch."

His pitching caught the eye of scouts. Both the Cardinals and expansion Colt 45s showed interest in him, but he chose the Colt 45s, figuring he would likely get to the big leagues quicker with the new club. He signed with them on June 16, 1961, and spent just one season in the minors before breaking into the majors in 1962.

His debut was on April 13 at Philadelphia, but as a pinch runner. He made his first appearance on the mound on April 22 against the Phillies in a start, which he lost 4-3. At 2-3 with a 5.62 ERA, his first taste of the majors was inconsistent. Following the season, he had surgery to remove bone chips from his right elbow.

He spent 1963 and most of 1964 starting at triple-A Oklahoma City. In 1965, the Astrodome opened, and thanks in part to Don Larsen getting traded to Baltimore, Giusti got the opportunity to be the Astros' fifth starter.

On August 13, 1966, at Candlestick Park in San Francisco, Giusti came within one pitch of throwing a no-hitter. Cap Anderson hit a two-out single up the middle in the second inning for the Giants' only hit of the game.

On October 21, 1969, Giusti was traded to the Pirates and his fate would be altered. Originally slated as a starter, Giusti had a terrible spring and was designated to the bullpen. On April 20, 1970, at Forbes Field in Pittsburgh, the Pirates and Doc Ellis were facing Denis Menke and the Astros. Menke smashed a ball up the middle and Ellis' hand got in the way. Giusti entered the game in the seventh inning and shut down the Astros, preserving the win, earning his first MLB save, and taking his first steps to becoming a closer.

When bullpen ace Chuck Hartenstein faltered, Pirates manager Danny Murtaugh decided to give Giusti a try as the closer.

The Early Years

At first, Giusti wasn't pleased with his new team's plans for him in the bullpen. "I want to be in the starting rotation. I think I am a better pitcher if I'm used in the rotation." His philosophy was "The way to make money in this game is to pitch a lot of innings. If you pitch enough innings, the wins will come. I've never set any victory goals for myself. I don't believe in worrying about a win-loss record. If you pitch enough and pitch well, you're bound to win. Of course, luck has a lot to do with it." Nevertheless, he accepted his new role.

Giusti went on to compile a 47-28 record in his seven years with the Pirates. He had a 2.94 ERA with 133 of his 145 career saves in 618 innings over 410 games with Pittsburgh. He led the National League with thirty saves in 1971 and earned his all-star bid in 1973.

But the highlight of his career was winning the 1971 World Series against the Orioles. "Being in a World Series is what you strive for and is why you get into this game," said Giusti. "And I was very fortunate to be in the first night game in World Series history during game four of the series, and get the save in that ballgame. That was a big thrill for me!"

His worst moment came the following year. "It was in 1972. We were ahead in the final ballgame of the year, and we were playing the Cincinnati Reds," Giusti shared. "Both us and the Reds were fighting for the playoffs. We were ahead going into the ninth inning, and I was called in to finish it up. The first guy up was Johnny Bench. The first pitch I threw to him, he hit a foul ball down the left-field line. I then said to myself, 'That's great because that was my fastball.' I figured he was all set up for the next pitch because I was going to throw him my palm ball as a change of pace. But all of a sudden, he double-clutched and took the ball over the right-center-field fence.

"That was so disappointing for me because I kind of lost my temper from that moment on, and the next few batters got on base, too, and my inning was over. The manager came out to pull me out of the game. So, the Reds won the game and headed on to the World Series. Johnny Bench has said on occasion that home run was one of the highlights of his career, plus his mother was in the stands to see him play. But that's how it was! It was very disappointing for me because I thought I had him with my best pitch."

Giusti added, "After the 1972 season, which we lost to the Reds, I remember we were headed to the airport because it was time to go home because our season was over. Steve Blass was my roommate for a few years in Pittsburgh before he started having problems getting the ball over the plate. We were all in a taxi headed to the airport. We ran into traffic and Steve decided that we should have a fire drill. So, Steve jumps out of the taxi and runs over to the other side of the car, and then the rest of us all moved, too. All Steve was trying to do was make me feel better after the game and inning I had. He was trying to make me laugh because I felt so disappointed, but that was the kind of guy he was. He was that kind of guy and he was very instrumental in helping me to get over the situation, even though I could never help him with his problem; even the psychologists couldn't even help him. Yet, this was the same guy who won two games during the 1971 World Series and only gave up one run in both of those games."

Giusti worked as a carpenter in his off-seasons. He believed it helped to strengthen his arm and added longevity to his career. So, Giusti did not think the physical challenges of closing were that great. "The closer role has always been more mental," he said. "First and foremost, you know you have the physical ability to get you where you need to be in this game. As a closer you better have some good stuff or those batters will find your weaknesses pretty fast. So, you have to get to where your best stuff is attacking their weaknesses. Even if a guy is a good fastball hitter and your best pitch is the fastball, you still have to throw it. Sometimes it works and sometimes it doesn't."

Giusti was always ready to pitch. "I would go down to the bullpen at the start of the seventh inning. But otherwise I stayed in the dugout because I wanted to learn as much as I could from my teammates about the batters I would be facing as the game went on. You had to be ready to pitch all the time because back then there was no such thing as a multiyear contract. You were given a one-year contract and if you had a bad year you might find yourself traded or worse—it might be pink slip time. You had to continue to pitch well all of the time, year in and year out."

Giusti went 100-93, with 145 saves and a 3.60 ERA in 1,716²/₃ innings over 668 games (113 starts) in his fifteen years. He was an all-star. He appeared in the postseason five different years, and won a world championship in 1971. Was anything missing?

"My only other regret was that I wish I could have been a closer from the start of my career. I loved the closer role and I was always curious to see how far I could have gone in the role. Half of my career was as a starter and half of my career I was a closer. But that is how it was back then!"

RICH
GOSSAGE
CHICAGO WHITE SOX

PITCHER

RICHARD "GOOSE" GOSSAGE
1972–1994

Richard "Goose" Gossage is a member of the old regime. Born on July 5, 1951, Goose made his major league debut in April 1972, at the tender age of twenty.

He played in the majors for twenty-two years with nine different teams (White Sox, Pirates, Yankees, Padres, Cubs, Giants, Rangers, Athletics, and Mariners). The nine-time all-star went 124-107 in 1,002 games, with 310 saves. Of those 1,002 games, only thirty-seven were starts. He finished his career with 1,502 strikeouts, which puts him behind only Hoyt Wilhelm for career strikeouts among pitchers who pitched mainly in relief, and his 115-win total in relief still ranks third all-time.

The right-hander retired following the 1994 season, but relievers were still slow to be recognized for their impact on the game back then, so it took until 2008 for him to be voted into the National Baseball Hall of Fame.

"The word *closer* wasn't even a coined phrase in my day,"

stated Gossage. "We were relief pitchers. We would pitch three innings on any given day. We weren't babies only pitching one inning. It takes three guys these days to do what we used to do. We were the setup man and the closer."

The save statistic did not officially come into effect until 1969. In Gossage's era of specialized relief pitchers—or multiple-inning closers—workload and resting bullpen arms was not thought of. "It was the sportswriter [Jerome] Holtzman who was instrumental in getting the save rule in place and for us guys getting credit for the save," explained Gossage. "He was really the guy who started the statistic for relief pitchers. Not closers. *Closer* is a brand-new name. I never heard of the word *closer* when I was pitching," said Gossage.

"Starters used to pride themselves on finishing what they started. That is no longer the case. You go five or six innings and that is considered a quality start when you go in and negotiate a new contract. You wouldn't be a starter with that behind you in my day. You'd be in the bullpen or in the minor leagues."

Further explaining the job of relievers in his day, Gossage exclaimed, "We were workhorses! It was a tough job, and on a scale of one to ten, it was a ten both on the mental and physical side. Today, it is a five. Back then, the mental and physical aspects of the game would grind you down. You were placed in tough situation after tough situation all year long. These modern day closers face very few guys with very few inherited runners. They start out in the ninth inning with basically no one on all of the time. We always seemed to come into the game in a jam . . . and you couldn't even allow the ball to be put in play, especially when it was a tie ballgame. No one thinks about it that way today. Everyone forgot what we used to do because some of these guys are so dominant in their one-inning role of today.

"We really never knew when the call would come down. We went into the game at times just to keep the game in check, maybe when the team was down by just one run. I would come into the sixth or seventh inning with bases loaded and one out, and the manager brought me in the game to keep it in check—so then we'd have the opportunity to win or stay in the game."

Gossage, a gruff and no-nonsense character, had a unique way of getting himself psyched for some of those appearances. "I used to have Thurman Munson back there [catching]. He used to come out to the mound and say to me, 'How are you going to lose this one?' I'd say, 'I don't know. Why don't you get your ass back there and we'll find out.' He'd say, 'Okay, asshole!' Then he'd be running back to home laughing as I was yelling at him."

Although Gossage believes the job was tougher in his day, he also has respect for the relievers and closers of today. "It is so specialized today. To me, Mariano Rivera is a great closer and so was Trevor Hoffman, who had a terrific career. You know three hundred saves used to be the benchmark for a great career for relief pitchers in the way they were used then. . . . The way we were used we were certainly abused. But, I loved being a workhorse. The tougher the situation I came into, the better I was. Bases loaded and nobody out—hey, that was when I really shined. I could get the chance to strike out the side or maybe get two strikeouts and a fly out to end the inning. That was the best situation for me to be in. Starting out the ninth inning with a three-run lead is hardly a challenge."

He continued, "Interestingly, I had 700 more innings than Mariano Rivera. I had fifty-two saves of seven-plus outs and 310 total saves. And closers today record a three-out save by coming into the ninth inning. Something's got to change because that is a misleading stat. Six hundred saves is great and all, but what percentage of those saves were just one inning and with their team three runs up? Any major league pitcher should be able to save a game that way, or he shouldn't be in the big leagues."

Gossage was a ninth-round selection for the Chicago White Sox in 1970. His debut came less than two years later with the White Sox and Manager Chuck Tanner. "Chuck Tanner was my first manager and he had the greatest impact on my career," said Gossage. "I was a young kid, he taught me how to act like a big leaguer and everything else. Tanner was also the manager who put me in the bullpen."

In reflecting on his great career, Gossage had a tough time picking a single moment that could be declared his greatest. "There were so many. There is not just one that stands out. I wouldn't even know where to start. Certainly the World Series Championship (1978 with the Yankees) stands out and was fantastic. But signing my first professional contract was big, too. Being able to pitch in my first big league game was up there. When I made the club for the first time was special. There was also the first time I got to try on a major league uniform. And I can't forget when I pitched in spring training and was invited to camp as a non-roster player.

"There were so many firsts. There are twenty or more firsts that stand out for me at different times during my career that were the greatest. When you play twenty-plus years in this game there are a lot of great things that are naturally going to happen. The longevity of your career lends itself to it."

JOHN HILLER

1965–1980

J ohn "Ratso" Hiller played his entire career with the Detroit Tigers, 1965–80. The left-hander grew up in Toronto, Canada, not New York, as his nickname would imply.

Hiller picked up the nickname Ratso completely by chance. "It was Pat Dobson and Jim Price who came up with the name during the 1968 season," Hiller explained. "It was after the Dustin Hoffman character from the movie *Midnight Cowboy*. Hoffman played this greasy derelict from New York who walked with a limp in the movie. I had a limp during that time because I was slightly injured. We were in New York during one visit and a bunch of us decided to go see *Midnight Cowboy*. As soon as Hoffman's character came on the screen the two of them shouted, 'There's Hiller; he's Ratso!' From that point on the nickname stuck."

Hiller was signed by the Tigers as an amateur free agent on June 16, 1962. He began his career in the minors in 1963, primarily as a starter, but before he debuted in the majors three years later, he was pitching more frequently out of the bullpen. He made his major league debut on September 6, 1965, against the Boston Red Sox, pitching the final inning of a 4-1 loss and striking out a batter. It was his first of five relief appearances for the Tigers that season.

Hiller made only one major league appearance in 1966, pitching the final two innings of a 10-4 loss to the Washington Senators.

From 1967 on, he pitched when called upon—whether it be in a starter or reliever role—as did all the relievers of his time. But then on January 11, 1971, something happened to him that has happened to no other major league player. He suffered a massive heart attack at the age of twenty-seven. He miraculously returned to the majors a year and a half later.

Initially, the Tigers were not sold that Hiller could come back to his previous form, so they offered him $7,500 to be a minor league instructor in spring training. He worked every free minute in spring training to impress the brass, and then worked on his own until July 1972 when he was called up. The long shot ended up pitching in twenty-four games that season, posting a 2.03 ERA in forty-four innings.

"I had the heart attack in June 1971, and I came back about the second half of 1972," stated Hiller. "By then, Chuck Seelbach was the right-hander in the bullpen and Freddie Scherman was the left-hander. By chance they had some physical problems with their pitching, so I signed a contract and later that night Billy Martin, the manager, put me into the game. There was no such thing as a rehab start, simulated pitching, or a stint down in the minors. I was facing my first batter in a year and a half. My only rehab came by throwing for myself in a gym in Duluth, Minnesota. No one could catch for me back then, so I was forced to throw against the wall. Billy put me into the game and Dick Allen was the first batter I faced, and he hit a home run off of me. I pitched three innings that night and didn't walk a batter. I remember Billy Martin saying to someone in the media, 'This guy came back from the dead, and he didn't even walk a batter!' From that day on I became the team's closer. I pitched against Oakland in the playoffs and continued in that role. I had my best season just a year later when I had thirty-eight saves and ended the season with a 1.44 ERA. It was the record at the time until Dan Quisenberry broke the record ten years later."

Hiller pitched so well the year following his return to baseball that noted baseball statistician Bill James described his 1973 season as "the greatest season for a closer in the history of baseball." Hiller went 10-5 with a 1.44 ERA in a league-leading sixty-five games and (at the time) a major league record of thirty-eight saves in 125 innings. He earned the American League Fireman of the Year Award, Comeback Player of the Year, and the Hutch Award, which is given to a player who best displays a fighting spirit and competitive desire.

Hiller never replicated that great season. However, he still pitched well in relief and in 1974 was selected to his first and only All-Star Game. He finished his major league career in May 1980 after having compiled an 87-76 record with a 2.83 ERA in 545 career games, with 43 starts, and 125 saves in 1,242 innings.

The six-foot-one pitcher compared his role as the closer to the closers of today. "The old days were so much different from today," Hiller said. "First of all, there was no such thing as a one-inning save. But there were a lot of factors back then as to how a manager would use you because he didn't have the choices he has today. Back then, how you were used depended on the team you were on. When I started in the bullpen in the 1960s, we had four starters: Denny McLain, Mickey Lolich, Earl Wilson, and Joe Sparma. You didn't relieve McLain and Lolich! So, there were not as many save opportunities. So, Pat Dobson and I [one left-hander and one right-hander] were spot starters more than anything, with an occasional save here and there. We'd end up pitching a lot of game-two doubleheaders, or maybe we'd pitch in long relief when someone got into occasional trouble. We never considered ourselves closers."

He continued, "In the 1970s, especially after the 1973 season, the Tigers didn't have a lot of great teams. The organization had to wait a few years to see players like [Lance] Parrish, [Lou] Whitaker, and [Alan] Trammell make their way through the ranks. So, because of the years we had and not winning a lot of games, I was often in the game from the seventh inning on, trying either to stop the bleeding or to hold the other team so we could put some more runs on the board. That is why in 1974 I went 17-14 as a relief pitcher. I had a total of thirty-one decisions out of the bullpen and I came one short of tying Elroy Face's record of eighteen victories as a closer. But that is why I also had fourteen losses, because Manager Ralph Houk kept putting me into every ballgame that last month of the year so I could match the record. Ralph said, 'Every tie ballgame we have I'm gonna get you into the game so you can get that eighteenth and ninteenth win!'. . . but I never did.

"And then every once and a while, Ralph Houk would turn to me and say, 'Hey, John, I don't have a starter for today's game. Can you start?' I'd reply, 'I'd love to!' So, I would start occasionally and then be ready to pitch three innings every night. I pitched a lot of innings. Also, the other thing that is different about the role of the closer of today and the closer in my day, we normally did not come in at the start of the inning with no outs and no one on. We always came in the game with runners on. But mentally, I preferred to have runners on the bases. It helped me to build up the adrenaline and get that going for me. I think I was a better pitcher, in fact, and threw a little bit harder based on those circumstances."

Like many pitchers of today, Hiller believes the closer role was also more of a mental challenge than a physical one. "I was blessed with a great arm," he explained. "I remember pitching thirteen games in fifteen days one time and I picked up eight saves. I would throw every day and never did I have arm trouble. I think it was always more mental to me. If I had a good outing, or if I went through an inning or two, then I went into the next outing or inning with a lot more confidence. On the other side, when you had a bad outing you had to let it go. The worst was when you had back-to-back bad outings and you started to question yourself and your own confidence level. You start feeling bad because you are letting your whole team down."

Unlike pitchers of today, who are more cautious with the amount of wear and tear put on their arms, pitchers in Hiller's day threw all the time. "I remember we were in Anaheim one day and Billy Martin asked Art Fowler to get me warmed up," Hiller recalled. "And because I threw every day, I was always ready and I could get warmed up quickly. That day I warmed up on two pitches in the bullpen, and then when I got to the mound I got only three warm-up pitches and I was ready," recalled Hiller.

"I will never forget one day I was sitting in the dugout ready to start a game," he went on, "and Johnny Sain [pitching coach] came up to me and said, 'John, are you gonna go down to the bullpen and warm up?' I replied, 'Johnny, I've got a whole fifteen minutes before the game starts. I just need two minutes.' And then I said, 'I only get two minutes to warm up as a relief pitcher, why should it take me any longer as a starter?'

"I was also very fortunate to be able to throw strikes all day. I never had great stuff, but I threw three pitches, all for strikes. I never had any gimmicks; I didn't pound the glove, or walk around the mound. They would just give me the ball and I would throw it. But most of all," he concluded, "you never let the other team see you sweat. I might have been scared to death at the situation or the batter up, but they never knew it."

Hiller felt Johnny Sain had the greatest impact on his career because he taught him how to throw every day. According to Hiller, the former right-handed pitcher turned pitching coach would say, "Throw the ball every single day, maybe not on the mound, but throw every day and you will condition your arm this way. If you are going to be a relief pitcher, you've got to be ready every day. Your team is going to depend on you."

TOM HOUSE
1971–1978

N ot only does it take a certain personality and ability to close for a Major League Baseball team, it takes a lot to remain in the role. Just ask lefty Tom House.

After turning down the Chicago Cubs in 1965, House signed a contract with the Atlanta Braves when he was selected in the third round of the secondary phase of the 1967 June draft out of the University of Southern California.

Like all the others from his generation, House began in the minors as a starter. He began pitching in relief in 1970 and made his major league debut the next year—in relief—on June 23, 1971, against the Montreal Expos.

The five-foot-eleven, young-looking, bespectacled pitcher ended up pitching in the majors for eight years with the Atlanta Braves, Boston Red Sox, and Seattle Mariners. He did things a little backwards, as he began his career as a reliever and finished it with twenty starts in his last sixty games over two years with the Mariners.

House was a teammate of Hank Aaron's in 1974, and on April 8 of that year, Aaron hit his record-setting 715th home run. House was in the bullpen and caught the ball on the fly. The game was stopped to celebrate the achievement and House ran out with his warm-up jacket over his uniform to present the ball to Aaron at home plate. At the time, Aaron, who was caught up in this legendary moment, did not even recognize his youthful teammate.

That was the best year of House's career. He went 6-2 with a miniscule 1.92 ERA over fifty-six games with a career-best eleven saves, which he duplicated in 1975.

"I closed for about a year and a half (1974–75) with the Braves," said House, "so I had a little experience and an idea as to what the role was all about. But, I was the low-end guy, and my best year happened to be the year I caught Henry Aaron's 715th home run."

He continued with a laugh, "If you pull the book on my playing career, I was marginal to horseshit for seven years, and I was really, really good for one year. It's like that expression, 'Those that can, play, and those that can't, coach.' I think it's because you have to know why you are good. There are guys that are really good because they are subconsciously confident, and then there are those who know how to grind it out every day who find themselves as that tenth or eleventh guy in the bullpen. So, to hang around the bullpen and in that role you better be able to figure things out in a hurry.

"I think the closer role came into its development during my generation," said the lefty. "The only consistent characteristic among all of the closers, from yesterday to today, is they seem to embrace the moment. No matter what their makeup is, whether they are hyper guys or if they go out there quietly or if they are a power pitcher or a three-pitch kind of guy, they all seem to embrace the moment. That is what connects them, whether it is a closer from thirty or forty years ago or from today's crop of closers. They live most comfortable on the edge. They don't run from any situation, rather they run towards it. For example, trying to talk a guy out of the role after they are in that role is like trying to talk them down from the cliff. Once you've been a closer it is nearly impossible to talk that same guy into another role in the bullpen."

When House finished his playing career in 1978, he had a bachelor's degree in management and a master's degree in marketing from the University of Southern California. By 1981, he had a second master's degree in performance psychology and finally earned his doctorate in psychology in 1984.

House turned to coaching in 1985, latching on with the Texas Rangers. It was there he connected with Nolan Ryan, among others, and his reputation as an extraordinary pitching coach blossomed. "Baseball has this beautiful way of evolving," House said. "It is the same game that they played a hundred-plus years ago, but the interpretation and the implementation is always changing. And the role of the closer is so much driven by the economics of the game, because if you are going to pay a guy to close, then he's gonna close. If the correct game-day situation comes up and it is a save situation, then he's gonna save the game. So, it's like the expression: what came first the chicken or the egg? That is where I believe we are right now. That is why there are other roles developing, too. Those seventh- and eighth-inning guys are now turning out to be just as important as that closer role. It's guys like Tony La Russa and Bobby Valentine who understand pitch count and the need to save arms.

"There are all kinds of factors," House continued, "but I am willing to bet if you put Goose Gossage and Jonathan Papelbon in the same room and profiled them or did a Rorschach inkblot test on them, they would look at those inkblots the same way. I think the closer has always been hard-wired to be the closer. It is the same genetic code that exists in all of them."

Like many others, House believes the closing role is more mental these days than physical, although for different reasons. "The closer of today has to be able to fire it up like a Saturn V rocket each time he goes out there. If you have a closer that you see out there for two innings, then that manager is probably in trouble somehow. In the Goose Gossage and Rollie Fingers generation, a three-inning save was commonplace. I think in my day I even had eleven or twelve saves that went three innings. That is the evolution of the game and the role of the closer in my mind."

Despite having more "fixed" roles on the club, House believes managers these days have more choices—until the end of the game. "But once they get to the closer, they really have no more choices left."

So, if Dr. House could create the perfect closer, what characteristics would he have?

"I would look for three things in a closer: makeup, a freak pitch, and durability," explained House. "For example, what I mean by a freak pitch is one pitch that stands out. Like a Mariano cutter, a Bruce Sutter splitter, a Lee Smith fastball, or even a Tom Gordon unhittable drop curveball. They are the freak pitches I'm talking about. I also teach; 'See it, feel it, do it!' Put the feeling in your body and do it. The best closers see themselves getting that double play when they need a strikeout. For example, Trevor Hoffman could always write a script in his head of how he saw himself getting a batter out. He would see himself getting the strikeout he needed with that change-up. The really good closers have this ability to write the perfect script for how they were going to achieve the save. And their script always has a happy ending!"

AL HRABOSKY

1970–1982

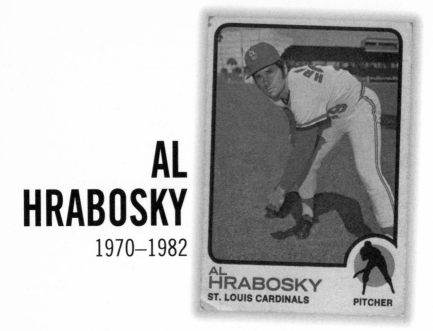

AL HRABOSKY

ST. LOUIS CARDINALS   PITCHER

A l Hrabosky was one of the middle generations. The Mad Hungarian, as he was known, played in the majors from 1970 to 1982. He made just one start in his thirteen seasons and witnessed, firsthand, the progression of the closer position.

"At the beginning of my career I was obviously a relief pitcher," Hrabosky stated, "but towards the end of my career, or at least in my heyday, I was a closer."

He expanded: "I think everyone knows now that you can't win without a good closer. And I truly believe you ought to have a good closer and you better have a few good setup guys to go along with that so you can use the closer effectively. But I think the evolution was a little later in my case.

"In the past a relief pitcher was in many ways a second-class citizen. He was either a broken-down starter—one who was aging and not good enough anymore to fill the role of a starter and now was in the bullpen—or he was a young kid who the club was looking to get more work for and not good enough yet to find himself in the rotation.

"I think when I came along, in the mid-seventies, there were a few guys like [Rollie] Fingers and [Goose] Gossage, who were figuring it out and understood what it meant to be a closer and that there was a niche to be filled out there. Then there were some of us who caught on to the closer role in time."

Hrabosky's professional career began in 1969, when he was drafted by the St. Louis Cardinals as their first pick (nineteenth overall) in the January draft. It could have started earlier, as the left-hander from Savanna High School in Anaheim, California, was All-League, All-City, and All-Orange in both baseball and football, and had been selected by the Minnesota Twins in the June draft. He opted to go to college instead.

He went on to Fullerton California Junior College, where he was twice named to the All-Conference baseball team before his January selection.

For the five-foot-eleven lefty, his major league career started quickly. One year after beginning his pro career, on June 16, 1970, he made his major league debut. He pitched relief against San Diego. After two relief appearances, he was slated for his first (and only) major league start on June 24, 1970, at Pittsburgh. He finished his first season in the majors with a total of sixteen appearances.

Despite the perceived reputation of relievers as being pitchers who just weren't good enough to start, Hrabosky craved the role. "Once I got to the big leagues and I started pitching on such a regular basis, I wanted to be in the bullpen. I loved it! And once I reached a certain level of success, I really thrived on coming into a game when it was on the line in the late innings. I felt like anyone could pitch in this game being five runs up or five runs down—and, really, that was no big deal—but I thrived on wanting to be on the mound when the game was on the line."

It wasn't always easy, however. Hrabosky made his debut in

1970, but he had to fight—and have someone fight for him—to get back up to the majors for good in 1974.

"Fred Koenig, who I played for in double-A, was one of the greatest influences on my career," recalled Hrabosky. "He would constantly put his neck on the line for me and try to convince the Cardinals to bring me back up. He called the Cardinals every day in 1972. . . . He was someone who believed in you even if the raw statistics tell you otherwise. Fred was able to look beyond the numbers and trust his own judgment."

Hrabosky got to the majors again in 1973, thanks to Fred, but needed someone else to speak up for him again in 1974. He got off to a horrible start (10.12 ERA in five appearances) in 1974, and the Cardinals almost were going to send him back down to the minors. "One day," remembered Hrabosky, "Jack Buck, the announcer for the Cardinals, came up to me and said, 'You know, Ted Simmons just saved your life.' I turned to him and said, 'What do you mean?' And then he said, 'You know, they were thinking about sending you down and then they asked Ted Simmons what was wrong with you. Simmons told them, 'Don't worry about it, Al will figure it out.' It's a great thing when the announcers know more than the players.

"So I knew I needed to start something that would be the key to my success and concentration. I don't know what I was doing prior, but I was having some problems with my concentration. My mind was wandering and I wasn't getting the job done. So that is when I devised this ritual of walking around the back of the mound and placing myself in an almost self-hypnosis state by projecting in my mind how to get the hitters out. I know other pitchers didn't have to do all that, but it worked for me. I was the first to get the audience and fans to be a part of the game and the action with that ritual."

After developing that ritual, which would become his signature, Hrabosky went on to throw scoreless innings in eleven straight appearances that year and was never in jeopardy of returning to the minors.

The ritual was not without controversy. Many opposing players did not like his antics, thinking he was making too much of a show; others thought it was just a ruse to intimidate batters. Not too many people in the game realized its true purpose.

The Mad Hungarian played the majority of his career for the Cardinals, and, whether it was due to his rituals that rallied fans behind him or the success he had as the team's closer, Hrabosky was a beloved member of the Cardinals organization from 1970–77, and continues to be today as part of the Cardinals broadcast team.

Hrabosky wasn't always the calm and thoughtful person he is now. He was a very animated pitcher. His antics—or ritual—had a tendency to aggravate his opponents, which led to some infamous brawls.

His first—and arguably most memorable—brawl came in 1974, shortly after he created his ritual. Bill Madlock of the Chicago Cubs came to the plate and just as Hrabosky was ready to pitch, Madlock returned to the on-deck circle, thinking he was breaking "The Mad Hungarian's" concentration. But Hrabosky was not to be outdone—as soon as Madlock was ready, he walked behind the mound to do his routine again. As soon as Hrabosky was on the rubber, Madlock returned to the on-deck circle. This time, home plate umpire Shag Crawford had enough and ordered Hrabosky to pitch, which he did and got strike one with no one in the batter's box. That brought Madlock, on-deck hitter Jose Cardenal, and Cubs manager, Jim Marshall, out to argue—all around the plate.

"My next pitch separated all three of them," Hrabosky said with a grin, "and for some reason that started a fight. And it was a good one."

He was involved in another classic brawl in 1978, when he was with the Kansas City Royals. He had not pitched well against the California Angels all season when Carney Lansford hit a three-run homer off him. Lyman Bostock came to the plate and "I wanted to send a message that next season would be a different story," recalled Hrabosky.

The next pitch went towards Bostock's head, sending him diving into the dirt and clearing the benches. Order was eventually restored and, astonishingly, no one was ejected. But Bostock continued to scream at Hrabosky. Royals Manager Whitey Herzog decided to take Hrabosky out of the game. At that point, since he was out of the game, Hrabosky charged Bostock, initiating round two.

Although Hrabosky had an intimidating presence on the mound, he feels he pales in comparison to the player he believes had the greatest impact on his career—Bob Gibson. "In my mind he was the most intimidating player I ever witnessed," confessed Hrabosky. "He was a monster on that mound. If I ever had to win just one game it would be Bob Gibson who would be on the mound. What the fans said in praise about Bob Gibson was always what I strived for them to say about me. Bob taught me a lot of little lessons. As a player you learn a lot from other teammates and you file the important stuff, and that is what I did with Bob, but it was all important when it came from him."

Mental toughness was one of Gibson's strongest qualities and is the key, according to Hrabosky, to being successful at the major league level. "From my standpoint, the role of being a closer was definitely more mental than physical. Obviously, you have to have to possess physical traits, but because of my mental toughness I was able to play this game. I kind of programmed my mind when I went to the closer role. I could handle it. I do remember losing a little bit on my fastball as I got older, and I should have reprogrammed myself and my mind and said to myself, 'This is what I need to do.' This game is so much more mental."

JIM KONSTANTY
1944–1956

C asimir James "Jim" Konstanty was a closer before anyone knew what a closer was. The right-hander pitched in the major leagues in 1944, 1946, and from 1948 to 1956.

It was never a certainty that Konstanty would pitch in the majors. He was the son of a farmer and a star athlete at Arcade High School in New York. He went on to Syracuse University and earned a degree in physical education in 1939. After graduating from college, the bespectacled athlete became a physical education teacher at St. Regis Falls in New York. It wasn't until 1941 that he began his professional baseball career with Springfield (Massachussets) of the Eastern League—and that first foray into pro ball did not open the eyes of any scouts, as he went 4-19 as a starter.

In 1942, he played for the Syracuse Chiefs (a Cincinnati Reds farm team), but only pitched in five games. He remained with the Chiefs in 1943 and 1944, with continued nondescript results. Midway through 1944, with the majors losing players to the war, Konstanty was called up to the majors and made his debut as a starter on June 18 in the second game of a doubleheader. He pitched mainly as a starter that season, with twelve of his twenty appearances in the starting role, and five of those were complete games.

In 1945, after trying for a military commission several times but being denied because of his eyesight, Konstanty was finally accepted into the navy. He returned to baseball in 1946 and was traded to the Boston Braves. After ten appearances, he was sold to Toronto of the International League. He remained there through the 1947 season, but it was a significant time in his career as he taught himself a couple of pitches—the slider and palm ball—that would give him the edge he needed to succeed in the majors.

The Philadelphia Phillies bought his contract prior to the 1948 season, and he appeared in six games in September for them. In 1949, he finally pitched his first full season in the majors, appearing solely in relief.

But at the age of thirty-three, Konstanty enjoyed a 1950 season that would be one for the record books.

Bob Miller joined the Phillies in September of 1949. His rookie season was 1950, and he was a solid member of a strong Phillies and Whiz Kids rotation that featured Robin Roberts and Curt Simmons. He also had a unique perspective on Konstanty's MVP season.

"We didn't have the closer as they do today. If they did, I probably would have won a few more ballgames than I did. I remember my first game in the majors. I beat the Boston Braves by a score of 2-1, and I went all the way, pitching the complete game. I may not have had a closer finishing the game up for me, but at least it gave me the confidence to go on."

Miller continued, "Back then, pitchers finished games and if they didn't, it was for reasons like something was physically wrong with them or because the starter was getting beat up out there on the mound. But Jim was unbelievable! Anytime we had a close game and it looked like the starting pitcher was getting into trouble the manager, Eddie Sawyer, would pull the starter and put in Jim Konstanty. He won sixteen games that year and saved a ton of games. He just had an unbelievable season. I think the only pitcher he never had to come in for was Robin Roberts, who I think finished every game he started."

Eddie Sawyer was the manager and the main reason Konstanty got in so many games. "I think he helped define the closer role," said the right-hander Miller. "Sawyer was a great player's manager and friend to us all. Sawyer was always smiling."

Konstanty appeared in a then-record seventy-four games in 1950 with sixteen wins and a National League-leading twenty-two saves (although technically that statistic was not kept then). But, surprisingly, he was named the starter for game one of the World Series against the New York Yankees. He did well, pitching eight innings, allowing four hits and one run, but lost 1-0 to a two-hit complete game by Vic Raschi.

For his efforts in 1950, Konstanty was named Most Valuable Player, Associated Press Athlete of the Year, *Sporting News* Pitcher of the Year, and he was a National League all-star. To this day, he is the only National League reliever to win the MVP award.

Konstanty was never able to replicate his 1950 season, but he continued pitching another six seasons—for the Phillies through 1954, for the Yankees from 1954 to 1956, and with the St. Louis Cardinals in 1956. He retired at the age of thirty-nine.

Following retirement, he became a minor league pitching coach for the Cardinals organization. From 1968 to 1972, he was director of athletics at Hartwick College in Oneonta, New York, near Cooperstown. In addition, he owned and operated a sporting goods store, also in Oneonta, from 1948 to 1973. He passed away in 1976 after a brief battle with cancer.

"Jim was a great guy," said Miller. "A true professional when it came to baseball. He never got drunk and he never got into trouble. We knew we could always count on him and his palm ball. And, being a veteran player, he was always there to share his knowledge. We used to call him Yamka because he used to stay at the YMCA all of the time. He was a leader for us all, leading by example. He was quiet and all business, and he really, really loved his role as the closer. That's for darn sure."

TUG MCGRAW
1965–1984

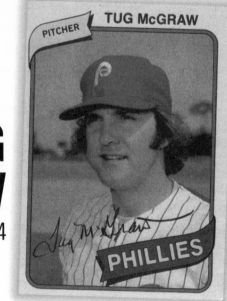

L ike the little engine that could, Frank Edwin "Tug" McGraw, became—and remained—a major league pitcher for nineteen years.

He was born on August 30, 1944, in Martinez, California, played baseball at St. Vincent's High School in Petaluma, and attended Vallejo Junior College for a brief period. But the almost six-foot lefty was never drafted by a major league team. With luck on his side, on June 12, 1964, he was signed as an amateur free agent by the New York Mets.

Like so many pitchers of his generation, McGraw began his minor league career as a starter. He made eight starts in eleven appearances in his first pro season. But on April 18, 1965, at the age of twenty, he made his major league debut in relief against the San Francisco Giants. He remained a reliever in the majors for most of the 1965 season, not starting until the second game of a doubleheader in late July, and proved himself enough that he ended up making eight more starts for the Mets that year.

McGraw returned to the minors in 1966, 1967, and 1968, pitching almost exclusively in the starting role and making brief major league appearances in 1966 and '67. Frequently likened to a leprechaun because of his height, Irish descent, and upbeat attitude, McGraw had a decent fastball and curveball, but when he developed a screwball after some time in the minors, he had the arsenal he needed to succeed—and a trademark pitch.

He returned to the majors for good in 1969, helping the Miracle Mets to become World Series Champions. But it was in August 1973, in the days leading up to the pennant race and ultimately a National League Championship, when he coined the phrase "Ya gotta believe." It was originally said in jest, but it caught on and became his signature phrase.

After the following season, on December 3, 1974, he was traded to the Philadelphia Phillies, where he helped his teams to the National League Championship in 1976, '77, '78, and the first World Series Championship for the Phillies in 1980.

McGraw's nineteen-year career ended following the 1984 season, but his career was as full as he was full of life. He competed in two All-Star Games and nine postseason series, and won two World Series Championships.

Former Phillies teammate Larry Bowa remembered one of the late McGraw's funnier moments. "There are a lot of stories," Bowa recalled laughing. "The one that sticks out in my mind was when we were in Chicago. I don't want to sound disrespectful; it's just funny. Again, Tug loved Chicago because of the nightlife but yet he hated to pitch at Wrigley Field. On one of those occasions we all went out to the bar, as we would often do just to unwind after the game, and have a beer or two. But after this one particular game I remember the next morning coming down to get on the bus that would take me to the ball park. I used to try and get to the ball park early, and as I was leaving Tug was coming in from the night before. I remember laughing when I heard Tug say to someone at the front desk, 'Can I get a wake-up call for 9:00 a.m.?' I think it was already

8:15 a.m. And I remember just scratching my head and saying, 'Are you kidding me!' Basically, Tug had a great time the night before and was just looking for forty-five minutes of sleep before he had to get up and go to the park. It was funny, because here I am getting a good night's rest and there was Tug looking for a forty-five minute wake-up call."

Following McGraw's career, he became a sports reporter in Philadelphia and wrote three children's books based on a screwball character. He was also a special instructor for the Phillies in spring training. It was during spring training in 2003 that it was discovered he had a brain tumor.

McGraw passed away from brain cancer the following January at the age of fifty-nine.

"The one memory of Tug that sticks out the most was watching him on the mound with the bases loaded in the 1980 World Series," recalled Bowa, a five-time all-star. "People don't realize how much Tug had pitched up to that point, in the playoffs and prior to that. He was literally out of gas, but he went out there with his guts and whatever he had left in his tank, and let it go and gave all he had to that at-bat against Willie Wilson. You could tell he was running on fumes for a long time, but that was the kind of pitcher Tug was. He never declined the ball. He was always available to pitch for his teammates and he'd find a way to get it done regardless of how many games he got himself into or that we got him into. He would always pick us up or we would pick him up. That stands out as my favorite memory of Tug and especially after he got that last strike to get us the world championship.

"It was a long drought for Phillies fans finally winning it in 1980. Once Tug got that strikeout of Willie Wilson and the win for us, it was like fifty elephants were off of our shoulders. I remember going to the mound that inning and visiting Tug and I said to him, 'Come on Tug! You gotta close this thing down' and 'You gotta throw it over the plate,' and he turned to me and in Tug McGraw fashion said, 'Don't you think I'm trying!' Tug was unbelievable in that series. I remember he didn't even look like he was caught up in the moment or like he was afraid of the situation. He always kept it real light, like he always did. I don't know what he was like inside his heart, but he never let anybody get the feeling from him, 'Oh, god, what am I gonna do now?' He'd always say 'Don't worry about it. I'll get us out of this!'"

McGraw still ranks in the top sixty with his 180 career saves, and there are only six relievers ahead of him with as many or more major league seasons: John Franco (21 years, 424 saves), Dennis Eckersley (24, 390), Jose Mesa (19, 321), Goose Gossage (22, 310), Hoyt Wilhelm (21, 227), and Gene Garber (19, 218). The only ones ahead of McGraw on the all-time list who started their careers before him are Wilhelm (1952–72) and Roy Face (who had 193 saves in sixteen years, 1953–69).

"Tug was a great reliever because he had great short-term memory," said Bowa, who retired as a player in 1985 but stayed in the game as a coach and manager, and currently works as a studio analyst for the MLB Network. "Relief pitchers have to have amnesia at times, and that is what Tug had. If Tug blew a save on Monday and you called him on Tuesday, anything that happened on Monday was the furthest thing from Tug's mind. He was able to clear the slate every time. And what a lot of fans and people don't realize is that many of Tug's saves were two and three innings long. If Tug was a pitcher today in today's closer environment of pitching, meaning just the ninth inning, he would have racked up a lot more saves."

Ninety-two of McGraw's 180 saves were more than one-inning outings, and even more impressively, seventy-nine of his saves were two innings or more.

"I think Tug considered himself more a relief pitcher than a closer," Bowa speculated. "Tug was ready from the seventh inning on. These guys nowadays, if they get the call prior to the ninth, they are shocked. In fact, I've been in situations as a manager where we've won five in a row and we've blown out the other team and I hadn't had a chance to use the closer in all of that time. I'd call down to the bullpen and say, 'Do you [the closer] want to get into the game and get some action?' And a lot of them would say back to me, 'No, this is a meaningless game for me.' I guess the mind-set can play funny tricks on you. Their mind is set for a save and to close the game out."

But McGraw was an old-school pitcher. "Tug was one of those rare pitchers who had three good pitches (fastball, curveball, and screwball) and very seldom do you see guys in that role who could throw three good pitches," said Bowa. "Tug could throw all three for strikes, and that was a rarity. Tug was one of those guys who had the ability and the arsenal to be a closer and a starter. When you have only two pitches it's hard to go through a line-up twice without the other guy figuring you out. But when you have more than two pitches, you can be a very effective starter. But Tug wanted to be a closer and thank goodness for us that he did, winning us a World Series. They often say, when you are a closer 'You never want to get beat on your third-best pitch.' That's a favorite line amongst closers today. You hear them say, 'I've got this third pitch, but I don't want to throw it and then we might not get the win.' But Tug didn't think one pitch was better than another and rather thought that he could beat you with any of them."

JOE PAGE
1944–1954

Like Elroy Face, Joe Page was considered one of the pioneers of the modern day closer.

One of the first forkballers, Page pitched for the New York Yankees from 1944 to 1950, and for the Pittsburgh Pirates for half of the 1954 season.

A native of Cherry Valley, a coal-mining region in Pennsylvania, the left-hander signed with the Yankees in 1940 and made his major league debut in relief on April 19, 1944. Of his nineteen games in his rookie season, sixteen were starts and his overall record of 5-7 and 4.56 ERA was deceiving, as he went 4-1 with a 1.60 ERA over the first two months of the season and earned his first of three all-star selections.

Page spent his first three seasons pitching mainly in a starting role, although he did make several appearances in relief.

He found his calling in 1947, when manager Bucky Harris had him pitch almost exclusively from the bullpen. Page led the majors that season with forty-four games finished, led the American League with seventeen saves, and went 14-8, with a 2.48 ERA. He finished fourth in the Most Valuable Player voting and was named the first World Series Most Valuable Player after the Yankees defeated the Brooklyn Dodgers for the title.

His success as MVP of the World Champion Yankees helped give recognition to the relief role. However, Page, who was also known as a man who enjoyed the nightlife, struggled for most of the 1948 season. He did lead the league with fifty-five games and thirty-eight games finished, but he won just seven games and his ERA ballooned to 4.26.

He rebounded with another stellar season in 1949, leading

the league with sixty games, forty-eight games finished, and twenty-seven saves. He went 13-8, and his ERA returned to a respectable 2.59. And he again helped the Yankees to a World Series Championship.

Jerry Coleman, currently a broadcaster for the San Diego Padres, signed with the Yankees out of high school in 1942 and after postponing his baseball career to join the Marine Corps, made his debut with the Yankees in 1949. He recalled the early days of his career with Joe Page. "I played with Joe on the Yankees for a couple of seasons. I joined the club in late 1948, and Page was already there. I was his teammate up to 1950," recalled Coleman. "In fact, I was there for his best years—1947 and 1949 were his years, and he kept the Yankees in the World Series. He helped us get there and he did a great job for us."

Like closers of today, Page was the "go-to" guy in the bullpen. "He was our guy!" confirmed Coleman. "But of course he didn't win them all. Today, they are expected to save them all because the closer of today is a specialist and he is expected to pitch just that one inning sometimes two or three times a week. It is a completely different style of pitchers from those in my day."

The word *closer* was not even used in baseball when Page pitched and relief pitchers generally were pitchers that couldn't handle the more prestigious starting role. Relievers could come in at any point. "In 1949, we were one game out of first with two games left in the season," recalled Coleman. "We went into that last weekend playing the Red Sox, who were the ones in front of us. We beat them on Saturday and Allie Reynolds started that game, and by the third inning he was a disaster and they brought in Joe Page. I think he pitched six and one-third innings that day and helped us get the win. That is something that would never happen today. Today, there would have been six guys in there before they would have gotten to Joe Page. He came into that game and stopped the Red Sox cold. We eventually beat them 5-4 on a John Lindell home run. But the classic part of this all was that Page was our closer and he pitched six and one-third innings and shot them down. The closer today is only a one-inning guy and that's it."

Coleman continued, "Joe Page was a good teammate and he was always ready to pitch when he was called upon. And I know in 1947 and 1949, he was the difference in winning or losing for the Yankees those years. Especially in 1949, he was "the guy" we all counted on. He came in anytime, the fourth, the sixth, the eighth, it didn't matter, he was ready. He was the guy we all counted on to close it out. He had some incredible years. Page was great and he was the reason why we won the pennant . . . especially in that final series against the Red Sox. If we didn't have Joe, then we wouldn't have won it!"

Coleman has seen the evolution of the closer first hand, so is in a unique position to point out the main difference. "Back in my day the big teams had four starting pitchers and everybody knew who they were. Now teams average five starters and they don't see action until that fifth day. Today, teams develop their bullpens just like they would develop their starting rotation. That is because the bullpen of today is about as important as the starting rotation. It is so specialized anymore."

RON PERRANOSKI
1961–1973

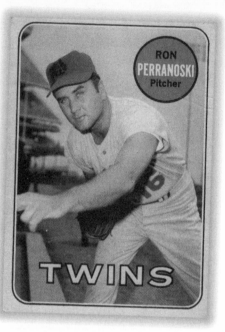

Ron Perzanowski (as he was born) or Perranoski (as he is better known) has been involved in professional baseball for over fifty years.

He is probably most remembered as the Los Angeles Dodgers' tremendous pitching coach under manager Tommy Lasorda from 1981 to 1994. During that time, he earned two World Series titles and had pitching staffs that ranked first or second in the National League in ERA nine times. But his career in Major League Baseball did not end there.

He has been working since 1995 in the San Francisco Giants organization, where he has held positions of coordinator of minor league pitching, major league bench coach, major league pitching coach, and senior consultant, player personnel.

What many people of the younger generation don't realize is that Perranoski had an impressive thirteen-year major league career as a reliever for the Dodgers (1961–67; 1972), Minnesota Twins

(1968–71); Detroit Tigers (1971–72); and California Angels (1973).

Born on April 1, 1936, in Paterson, New Jersey, the left-hander graduated from Fair Lawn High School and then attended Michigan State University (1956–58). He was signed by the Chicago Cubs as an amateur free agent on June 9, 1958.

Perranoski began his career mainly as a starter. After just two years in the Cubs organization, he was traded to the Dodgers on April 8, 1960, and began his transition to a relieving role.

One year later, on April 4, 1961, Perranoski made his major league debut, pitching the final one and one-third innings in the Dodgers' 6-3 loss to the Pittsburgh Pirates.

In 1962, he became his team's closer, a role he would hold throughout the rest of his Dodgers' career and during his first three seasons with the Twins.

"I was very fortunate to play for Walter Alston with the Dodgers for most of my career," said Perranoski. "And then I had Billy Martin when I went over to the Minnesota Twins. They gave me the ball, and that is all I ever asked for. They knew it was my game when the game was on the line from the seventh inning on."

The Polish pitcher led the league in games played three times (70 in 1962, 69 in 1963, and 70 in 1967). He also led the league in saves twice (31 in 1969 and 34 in 1970). He finished his thirteen-year major league career with a 79-74 record, a 2.79 ERA, 179 saves, and 1,174²/₃ innings in 737 games.

Two of his finest seasons were 1963 (with LA), when he went 16-3 with twenty-one saves and a 1.67 ERA in 129 innings over sixty-nine games, and 1969 (with the Twins), when he saved thirty-one games with a 2.11 ERA in 119²/₃ innings over a career-high seventy-five games.

"I came to the ball park ready to start pitching, no matter what inning I came in," said Perranoski. "I knew if we were in a close ballgame, from the seventh inning on, it was going to be my game. I even pitched six-plus innings several times in my career. I pitched to left- and right-handed batters. That game was mine from the seventh inning on and I knew it. I think I used to hold the record for most saves of over three innings or more at one point."

Perranoski is grateful for the career he had and has no regrets. "I was fortunate to pitch for thirteen seasons and in those thirteen seasons I got to pitch a lot of those innings," stated Perranoski. "During my coaching career, I got to work with a lot of great guys: Rick Sutcliff, Steve Howe, Fernando [Valenzuela], Alejandro Pena, Orel Hershiser, Dave Stewart, and Bob Welch.

"I remember this game we played in 1963, in late September. The season was on the line. In 1962, we had lost to the Giants in the World Series, and everyone was waiting to see how the Dodgers were going to blow it again in 1963. We had a game and a half lead on the Cardinals, who had just won nineteen out of the last twenty games. And we ended up playing them in the upcoming series. Sandy Koufax got us the win in the first game of the series, and then we were headed into game two. We were losing late in the game by the score of 5-1. By the eighth we got back in it to run the score to 5-4. In the eighth inning Dick Nen came up to bat in his first game as a rookie. He was just called up. He was the father of Robb Nen, who I coached as a closer in San Francisco. Nen hit a home run to tie up the game. I pitched a scoreless ninth and then in the tenth I gave up a leadoff triple to Dick Grout. Walter Alston came out to talk with me and asked if I wanted to walk the next two batters. I said, 'Let me try and strike out Gary Kolb [the next batter], and then I'll walk the next two after that, Kenny Boyer and Bill White.' So that is what happened. I got Kolb on strikes and I walked Boyer and White. The next batter grounded into a double play to end the inning. I eventually pitched until the thirteenth inning, and that is when we got the lead and won the game. Sometimes those are the games that decide your season. We won the pennant that year and went on to beat the Yankees 4-0 and win the World Series."

In Perranoski's era, it was the norm that the pitcher who finished the game would pitch multiple innings, but it was not the norm that the name *closer* was used. "I considered myself a closer.

Absolutely!" said Perranoski. "The only difference was that I pitched more innings back then. Today, if a closer comes into seventy games a year, they usually average seventy innings. In my day, if I was coming in to seventy games, we were pitching 130 to 140 innings a year. It was a very different approach back then."

Blown saves were handled differently as well, mainly due to the innings pitched. "If you are only pitching one inning and you blow the save, it is really going to affect you," explained Perranoski. "But, if you are pitching two or three innings in nine straight games, you know in your mind that you're still busting your ass out there and it just happens. The person I felt bad for was the closer if it wasn't me, because I knew he just busted his ass, too. I never worried about myself.

"If things do go bad, they can affect you mentally," he added. "I remember I had this pretty bad stretch of losing ballgames, and yet I thought I was pitching pretty well. It was a soft line drive here and a ground ball up the middle and those were the hits that lost me the game. And then, I thought I threw this really bad pitch and I thought I was going to lose another game in Chicago, and I somehow got Billy Williams to pop it up to end the game. I then went on to save the rest of my ballgames that year. It's a funny thing, this game."

Perranoski concurs that the closer's role is more of a mental strain. "Physically, I never really had any problems until later in my career. I pitched thirteen seasons and I basically had no problems. I was pretty durable. Yet the mental approach to the game was probably the most important part for me."

Sometimes a little laughter helps ease the mental strain. "I always loved the challenge of the game," shared Perranoski. "Once I got the ball I was very serious, but before the game I'd sit in the bullpen and do a crossword puzzle or two and we'd fool around. If it was a tight ballgame, I would prepare myself to pitch.

"I remember I used to room with John Kennedy, a third baseman we got [from the Washington Senators] in 1965. One day in May, I came home from a game and he was already there and he was looking pretty dejected. I saw that the phone and the shower curtain were both pulled out of the wall. I said, 'What's the matter with you, John?' He said, 'I got this letter from the scout that signed me.'

"I then read the letter and it said basically that he was proud of him and that he was doing a heck of a job. But it also said that late in games, when the game is on the line, that he should go in and talk with the pitcher. I said, 'John, forget about it! You're doing a great job. Leave the pitching to me.' That was in May, as I said . . . later in September I had this tough game going with one out and the bases loaded and here comes John in from third base. I said to him, 'John, I read that letter in May and said that I would handle the pitching and you handle third base. Now get back to third.' He said, 'How the heck did you remember that letter?' The next thing you know I got the next batter to ground the ball to third and we turned the double play to end the game. Sometimes a little sense of humor can help!"

DAN QUISENBERRY
1979–1990

Dan Quisenberry pitched for twelve years in the major leagues, and although he pitched for the St. Louis Cardinals and San Francisco Giants at the end of his career, he was primarily known as a Kansas City Royal.

Quisenberry, or Quiz, as he was called, was born on February 7, 1953, in Santa Monica, California. He received very little interest from pro scouts in high school, so he went on to Orange Coast College for two years (1971–73), where he threw a school record 254²/₃ innings. Following OCC, he attended the University of La Verne and was finally signed by the Royals as an amateur free agent on June 7, 1975.

By his own admission, Quisenberry thought of himself as a marginal player at best, so just being signed by a big league team was an accomplishment. Scouts didn't think he had "the stuff" to be a dominating pitcher in the majors, so he went straight to the bullpen. After four years in the minor leagues, the "marginal player" made his major league debut on July 8, 1979, against the Chicago White Sox, pitching the final two and two-thirds innings, allowing just two hits in the Royals' 4-2 loss.

Quisenberry pitched in thirty-two games for the Royals his first year, but everything turned around the following spring training when manager Jim Frey suggested that he throw sidearmed, or submarine style, like Kent Tekulve. Once he changed his style, his career took off.

The beloved closer for the Kansas City Royals led the American League in saves in 1980 and from 1982 to 1985. He enjoyed a then-record forty-five-save season in 1983; he led the AL in games in 1980, '83, and '85; and he led the AL in games finished in 1980, '82, '83, and '85. He was a three-time all-star (1982–84) and pitched in four postseasons, including 1980, when the Royals lost the World Series to the Phillies, and 1985, when Kansas City won the World Series over the Cardinals. Of his 244 career saves, all but six came with the Royals.

Quisenberry was inducted into the Royals Hall of Fame in 1998.

The prior December, just a few months before his induction, Quisenberry had been diagnosed with a very aggressive cancerous brain tumor. On September 30, 1998, he passed away.

John Wathan was a catcher for the Royals from 1976 to 1985. Following his retirement he was named manager the Omaha Royals, Kansas City's triple-A affiliate. On August 28, 1987, he was promoted to manage the big league team (which he did until early in the 1991 season).

"I had the unique pleasure of playing with and managing Dan Quisenberry for about ten years," said Wathan. "Dan was a good friend as soon as he came to the team in 1979. As a catcher, what surprised me the most was the fact that Dan never really threw the ball more than 84 mph, and then he had this unusual way of throwing the ball with this quirky delivery. You would think to yourself, 'How is this guy ever going to get out a major league hitter?'"

Wathan said with a laugh. "But then after you saw him pitch, you quickly said to yourself, 'Wow! Was I wrong.' Especially after you watched all of that movement on the ball, and how it sank and then to watch how deceptive he was with the delivery, you realized that this guy was going to be a great major league pitcher. And who would have ever imagined that this guy was going to be a part of Royals history, the way he was?"

Wathan went on, "He was always good with those one or two liners. I remember him saying after one game he gave up a home run to Reggie Jackson, 'That ball is still burning its way to St. Louis.' Then he said, 'I think I have a delivery in my flaw today.' Dan was also such a great team player. He cared about every guy out there. And needless to say, he was a great leader. I remember we went out to dinner, us and our wives, one day shortly before he passed away. I said to him, 'Did you ever wonder why this happened to you?' And then he said back to me, 'Why not . . . why shouldn't it be me?' He accepted his fate better than anyone I ever met. He was remarkable."

Steve Farr is a right-handed pitcher who signed with Kansas City in 1985, after just one year in the majors. He joined the Royals as Quisenberry's career was winding down and became the new Royals' closer when Quisenberry moved on.

"I learned a lot from Dan Quisenberry and several of the guys on the Royals pitching staff," said Farr. "I really admired how they got hitters out, especially Dan. I thought he was a great guy. He was never flashy. He was just a down-to-earth kind of guy. I kind of molded my own pitching style and my own approach to the game to resemble Dan Quisenberry. It was amazing how many ground balls he got. Dan was like clockwork and I don't ever remember anyone ever hitting a ball into the outfield on him."

Farr continued, "Dan Quisenberry was such a professional and he was always willing to share his knowledge with the younger players. I remember him coming up to me one time when we were in New York and saying to me, 'Hey, what are you doing today?' I said, 'I don't know.' So he said, 'Then I am going to take you to a Broadway show!' And he did, and he also took me to my first German restaurant in Kansas City. But he was like that. And I was just a rookie, and he certainly didn't have to do all of that with just a rookie, but he did that to everyone."

"The fans just loved Dan," added Wathan. "I still remember how he used to hose down fans in the general admission seats in right field near the bullpen in Kansas City. The fans loved it and most of the time they were begging to get wet on those really hot days. I guess Dan took the 'fireman' description for the closer literally."

Like every pitcher, Quisenberry had his own routine before entering a ballgame . . . although his was a little unusual. "For the first few innings of every game we would be down in the bullpen and we would get a copy of that day's Kansas City paper and do the jumbo crossword puzzle," Wathan explained with a laugh. "Dan was not like the rest of the closers. He was always down in the bullpen at the start of every game. Dan was there the whole game. Once the fifth inning would come around he would then start getting ready. He first would visit the bathroom and do his business. And then he would finish and be ready to go in and close out the game. From that point on, he was completely focused on the game."

Wathan explained the importance of Quisenberry to his team. "When Dan came in we used to say, 'Lights out!' There is an old saying, 'Does confidence breed success or does success breed confidence?' Once Dan became our closer we pretty much knew as a team that this game was over. We knew he was going to lock it down, especially during that 1980 season. He was awesome. Whitey Herzog and the rest of the team had such tremendous confidence in him. It was unbelievable. He wasn't that traditional closer that was known for the big strikeout, but rather he knew he was going to get you with a ground ball or a double-play grounder.

"Dan was always a two- or three-innings save guy," said Wathan. "He was a workhorse for us. Think about some of those games he was involved in, especially given all of those intense rivalries against the Yankees. That is why it is so tough to compare the Dan Quisenberrys and Goose Gossages to the closers of today, who are just one-inning guys."

Quisenberry's greatest moment on the mound most likely came in 1980, during the American League Championship Series against the New York Yankees. "Probably, it was striking out Willie Randolph to end the game and win the 1980 playoffs against the Yankees," said Wathan. "That was such a great victory for the organization, considering we lost to the Yankees in the playoffs in 1976, 1977, and 1978. Beating the Yankees that year was like winning the World Series for us. And I'm not looking to make any excuses, but that is why many of us believe we had a little letdown in the World Series against the Phillies. Being able to get past the big, bad Yankees was the ultimate.

"I remember I was playing right field when Dan got that last out and I started to run into the infield to celebrate. It was the only time in my career that I had tears in my eyes and rolling down my cheek. It was so emotional for us to beat the Yankees that year, and I know it was pretty special for Dan!"

KENT TEKULVE
1974–1989

Kent Tekulve was a sidearmed, right-handed pitcher who played in the major leagues for sixteen years for the Pittsburgh Pirates (1974–85), Philadelphia Phillies (1985–88), and Cincinnati Reds (1989). He pitched during the transitional era of the closer, before it became the norm to have a closer pitch just the final inning.

Tekulve was born on March 5, 1947, in Cincinnati, Ohio. "I was a big Reds fan growing up, but I did like watching Don Drysdale because he, too, was a sidearmer like I was at an early age," said the lanky reliever. "Later on, I actually got to know him when he spent a few years helping with the Expos. And that is when I really liked him."

Tekulve went to Catholic High School, where he made the baseball team his freshman year, but was cut his sophomore season. He worked hard and made the varsity team in his junior and senior years. After high school, he went on to Marietta College, where he played baseball from 1966–69. He recorded the fifth lowest ERA (0.94) in the school's history during his senior year and was selected to the All-Ohio Athletic Conference Second Team.

Although Tekulve was not selected in the major league draft, he was invited to a tryout camp at Forbes Field, home of the Pittsburgh Pirates, on July 16, 1969, and was signed by the Pirates on the spot. Two days later, he began his professional career for the Geneva Pirates. The following season, he was moved into a relief role and he never looked back.

In 1972, he began experimenting with what would be his trademark submarine delivery. He mimicked Ted Abernathy, whom he had watched in Cincinnati when he was growing up. By 1973, he had mastered the delivery and ended up leading the Eastern League with twelve wins.

Tekulve made his major league debut on May 20, 1974, when he pitched the final inning in the Pirates' 4-2 loss in Montreal.

The 1977 season was the most impactful on Tekulve's career, when the Pirates hired a new manager, Chuck Tanner. Looking back, Tekulve recalled, "Chuck Tanner really knew me better than anyone. He was also the only guy I could ever think of that would have given me the chance to pitch as much as I did. No other manager would let someone six foot four and 155 pounds pitch ninety games in a year. No one else would have done that. But Tanner was actually the manager I needed to have to be effective and could do as much as I could for my team and for myself. Chuck was great at thinking out of the box!

"I really had great rapport with Chuck Tanner," he went on, "and therefore I pretty much knew when I was going to pitch. Especially if I went a long period of time without pitching, like two or three days, he found a way to get me in the game to get some work. There was also two streaks in my career that I can remember, I pitched one time nine days in a row and during that same streak I pitched nineteen out of twenty days."

It was also 1977 when the Chicago White Sox traded Goose Gossage to the Pirates to be the new closer. Tekulve spent the season setting him up. "In 1977, I was pitching for Pittsburgh and the record for a right-handed pitcher for appearances was seventy-one games and we were entering the final game of the year," Tekulve recalled. "Both Goose and I were tied for seventy-one games leading into that final game. I ended up pitching the eighth inning and Goose pitched the ninth inning. The game finished and we went into the clubhouse and we both finished the year with seventy-two games. Goose came up to me and said, 'Wow! We both set the new Pirates' record for appearances.' I looked at him and said, 'Goose you gotta remember one thing . . . I pitched the eighth inning and you pitched the ninth inning. I set the record and you tied *my* record!' It was one of the few times anyone would one-up Goose.

"I loved playing with Goose, even though our personalities were so different," he continued, "but they were the things that go on in a professional clubhouse. I also remember those guys back then used to rib me all of the time, but again that is what it was all about being in a professional locker room. You learned to survive. Yet those same guys that would rib me would always show the greatest respect to me when it was my time to get out there on the mound. And keeping their respect was a great motivator for me, and I always wanted to do my best for them and the team."

Tekulve, who was not a great runner, actually played left field for one out in 1979. "I remember Chuck Tanner coming out to the mound one day and saying, 'I'm putting you in left field!' And then I said, 'Are you nuts?' Tanner replied, 'No, I am putting you in left field for this next batter, Darrell Evans, and then this way I can put you back on the mound for the next batters. This way, I don't have to take you out.' I thought he was crazy."

The gregarious pitcher continued, "I also remember Chuck Tanner coming out a few times and saying, 'You're pitching pretty well and . . .' this and that. And then he'd talk to me about the situation and what to expect. Like 'You've got Luzinski and Schmidt coming up, and I think we should do this.' I'd then say to Chuck, 'Just have someone fill up my beer mug and have it waiting on my chair in the clubhouse.' I used to have this thirty-two-ounce beer stein in my locker, and sure enough the cold beer would be waiting for me. I said it that way to Chuck because I didn't want him to worry about me or the situation. Most of the time it would work out and sometimes the beer would be warm. I remember Tanner would always reply back to me, 'What am I going to do with you?'"

Tekulve explained how different the role of the closer was in his era. "Over the years the role of the closer has evolved. The closer in our day still worked two or three innings. Therefore my job as a closer started in the seventh inning," he said. "So, I knew I'd see action if we were up three runs or down two runs. I wasn't in games only when we were ahead. My job as the closer was sometimes to stop the bleeding or keep it close for our team so we could come back, and we did come back quite a bit given the tremendous talent we had on that team during those years. I remember I was 10–1 in 1977. I still don't remember how I ever lost that one game!

"Yet, the more I worked the better I got. If I went more than two days I knew I didn't have my best stuff. Eventually, I became the closer after Goose moved on. Prior to that I would pitch the eighth and Goose would pitch the ninth inning."

Tekulve played in the National League Championship Series in 1975. The Pirates lost to the Reds in that series, but they were not to be denied in 1979, as the Pirates became world champions that year, with the theme song of "We Are Family." The Rubber Band Man, as Tekulve was being called as he entered the game, was on the mound for the final out of that series, the greatest moment of his career. "By then I had learned so much that it prepared me for that moment," Tekulve shared.

The 1980 all-star never led the league in saves, although he finished second twice (in 1978 and 1979, with thirty-one saves each year). Tekulve did lead the NL in games played four times (1978–79, 1982, and 1987) and games finished three times (1978–79 and 1983). His ninety games in 1987 with the Phillies still stands as a club record.

"What separates us closers is really what connects us," Tekulve philosophizes. "We all have different personalities and there is no mold for us, but what connects us is that we can all pitch that ninth inning and we can get it done. It is that bond that connects us all. Yet every pitcher who might have tremendous talent may not be able to pitch that ninth inning."

It is likely the ability to handle the mental strains of the game that makes the successful closer. "The physical part of the game was never a problem for me. I could physically throw a lot of innings. At least for me, the mental part was more prominent to me. As time went by I learned so much about what my body was capable of doing."

For example, "My arm was always tired, but that is how I wanted it to be. One of the biggest lessons I learned in this game was knowing the difference between a stiff arm and a sore arm," Tekulve explained. "So, if your arm is stiff, then you don't want to pitch, otherwise if you continue it could lead to a damaged arm, and at that point I knew I needed to give it a break. If it was sore, then I learned what to do to get through it and pitch."

Tekulve was proud to pitch for the Pirates, a team with a rich history. He once mentioned that some cities have had a greater history when it came to the closer role. He explained, "In a city like Pittsburgh, it seemed like it had a higher bar when it came to the closer role, primarily because it had such a tremendous history when it came to the role. For example, before I got there we had Elroy Face and Dave Giusti. Since the late 1950s, when Elroy started the role in the city of Pittsburgh, the Pirates had a great tradition in the role of the closer."

When Tekulve ended his career in 1989, he had compiled 184 career saves, but his 1,050 games pitched were second only to Hoyt Wilhelm's 1,070. He currently ranks ninth on the all-time list, but of the top ten pitchers on the list, he pitched the fewest years (sixteen). Tekulve also held the record for more appearances strictly in relief. At the time of his retirement he said, "After all those years of being in the middle of things, I wasn't enjoying being on the fringe."

HOYT WILHELM
1952–1972

Knuckleballer James Hoyt Wilhelm was born in Huntersville, North Carolina, on July 26, 1922, and passed away on August 23, 2002. He began his career at Mooresville of the Class D North Carolina State League in 1942, served his country with the US Army in World War II for three years, then returned to Mooresville from 1946 to 1947. Old Sarge, as he was nicknamed because of his service, was purchased by the Boston Braves following the 1947 season and shortly thereafter was drafted by the New York Giants in the 1947 minor league draft.

Wilhelm made his major league debut with the Giants on April 18, 1952, and pitched the entire season in relief. It was the beginning of a twenty-year career with the Giants, Cardinals, Indians, Orioles, White Sox, Angels, Braves, Cubs, and Dodgers. Although he pitched in relief for the majority of his career, he did make a few starts with the Indians and Orioles. With the Orioles, he threw his only career no-hitter, on September 20, 1958, versus the

Yankees, winning 1-0, walking two and striking out eight.

In his storied career, he was also a World Series Champion in 1954 with the Giants and an eight-time all-star. He was one of the oldest players to appear in a game, pitching his final game on July 10, 1972; just sixteen days shy of his fiftieth birthday. The right-hander was the first pitcher in major league history to earn two hundred saves and to appear in one thousand games. In 1985, he became the first player to have pitched mainly in relief to be elected into the Hall of Fame.

Wilhelm recalled his early years in his Hall of Fame induction speech on July 28, 1985, "When you consider all the players over the years and years that have played the game of baseball and then you think of the number that has been elected here, and then it really makes you start thinking. And I guess I think back to a time, my first year in the class B league, which at that time was the bottom of the rung of baseball. And I did get released from a class B club, but I didn't give up. I still thought I could play, and I did get back in the game, and then to think, after being released off a class B club, I wound up pitching a little over twenty years in the big leagues and being elected to the Hall of Fame. That is unreal and it's pretty hard for me to contemplate."

In his speech, Wilhelm also thanked two baseball people in particular—his first manager, Leo Durocher, and Paul Richards, his pitching coach with the Orioles and Braves. "I'd like to give a little bit of special thanks to Leo Durocher; he was my first manager and gave me the chance. After many years in the minor leagues, it didn't look like I would ever get to the big leagues, but finally did, and Leo gave me the chance to see and prove that if I could pitch in the big leagues and I thank him to this day.

"Paul Richards was a man that I consider to this day to be one of the greatest pitching coaches that I have ever run into—even though he was a catcher, and maybe that's where he learned it. But he had a knack of taking older pitchers—and he did it with several of them that were kind of over the hill or losing their stuff—and rehabilitate them and get them to go on, and he got several good years out of them after that. And in my case, after I went to Baltimore in early September [1958], the results were almost instant, because after a couple of weeks, that's when I pitched a no-hitter and I give Paul Richards a lot of credit for turning my career around right there. It could have been the end of the road the way I was pitching in Cleveland, but I wound up there and pitched about five years in Baltimore, went on to Chicago and had a few good years there."

Wilhelm hooked up with Richards again when he was traded to the Atlanta Braves in September 1969, and helped the Braves to their first National League West division title, and again extended his career for a few more years.

Art Kusnyer was a catcher in the 1970s for the Chicago White Sox, California Angels, Milwaukee Brewers, and Kansas City Royals. Following his playing career, the six-foot-two Ohio native spent twenty-seven years as the bullpen coach for the White Sox and A's. Born on December 19, 1945, he is one of a very few guys who can say he caught Hall of Famer Hoyt Wilhelm.

"I remember I was just a kid who was just called up and he (Wilhelm) was nearing the end of his career, but I got to catch him," Kusnyer said. "I remember when I caught him I never had seen a knuckleball before. I went through high school and then through college and no one threw a knuckleball. When you caught a pitcher back then you never wore any equipment. But I remember someone saying to me before I caught Wilhelm, 'If you are going to catch a knuckleballer, you better wear some equipment . . . like a mask, kid!' I'm thinking to myself, 'Why do I need a mask? I never wore a mask before.' But I found out quickly why they said what they did. Wilhelm threw that first pitch and I said to myself, 'Geez!' That ball was going there and here and everywhere!"

He continued, "I remember the first time I caught him in a game, it was spring training and I had four passed balls and I was even wearing one of those oversized gloves at the time. I would try and catch the ball this way and then the ball would go the other way. They would often say Wilhelm had this ability to throw the knuckleball for a strike on the right side of the plate and then on the left side of the plate. I remember catching Hoyt one day and his knuckleball never did the same thing twice. I remember he would throw that pitch and it would float and then all of a sudden it would just drop," said Kusnyer.

"Hoyt was like the rest of the closers back then; they were such great competitors and when they came into the game there was never any doubt what they were going to do out there on the mound," Kusnyer continued. "They would always throw their best pitch and challenge the opposition and batter, daring them to hit it. Their control was always so good. For example, the five years I played alongside Dennis Eckersley, I don't ever remember the guy giving up a walk. Because when he did walk a guy the papers would usually say the next day, 'Flash! Dennis Eckersley walked a guy!'

"Hoyt was a great competitor and he was always ready to pitch. It never mattered what the situation was—whether the team was up by three runs or down by four. It didn't matter to those guys back then. Those guys were the real professionals. You have a lot of professionals out there and then you have those like Hoyt that stood above the rest and everybody else. There is an old saying, 'When you shake that baseball tree you start seeing all of the gloves falling out of it, but when the reliever or bat falls from the tree then you grab it!'"

Wilhelm retired following the 1972 season. It took until 1985 for him to be inducted into the Hall of Fame, mainly because relievers weren't as respected as starters, nor were knuckleballers. It would take seven more years for another reliever to join the Hall, when Rollie Fingers entered in 1992, and another twelve years after that for Dennis Eckersley (2004) to join the ranks. Bruce Sutter entered the Hall in 2006, but Gossage waited even longer, entering the Hall in 2008.

"Every closer has a certain mentality," concluded Kusnyer. "I've caught them all at one point; Eckersley, Goose, and Hoyt

Wilhelm. You can immediately see it in these guys that they were made for the closer role, because some guys can't pitch in that situation no matter how good they are. When you get to that ninth inning it really does take a certain personality and mentality. Those that are in that role really want to be the one with the ball and in that situation. I hear it from so many in this role how their teammates busted their ass for eight innings and it was up to them to close it out. They take it very seriously. But, that is how the greats were, including Wilhelm. They were so competitive and they wanted to be out there to get the job done. Those old timers went into a game with the mentality of not looking to trick anybody, but rather they would say, 'I'm gonna throw you my best stuff and here it is . . . and if you get the best of me, then my hat's off to you.'"

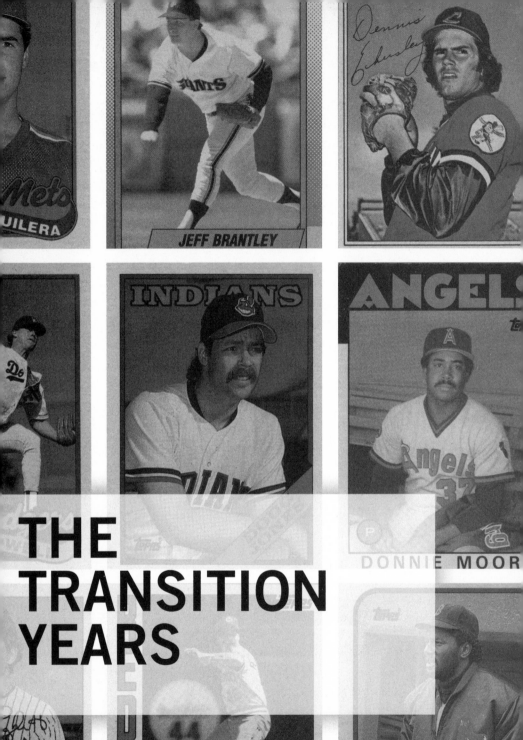

THE
TRANSITION
YEARS

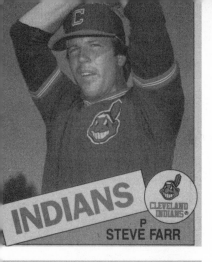

INDIANS
P
STEVE FARR

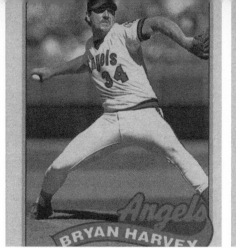

Angels
BRYAN HARVEY

RIC

Topps

JESSE
OROSCO
PITCHER
METS

Topps
DAN
PLESAC

Topps
JA

CUBS PITCHER
BRUCE SUTTER

CHICAGO
42

Topps
WhiteSox
BOBBY THIG

RICK AGUILERA
1985–2000

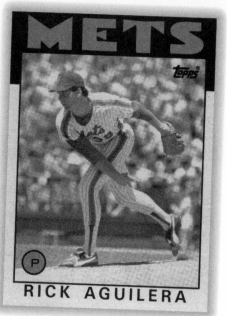

RICK AGUILERA

ick Aguilera had a very good career, playing sixteen years in the majors with the New York Mets, Minnesota Twins, Boston Red Sox, and Chicago Cubs. He was fortunate enough to accomplish things that many players, who have had even longer careers, never accomplished. The three-time all-star was a two-time world champion—in 1986 with the Mets and in 1991 with the Twins.

The right-hander was selected by the Mets in the third round of the June draft in 1983 out of Brigham Young University. (He was also selected by the St. Louis Cardinals in the thirty-seventh round in 1980, his senior year of high school, but he opted for college.) Aguilera began his pro career at Little Rock of the New York Penn League—as a starter.

Aguilera, a California native, started throughout his minor league career. He made his major league debut two years after being drafted, on June 12, 1985. He was the winning pitcher in relief, a 7-3 win in Philadelphia, pitching two innings with one walk and two strikeouts. But he quickly moved into a starting role, making nineteen starts for the season

Aguilera spent most of his first three major league seasons as a starter, although in the postseason he pitched in relief. In 1987, he was plagued by injuries, but still managed to post an 11-3 record in seventeen starts. In 1988, he moved into the bullpen and was still plagued by injuries. He pitched exclusively out of the bullpen for the Mets in 1989, until he was traded to the Twins on July 31, at which time he moved back into the starter's role, going 3-1 in eleven starts.

In January 1990, Twins' closer Jeff Reardon left the team via free agency. Twins manager Tom Kelly called Aguilera and told him the closing role was his.

"I think I would have not had the success I did in this game if I was never told by Tom Kelly that I was going to be the team's closer," said Aguilera. "Tom Kelly stuck with me through thick and thin. I learned a lot from him, and not just about pitching, but about being a ballplayer, and respecting the game and what that meant, and that the game will be here a lot longer than you and I will be playing it, and that is what I mean by respecting the game."

Aguilera believes the closer's role is tougher mentally than physically. "I remember over my career, people often asked me, 'What were you thinking about when you were on the mound during the World Series?' I remember I was always so impatient, and then there was a lot of stress just waiting for the call to come down to the bullpen," he recalled. "When the phone would ring and I got to the mound, all of the nervousness and the anxiety usually went away, because I was able to do something I worked for my entire career—being a pitcher and preparing to get the hitters out. So as a closer you have to stay focused, and if you find yourself thinking about other things, then you are probably not completely prepared to pitch.

"I give a lot of the credit for my success to Tom Kelly, my

manager with the Twins," said Aguilera. "I doubted myself at first, questioning if I had the mental ability to do the role. But even when I struggled, he would continue to give the ball back to me and he stuck with me, and then my team started to have the confidence in me that I did have the ability to get the job done. That meant so much to me! So, as time went by and the phone continued to ring, I was able to build up the confidence I needed that I could do the job."

Aguilera pitched with the Twins for eleven seasons, during which time he compiled a 3.50 ERA and 254 saves in 490 games, thirty of which were starts.

Despite injuries, Aguilera was always prepared to pitch as a closer. "I was always aware of the situation, and again, it was Tom Kelly who encouraged me to come up with some type of routine," he explained. "I remember though, the first few times I was in the role when our team went up by one or two runs in the first, I would be a basket case, thinking that it will be two or three hours from now that I will be able to pitch. That is why it was so important for me to have the routine. It eventually went away, but initially it took a while for me to calm down and not be so anxious."

The worst moment Aguilera had in his baseball career was in game six of the 1986 World Series. The Mets were down three games to two in the series. Aguilera came in to pitch the tenth inning with the score tied and allowed two runs. The Mets were down to their final out in the bottom of the inning when they staged a remarkable comeback to win the game, and ended up winning the series in seven games.

"It was very tough for all of us until—I hate to bring it up— the ball went through Bill Buckner's legs. That was a tough moment because for that brief moment our dreams of winning a World Series seemed to be over and we thought we were going to lose. But that is baseball; it's filled with so many highs and lows."

Another significant low in his career came in 1995. The Twins traded Aguilera to the Red Sox as a cost-cutting move. The trade was made on July 6 and the Red Sox were in town, so he packed his bag and walked over to his new clubhouse. "That was the toughest day of my career, maybe the toughest day of my life," Aguilera said. "To walk twenty feet down the corridor and pretend that I was happy about it — to try and put the smile on my face — well, I wasn't very convincing, I'm sure."

The Red Sox called on him that very night to pin down a victory, although Aguilera admitted he could have used a little time to compose himself. When his name was announced over the PA as he entered the entered the game, the Metrodome crowd showered him with adulation.

Somehow, he gathered himself and earned the save, striking out Kirby Puckett. "It was very emotional," Aguilera said. "Other than the birth of my children, that was the most emotional day."

Not surprisingly, his two World Series appearances are the high points of his career and in his memory banks. "On the mound, I would say 1986 was a great experience for me, but I didn't contribute as much as I did in the 1991 World Series for the Twins. So if I were to take a moment in my career and call it the greatest, it would have to be the 1991 (Worst to First) World Series Championship."

JEFF BRANTLEY
1988–2001

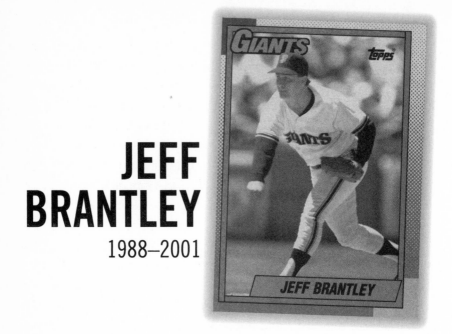

J eff Brantley pitched in the major leagues for fourteen years, from 1988 to 2001. In that time, the gregarious reliever compiled 172 saves in 615 games with five major league teams—the San Francisco Giants (1988–93), Cincinnati Reds (1994–97), St. Louis Cardinals (1998), Philadelphia Phillies (1999–2000), and Texas Rangers (2001).

Brantley went to Mississippi State University after graduating from W. A. Berry High School in Alabama. A starter for the Bulldogs, he went to the College World Series in 1985, the same year he was selected as an All-American, and he still shares the SEC record with forty-five wins over his four-year career (1982–85).

The five-foot-eleven right-hander was selected by the Giants in the sixth round of the June draft in 1995, and continued as a starter when he began his pro career at Fresno. He didn't really begin relieving until he made it to the majors. He made his major league debut on August 5, 1988, pitching two innings in relief.

"If you were a pitcher in the past, then you wanted to be a starter," admitted Brantley. "No one wanted to be the closer, and you certainly don't get a boatload of reporters wanting to talk to you as the closer after a game *unless* you blow that save."

Brantley had his most success as a closer with the Reds. He went 11-11 with eighty-eight saves and a 2.64 ERA in 185 games in his four years with them, including a stellar 1996 season in which he earned a National League leading forty-four saves with a 2.41 ERA in sixty-six games.

"My preparation was probably a little different from some of the other closers during my day," Brantley admitted. "I was never a flamethrower or that one-pitch specialty guy, like Mariano [Rivera] or Trevor [Hoffman]. I was just a pitcher and that is how I approached the role. There is nothing wrong with being a pitcher, but because I was just a pitcher, I had to know a lot more about the game of baseball and who I might be facing when the game got closer. I was a student of the game because of my knowledge of the hitters. I would sit with the hitting coach for the duration of the game until about the seventh inning, and that is when I'd make my way down to the bullpen.

"I didn't want to sit near the pitching coach, but rather I wanted to sit near the hitting coach because I wanted to know exactly what he was telling our own hitters what to look for in the opposing team's pitcher. That is how I learned the majority of the ins and outs of this game. I was a student of watching the hitters and paid attention to them because they were the guys I would eventually face. For example, when I was in San Francisco, we had Dusty Baker as our hitting coach; I talked with Dusty as much as anyone. When I was in Cincinnati, we had Ray Knight and when I was in Texas, we had Hal McRae. I had some of the best in the business in that role to learn from. They were all a tremendous source of information for me, and trying to figure out what was going through a hitter's mind and the given situation and all of the elements that go into this game. I was a pitcher and I wasn't a thrower. Outfielders throw, but pitchers pitch, and you have to understand that if you want to be successful."

Brantley is currently a broadcaster for the Reds and he sees some young, talented pitchers in his travels. "I love watching Craig Kimbrel pitch and his animal instincts and how he approaches each game." He added, "I have also been very fortunate to play and watch some of the best closers that have ever been in the role of the closer. I played and watched closers like Dennis Eckersley, Goose Gossage, Lee Smith, Mark Davis, Dan Quisenberry, Steve Bedrosian, and Dave Righetti. I learned so much from these guys and they all helped me to do my job better. These guys were so good and did their job so well because they played their hearts out for this game and had so much guts along the way."

Brantley had a lot of confidence in his abilities—something necessary to succeed as a closer. He shared a great example of that confidence in a story that occurred in his lone season with the Cardinals. "I remember we had this one run game against the Cubs back in 1998. I was playing for the St. Louis Cardinals at the time, and Tony La Russa was the manager. Tony never liked the catcher standing up to receive four balls in the form of an intentional walk. He didn't like it. He didn't like seeing the catcher because he believed that it helped pump up the other team or even the guy in the on-deck circle. He would tell the catcher to set up six inches off of the plate and then instruct the pitcher to throw four fastballs off the plate. So, it was really an unintentional intentional walk. That way, too, the game was out of his hands and so was the blame, and it rested all on the back of the pitcher.

"In my mind," Brantley continued, "if you wanted to walk a guy, just have the catcher stand up and walk the guy! So, I came into the game with two outs and no one on with Mark Grace due up. I knew Mark could hit the ball off of me, but he wasn't going to hit the ball out of the ball park on me. On deck was Sammy Sosa, and I had a lot of success with him. I think he was one for twenty-five off of me. I could tell him exactly what I was going to pitch to him, and he still couldn't hit off me and he knew it! But the all-knowing Tony did not know this. So, eventually, Grace worked a 3-2 count on me and then he checked his swing on the next pitch. The appeal went down to third and still no swing and off to first he went on a walk. So it's still 4-3, and we're up and there were still two outs. I'm also ready to face the guy who is chasing the all-time home run record in a year with Mark McGwire.

"Then all of a sudden, here comes Tony out for a visit to the mound. He turns to the catcher and says 'I want you to set up six inches off of the plate.' He then turns to me and says, 'Jeff, I want you to throw four fastballs off the plate and walk him.' I said, 'Tony, I'm not going to do that. This guy has no chance against me.' Tony then says, 'Do you know how many home runs Sammy Sosa has hit?' I replied, 'I know that, and I also know that the guy behind him, Glenallen Hill, that .200 batter, is hitting about .800 off of me for some reason. If you put Sammy on, then there is a good chance they are going to tie this game up.' He finally turned to me and said, 'Just do the right thing!' Tony then ran back into the dugout.

"So, after he left, I called the catcher back to the mound; the catcher at that time was Eli Marrero. I said to Eli, 'We're not going to do that.' He then said, 'Oh, no, you're going to get me released!' It was so comical. I then said to Eli, 'Just set up your mitt just off the plate and I'm going to throw the first two pitches at your catcher's mask. Then I am going to throw the third pitch up and off the plate and we are going to put this guy [Sammy Sosa] in the book.'

"He went back and I threw the first pitch on that outside corner and Sammy took it for a strike. I can now hear the turning over of trash cans and water coolers in the Cardinals dugout. Tony was livid. The second pitch was almost in the same location and Sammy fouled it back to the screen for strike two. I could then see all of hell breaking loose in the dugout with Tony. The next pitch Eli put the mitt up and then he came out of the crotch position, and

Sammy swung and missed. Game was over and everybody loved me. So here comes Tony. He said, 'Great job . . . great job. Way to go!' He then gave me this big old bear hug and I said, 'It ain't going to be like this from now on.' That is the essence of what I did as a closer. I knew what I had to do on any given day and I wasn't afraid to throw my pitches, despite my strengths and weaknesses."

Brantley laughingly added that things didn't really change with La Russa from that point. "He still didn't trust me at all. He probably did think, though, from that point on, that there was no need to talk with him on the mound, because he ain't gonna listen to me anyway!"

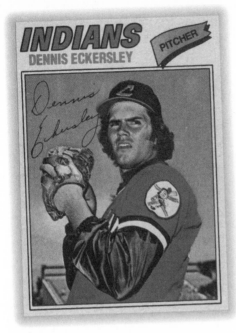

DENNIS ECKERSLEY
1975–1998

D
ennis Eckersley is unique in that he began his career as a very successful starter, but finished as an incredible closer.

The right-hander was born on October 3, 1954, in Oakland, California. A big prospect when he was selected by the Cleveland Indians out of high school in the third round of the 1972 draft, he made his major league debut less than three years later.

"My earliest memory of the game was trying to keep up with my brother," recalled Eckersley. "A two-year gap when you are little is huge when it comes to playing ball. That is what I remember and it helped push me that much harder to keep up. I think that had a lot to do with me getting and going professional and then eventually making it to the big leagues that much quicker, because I was always in that situation of having to keep up and be better."

He was a major leaguer who played for the Indians, Boston Red Sox, Chicago Cubs, Oakland A's, and St. Louis Cardinals in his twenty-four-year career. With a twenty-win season in 1978 with the Red Sox and a fifty-plus-save season in 1992 with the A's, he became the first (of just two; the other, John Smoltz) player to reach both plateaus in his career.

The six-time all-star was also the American League Rookie Pitcher of the Year in 1975, and the American League Cy Young Award winner *and* MVP in 1992. He compiled a record of 197-171 with 390 career saves. A superb control pitcher, Eckersley walked just 738 batters (91 intentionally) in 3,285^{2}/$_{3}$ innings over 1071 games. His career culminated with his induction into the Hall of Fame in 2004, his first year of eligibility.

In Eckersley's early days if you weren't a starter, you weren't a great pitcher. He was mainly a starter for eleven years (1975–86), twice making the all-star team; but moved into a relief role from 1987 until he retired following the 1998 season. As a reliever, he was selected to four more all-star teams and was named the American League Cy Young Award winner in 1992.

He found both roles challenging in different ways. "Obviously, throwing 100 to 125 pitches in a game is more physical than throwing fifteen or so pitches," said Eckersley, "so you would naturally say that the starter is more physical, but then the mental side is more adrenaline and I think that is what relieving is all about. It's all about the adrenaline rush and then being able to handle it. There is always adrenaline but sometimes it is more intense than other times, and that is when it is hard to slow down."

Eckersley believes the starter role is more about physical preparation. "You really have to be in good shape to throw 100 pitches or more in a game," he explained. "And there is always a physical program you have to stick with as a starter. It is so difficult for a starting pitcher to come out of their habits. Any change could throw them off their game. The same could be said about closers to a degree; for some relief pitchers it's all about superstitions, because in some cases you don't have to be in the greatest shape to be in that role. For a starter, you have to program yourself to do the same thing day after day, or do this after the day you pitch and then this the next day and so on. You don't want anything to disrupt that routine. For relief pitchers you follow a routine as well and when you don't follow it from day to day, then you never feel like you are ready to pitch—especially for those guys who have superstitions about their game. You never want to deviate from that routine, if you have a routine any day. But that is what baseball is all about, and don't be surprised how many guys are motivated by superstitions."

Regardless of the success or failures of regular routines, Eckersley staunchly believes the relieving role is totally mental. "The anticipation and buildup was incredible," he said. "But then you see different personalities on the mound and not one is the same. I was emotional, and then you see Mariano Rivera and he is like the Ice Man. He is very, very unemotional. He repeats his delivery the same every time and throws the same pitch. He never gets excited from pitch to pitch, regardless of the situation or the importance of the situation. I wish I had that. I don't know how he does it, remaining as calm as he does. I always had to let it go. I was so penned up all of the time. I needed to demonstrate my emotions, which were tough for me to control at times."

Eckersley admitted he was an alcoholic in the first half of his career. By facing the truth, he was able to recover and pitch in three World Series.

"I changed my own life before I went to the bullpen," admitted Eckersley. "The timing couldn't have been better. It was meant to be. It changed my life and it changed my career. I am convinced things do change for a reason. It's like life. Change comes around and you don't understand the meaning or importance of it at the time, but then things eventually fall into place. And sometimes all it means is being in a good place and I was in a good place when change came around for me, and to accept what was happening.

"When things changed for me in baseball I didn't go directly to the closer role, but rather I went to the bullpen. And for many

that is a demotion. But I accepted it and embraced it. I was sober
and ready for it both mentally and physically. If I didn't accept it, I
doubt that I would be in the Hall of Fame right now. I didn't know
it at the time. I was just happy to be where I was at that time. I don't
even think I would have been ready for the change that took place
any other time in my career except when it did happen. Sure, I
kicked at it a little when I first went to the bullpen because there is
always ego involved. I know I would have never accepted the role
if I was younger or just breaking in to the game in my twenties. But
I also knew I had to accept it, because physically I had nothing left.
And the combination of facing nothing but left-handed hitters was
driving me crazy."

Eckersley's move to the bullpen happened in 1987. On April
3 of that year, he was traded from the Cubs to the Oakland A's.
Oakland Manager Tony La Russa intended to use him in a limited
role in the bullpen, but when closer Jay Howell was injured, an
opportunity arose for the right-hander.

"Without a doubt, La Russa had the greatest impact on my
career," said Eckersley. "He understood the role of the closer before
anyone else; he knew how important the bullpen was to a club. No
one could have foreseen back then what it would evolve into one
day. But I do believe it is what it is because of La Russa. La Russa
had the vision, and I am glad I was a part of it and he certainly took
care of me.

"As soon as that phone rings when you are a relief pitcher,
the most important part is knowing that the call is for you,"
Eckersley shared. "You don't want to be surprised. And you can
never be surprised when you are the closer. Again, it's all about the
adrenaline. You can never get too used to it, but if you can channel
it, you can be better than you can be. I'll tell you what; it makes you
better than you are. Without the adrenaline I don't know how you
can pitch."

The six-foot-two pitcher once said he used fear as his
motivator. "I think a lot of people get the quote confused, thinking

that I am scared and it's not that at all," explained Eckersley. "The fear of failure was for me a major motivator. Knowing that every situation was all on me, and the more pressure I put on myself meant more adrenaline and I performed better like that. I probably would not have been able to do that when I was in my twenties or so because it may not have worked back then. When I was younger I threw so hard and I was confused and didn't know where I was going."

After a successful twenty-two years in the game, Eckersley had many interesting stories. "But sadly," he shared, "you don't always remember the good stuff because there is so much good stuff. After a while it all blends together. For example, you pitch about 85 percent efficiency when it comes to performances, and then what you are left with is remembering all of the failures and you are consistently reminded of them. And that is what you are left with. The failures are what got scorched in your brain and memory. That is the toughest part of the whole closing gig . . . is the failure. God knows that I've seen my share of failure. Today, I think to myself, 'I'm glad I don't have to do that anymore' because that is how much it stung when it came to remembering the failures."

He has a deep-rooted respect for the game, something ingrained in him since he was a child.

"But, I think what happens is when you get out of the game, especially when you've been in this game as long as I have, there is an even greater appreciation for things when they are gone," Eckersley analyzed. "When you are in the middle of it [the game] I don't think you ever realize it. You just don't, but then when it is taken away, I think it is then that you realize how much you really loved it."

STEVE FARR

1984–1994

INDIANS

P
STEVE FARR

CLEVELAND
INDIANS

N ot every closer in major league history is a household name. There are many pitchers who live life on the edge, but do so quietly. Steve Farr is one of those.

"I was a long reliever when I first got to the big leagues and then eventually I worked my way up to setup man and then I finally worked my way into the closer role," Farr explained. "I went to the closer role after Dan Quisenberry reached the final years of his career."

Farr was born in Maryland on December 12, 1956. He went to DeMatha Catholic High School and to American University in Washington, D.C. The right-hander was not drafted, but he did celebrate his twentieth birthday in style, as he was signed by the Pittsburgh Pirates as an amateur free agent on December 13, 1976.

The five-foot-ten pitcher spent over seven years in the minors, pitching primarily as a starter, before getting the call to the majors on May 16, 1984. During his time in the minor leagues, he was traded by Pittsburgh to the Cleveland Indians, on June 8, 1983. It was with the Indians that Farr made his major league debut, in a start against the Boston Red Sox, losing 5-2 to starter Dennis Eckersley while allowing four runs, two walks, and six strikeouts in his five and two-thirds innings.

Farr's rookie season was very inconsistent and ended with him posting a 3-11 record, with a 4.58 ERA. Following spring training, he was a late cut by the Indians, and he did not immediately find a job. Fortunately, Kansas City came through and signed him as a free agent on May 19, 1985.

"I got called up when I was with Cleveland my first year. I thought I pitched pretty well, but I guess they didn't think so, and they released me at the end of spring training after just five innings," said Farr. "But I guess it was meant to be, because Kansas City picked me up after the Indians released me. And what should have been a bad time in my career, actually turned out pretty well for me. By the end of that season I had a World Series ring."

After signing with Kansas City, he reported to triple-A Omaha and had an outstanding season as a starter, going 10-4 with a 2.02 ERA in seventeen games (sixteen starts). It was in Omaha that Farr met Jamie Quirk, a catcher who had a great influence on his career.

"It was Jamie who taught me how to get out left-handed batters," Farr explained. "He always gave me a target to hit, and I was finally able to get out left-handed batters. That allowed me to further my career, because I wasn't being lifted when a left-handed batter would come up. That was a big swing point in my career. Eventually, both me and Jamie went up to the majors. And it was Jamie who told the Royals catcher at the time, Jim Sundberg, how to catch me, and it just kept working."

When Farr returned to the major leagues in August of that year, it was not as a starter, but in relief. "Dick Howser, the Royals manager, really impressed me," recalled Farr. "I remember when I first got called up he came up to me that day and said, 'You're going to pitch today and then you are going to get two days off.

And today you're coming in during the fifth inning and face the fourth, fifth, and sixth hitters.' I'm thinking, 'How the hell does he know all this?' Sure enough, that was actually when he put me in the game, and it was exactly the scenario. That was how Howser was; he was funny like that, but it seemed to work. I guess he liked to take the guess work out of the situation. I also remember him saying to me once during a visit to the mound, 'I want you to throw nothing but curveballs until you walk someone or strike them all out and then I'll take you out.' Howser then turned to the catcher and said, 'You got it?' He replied, 'Yeah, I got it!' And sure enough, I threw the curveballs and got the strikeouts.

"In 1985, I remember getting the first playoff win for the Royals against Toronto [game three in Kansas City]," said Farr. "That was my favorite and most memorable game. [Bret] Saberhagen started the game and then I went in during the fifth inning when he got in trouble. We then were able to come back and win the game and I was the pitcher of record. I remember thinking the whole time I was in that the Blue Jays were probably thinking when I came in, 'Who is this guy? Where did they get this rookie?' Even after I came into the dugout after retiring the Blue Jays in the eighth inning I was waiting for high fives from the rest of my team because Dan Quisenberry was coming in. He had forty-plus saves that year and I couldn't imagine him not coming in the ninth during a one-run game. But, Howser never took me out. I stayed in during the ninth inning and got the final three outs. I was amazed Quisenberry didn't come in, because if we lost that game we would have been in trouble. Maybe Howser was thinking, 'He's a rookie; he doesn't know any better. So I'm going to leave him in.' Whatever he was thinking it did work!"

By the end of 1986, he was sharing the closing job with Quisenberry. He continued with random relief roles in 1987. In 1988, his versatility was the reason he made the opening day roster. By late June, Quisenberry and Gene Garber had lost the closer roles and Manager John Wathan gave Farr the chance to close. He did well, compiling twenty saves, despite starting the role halfway through the season, and a 2.50 ERA in sixty-two games.

In 1989, the Royals again settled on Farr to close games, but by July and eighteen saves later, he had lost the job to a young pitcher, Jeff Montgomery. In 1990, the jack-of-all-trades Farr earned just one save, but also made six starts. In November 1990, as a free agent, he signed a three-year deal with the New York Yankees.

With the Yankees, Farr earned twenty-three, a career-best thirty, and twenty-five saves, respectively, in 1991, 1992, and 1993. Farr finished his career when the labor strike hit in 1994, after starting the year with Cleveland and then being traded to Boston.

"I was both mentally and physically done when I ended my career," stated Farr. "I had enough. You have to remember I spent eight years in the minors, so that had a lot to do with it, too. I absolutely exceeded my expectations as to what I had ever imagined I would do in this game. I wasn't someone who ever threw 100 mph, but I had good control and I became a pretty crafty pitcher over the years."

Farr earned 132 career saves in his eleven-year career. He believes the closer role was nearing the end of its transition into the closer role of today by the time his career ended. "When Dan Quisenberry and those guys were pitching, it was still two- or three-inning saves," Farr began. "I was a little less, but it was still not the closer of today. I guess I was still in that transition phase."

One of Farr's favorite stories he likes to share, "I have the distinction of giving up Jim Thome's first home run during his rookie year [1991]", said Farr. "Thome was with the Indians and that homer won the game against us when I was pitching for the Yankees. Every time he would hit a memorable home run; his one hundredth, his two hundredth, and so on my phone would start ringing from reporters wanting me to reflect on his first home run. I remember getting calls at the end of the 2011 season and I said to myself, 'What did Thome do now?' Then sure enough I read that he hit his six hundredth home run. I guess you shouldn't mind giving up a home run to a guy as long as he is going to hit six hundred more!" he said with a laugh.

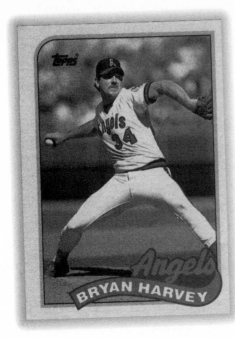

BRYAN HARVEY
1987–1995

B ryan Harvey was a late bloomer. He went to Bandys High School in North Carolina, and then to the University of North Carolina at Charlotte.

The right-hander loved to play baseball, but baseball scouts did not love him. He was not drafted.

"It really was tough for me at first," admitted Harvey. "My wife and I were living day to day. I had a new wife, a new baby, and I was doing my best to support them. It all turned around for me the day I got this call at 8:00 a.m. from the league I was playing for. They said they had a game they were playing at 10:00 a.m. that day and asked if I could pitch. I dropped my hunting gear and picked up my baseball stuff and I went to the field to play. I lost 1-0 but there was a Mets scout in the stands. They didn't have any room for pitchers, but he called his friend, a scout with the Angels. That scout called me and asked to see me pitch. I got through about twenty pitches and he signed me right then and there to a contract."

That occurred on August 20, 1984.

"I went into the Angels organization as a starter," he continued. "I was good for about three innings and then by the fourth inning the batters were getting to me. So that is when my pitching coach, Joe Coleman, said, 'We're going to put you into the bullpen.' I was also fortunate because I could never throw a split-finger until I met Joe Coleman, who knew how to throw it and teach someone like me. So in 1986, Joe Coleman helped turn my whole mechanics around by teaching me the turn I needed to throw the split-finger. Once I learned the split-finger, that pitch went berserk."

Harvey made his major league debut a few weeks shy of his twenty-fourth birthday on May 16, 1987, pitching the final inning of a 4-2 loss against the Baltimore Orioles. He pitched a scoreless ninth inning, walking one and striking out one. He made just three major league appearances that first season; but in 1988, the rookie had an impressive year, earning a 2.13 ERA with seventeen saves in fifty games. His efforts earned him the *Sporting News* Rookie Pitcher of the Year award and a second place finish in the American League Rookie of the Year balloting (Walt Weiss finished first).

Harvey pitched for the Angels from 1987 to 1992. During that time, he met some very memorable people. "I would say for me it was the opportunity to be around Jimmy Reese, who would be on the field for us during home games in Anaheim for batting practice. To hear from him the stories he would tell about being Babe Ruth's roommate were very special to me. I remember him telling us that he was more Babe Ruth's bags' roommate, because Babe was never in the room a lot," recalled a laughing Harvey. "And then there was Mr. Autry, the owner at the time of the Angels. Mr. Autry was always coming into the clubhouse, the locker, or even the tunnel, and there was no telling who would be with him. One day it might be Bob Hope, then Roy Rogers, or even Buddy Ebsen. It could be anybody. To hear the stories Mr. Autry and Jimmy Reese told was probably my favorite part of playing for the Angels. It was pretty awesome.

"My greatest moment on the mound would have to be August of 1989 in Anaheim," Harvey recalled. "It was a playoff run against the A's and we had this very important series against them. They had already beaten us the first two games of the series and game three was a must win game for us. And when Sunday came around there were sixty-four thousand people in the stands and we went up late with a 2-1 lead. I came into the ninth inning. I struck out Jose Canseco and the crowd went crazy, then I got the next batter out on strikes, the Angels killer Dave Henderson, and again the crowd went crazy. And finally, I got the next batter out, we got the victory, and the crowd erupted.

"The worst moment I had on the mound was every time I blew a save," he confessed. "For example, a pitcher in my day like Jim Abbott could have pitched his heart out and battled for seven or eight innings, and then I could come in and give up a two-run homer and lose the game. That is the worst part of being a closer when a blown save ruins all the hard work of your starter."

The pinnacle of the six-foot-three right-hander's career came in 1991. An all-star season, he led the AL with 46 saves and 63 games finished, while compiling a miniscule 1.60 ERA. He struck out 101 batters and walked just 17 in 78²/₃ innings. The season was his first of two all-star years (1993 was the other).

In 1992, Harvey was off to a great start when elbow injuries cut his season short after June. With a large contract and coming off an injury, the Angels did not protect him from the expansion draft; so on November 17, 1992, the Florida Marlins took him as the twentieth player selected in the draft.

Harvey proved to be a great selection for the Marlins, as he had a 1.70 ERA, with 45 saves and 73 strikeouts in 69 innings over 59 games. The Marlins won only 64 games that year and Harvey saved 70.3 percent of the team's victories, a major league record.

Harvey's career occurred towards the end of the transition of the closer role from a multi-inning job to a one-inning job. "Most of my saves were one inning, but I did have quite a few two-inning saves and even a three-inning save. I guess you can say I was a part of that generation of closers when things did start to change, which eventually helped define and identify the present-day closer."

Even during the transitional period, the role of closer was more of a mental challenge than a physical one. "It is mental because of the aspect of the blown save," explained Harvey. "Fortunately, I didn't have that good a memory two days in a row. For example, when you blow a save you can't think of it the next day, even though you might be in the same exact situation.

"I remember I played for the Marlins that first year they were a ball club back in 1993. I was going for my second save of the season and it was only the second series of the year, and then Gary Sheffield of the San Diego Padres hit a home run off of me and won the game and I blew the save. Then, wouldn't you know it, the next day we were in a similar situation, up in the ninth, I was in to close and Gary Sheffield was up to bat. I could have dwelled on it, but when you do [that] as a closer, that is when you're dead as a pitcher, especially a closer." (Harvey got Sheffield to ground out that second time, and picked up his second save of the season.)

In his nine major league seasons, Harvey compiled a 2.49 ERA and 177 saves in 322 games, and he was always ready for what came his way. "I was always prepared and ready to pitch."

Harvey says he didn't have too much of a routine, "but once I crossed that white line on the field I was ready to go as a pitcher and knew what I needed to do. I knew I needed to get the hitter out, and that was motivation enough. The biggest competition I had was against myself, and that is all I needed."

JAY
HOWELL
1980–1994

J ay Howell pitched during the end of the transition to the modern-day closer. He compiled 155 career saves in his fifteen-year major league career, which began in 1980 and ended following the 1994 season. "I was on the cusp of the closing transition," said Howell. "I had my share of saves the way they are achieved today and yet I had a good share of my saves when I went two innings. I think it was the late 1980s when it all turned around."

Howell grew up in Colorado. He was selected by the Cincinnati Reds in the twelfth round of the June draft at the end of his senior year at Fairview High School in Boulder. But the right-hander chose not to sign, and instead went on to the University of Colorado. Three years later, in 1976, the Reds selected him again, this time in the thirty-first round, and this time Howell chose to begin his professional career.

Like the majority of pitching prospects in his era, he began his career as a starter. However, he never really made an impact in the starting role in the majors. Howell made his major league debut with the Reds on August 10, 1980, pitching the final inning in relief in a 7-1 loss against the Los Angeles Dodgers. He was traded to the Chicago Cubs in the off-season and was recalled to the majors in August, when he made his first major league start on August 16, the second game of a doubleheader against the Pittsburgh Pirates. He won the game, 6-4, but it was a mediocre outing for him. He didn't start again until his final outing of the season, on October 3 against the Philadelphia Phillies. It was another win, 8-4, but another average outing for Howell.

Howell kept fighting to stick in the majors. In 1982, he was traded to the New York Yankees in August. It was a good move for him, as he was recalled in September and went 2-3 with a 7.71 ERA in six MLB starts. In 1983, he did it all, starting and relieving. "I remember I was starting this game against Dennis Eckersley in Boston," Howell recalled. "It was July [1,] 1983, and it was a big series. I remember we got to the second inning and Eckersley gave up a few bombs and we took a 7–0 lead. I then gave up a few runs myself, and Billy [Martin] pulled me. I went to the trainer's room, and then all of a sudden here comes George [Steinbrenner] and he started to rake me over the coals and ripped me a new one. George said to me, 'We're going to get someone else in here from Columbus that can hold a f---ing seven-run lead!'" Then all of a sudden Billy comes running in to the clubhouse, probably hearing that George was there. Billy walked right up to George and was as calm as could be, just like he was going to a tea party, and said, 'George, I told you a thousand times, please do not come into my clubhouse and beset my players. I respectfully ask you to leave.' George spun like a dime, didn't say a word, and walked right out of the clubhouse. It was so surreal! Billy then turned to me and said, 'Don't you ever let that son of a bitch yell at you again!' Fortunately, we came back and won the game.

"After the game, Billy calls me into his office while he is on the phone. He says to the person on the phone, 'I've got the kid right here with me.' He then put the phone down and said to me, 'Go upstairs and see George. He owes you an apology.' I said, 'No, man, I can't do that.' Billy then said, 'Just go. He owes you an apology, and then tell me what he says to you.' I go up, and then George proceeds to rip me another one, but I then remember what Goose [Gossage] told me about him—that he had a football mentality when it came to dealing with people. I would have to stand up to him. So I stood up and said, 'George, we win together and we lose together, and that is how it is, and that is why we are a team!' George then jumped out of his seat and hugged me. He then led me out of the room and said, 'Son, that is exactly what I wanted to hear.' I am leaving the room saying to myself, 'What the f--- just happened here?' I then got back on the elevator and went right to Billy's office. Billy asked, 'What did George say exactly?' I answered, 'I don't know what happened, we had this little talk, I didn't back down from him, and he said something like, I was going to be the next Allie Reynolds on the club.' Billy then got this big f---ing grin on his face and then said to me, 'Son, I think we are going to work you out of the bullpen from now on.' So, I went to the bullpen and that is when I was able to work with Goose."

Howell pitched exclusively in relief (with one exception) from 1984 through the remainder of his career. Gossage helped him to become an effective reliever, and in 1985, after an off-season trade to the Oakland A's, he became an effective closer.

"There was no doubt it was Goose Gossage who had the greatest impact on my career," said Howell. "I remember when I went over to the Yankees I had three pitches. I had a hard slider, hard curveball, and a fastball. I didn't have a change-up. I knew I wasn't going to ever be a Goose, but I just loved how he embraced every day. I took what he had, and from a few other guys like Don Sutton when I went over to Oakland. But I remember asking them both a lot about pitching and would often ask what hitters are looking for. It was a completely different way for me to pitch."

He continued, "I watched Gossage when we were on the

Yankees together. His attitude, from top to bottom—in my book, he was the quintessential closer. I was very fortunate that he took me under his wing at a very early age. I was going to be his pet project. So when he spoke, it was like the angels were singing. You better be paying attention. There were just a few that I would feel this way about. Don Sutton was another one of those guys. I remember how I learned how to scout teams from Don Sutton. But in Goose's case, his attitude was, 'I have this bazooka for an arm and I don't give a rat's ass, but if you can hit that f---ing ball, then I'll tip my hat to him.' That was his philosophy and that is what always worked for him. Because when you have that drop-dead dominant s--- like Goose, and even like Aroldis Chapman in Cincinnati, location doesn't matter.

"Here were Goose's criteria for pitching: catcher gives the sign; if you need to change speeds, you throw harder; and there is no such thing as a change-up; if you want movement, just keep throwing it harder, but twist your wrist a little before you let it go. It is a completely simple philosophy because you get to go after the hitter each and every time. Goose would always tell me, 'Don't get beat on your second-best pitch.' That is what I learned from him. But every pitcher goes through the other side of the wormhole, too, when your stuff is no longer dominant or his pitches don't really cut the way they used to."

Goose Gossage was not the only closer that Howell admired. "For me, Dennis Eckersley was one of the best I ever witnessed in this role," stated Howell. "Eckersley was just so damn good and was so dominant. I believe he is the godfather of the one-inning or modern-day closer. He was in the role, as such, before anyone else. He had one of the greatest makeups for a pitcher, and was so overpowering and dominant. Goose and Dennis Eckersley were the best two I ever saw. When they came in, you knew the game was over. Their philosophy was, 'I will conquer and I will succeed,' and that was huge. They had so much more confidence than anyone else."

After three years with the A's, Howell was traded again, this time to the Los Angeles Dodgers, where he remained for five years, picking up eighty-five of his career saves.

In his experience, Howell believes the closer's role is 50 percent mental and 50 percent physical. "I had a down breaking ball and a good fastball that I threw right out of my curveball. My out pitch was my high fastball. But as you get older and you don't pitch at 100 percent any more, what you are missing you have to sell as though you do. In other words, it came down to the salesmanship of the role. So when that did happen, the physical became so much a part of me. My elbow had issues and yet when they said to you, 'How do you feel?' And if you didn't reply, 'I feel great!' their attitude was, 'Heck . . . if you can't do it, then we'll get someone else in here then.' Back then, that was the philosophy. So in some cases, you battled every day, you battled with the physical and you battled with the mental. Mental was really taxing at times, especially when you started to doubt yourself."

The three-time all-star finished his career with Atlanta (1993) and Texas (1994). During his fifteen years in the majors, he witnessed the final transition of the closer's role, but unlike many others, he does not believe there are a whole lot of differences from today to the time he began. "There is no doubt. They are the same," Howell said confidently. "They are all a part of this certain mold, no matter if we are talking about today or thirty years ago. You are still subject to giving up that walk-off home run or bloop single down the line to lose the game. The door slams just as hard on a blown save, no matter what the year. Yet what has changed is the expectation of today's closers. There is a higher expectation to get the save. But again, the blown save is just as demoralizing and punishing today as it was in my day."

The expectation for closers these days is perfection. "I think it is the greatest description of the role," said Howell. "I say that all of the time . . . and I'll take it a step further: it demands perfection every day.

"I got way more out of this game than I ever expected," said Howell, who went 58-53 with 155 saves and a 3.34 ERA in his career. "I have no regrets. I gave it my all and I could have never imagined not going out there and helping the team. I am very happy with what I got out of this game."

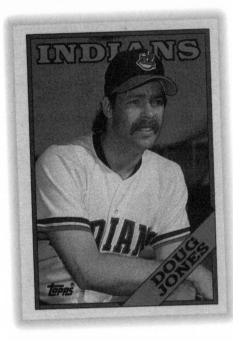

DOUG JONES
1982–2000

Doug Jones, although six foot three, was not your stereotypical closer . . . he was a reserved, thinking man, not a showy character. He was never expected to amount to much as a pitcher, much less as a closer; however, the unassuming closer finished a sixteen-year major league career with 303 saves.

Drafted by the Milwaukee Brewers in the third round of the January 1978 draft, Jones did not make his MLB debut until a brief stint with the Brewers in 1982. It took him another four years to return to the majors, this time with the Cleveland Indians in 1986, at the age of twenty-nine, but he finally stuck thanks to determination and a fastball and change-up that left his hands looking identical to one another.

His 1988 season was his breakout year. After struggling to stay in the majors the previous year, Jones had an all-star season, earning thirty-seven saves (second-highest of his career) in fifty-one games for the sixth-place Indians.

The right-hander was named to the all-star team four more times (1989, 1990, 1992, and 1994) and remained in the majors through the 2000 season, retiring at the age of forty-three. He pitched for seven different major league teams over his career—the Brewers, Indians, Astros, Phillies, Orioles, Cubs, and Athletics.

"Just the fact I was able to play as long as I did was an achievement enough for me in my mind," said the soft-spoken Jones. "I wasn't always the first choice of anyone. So often I would be the fill-in guy until . . . that young kid coming up could develop and be the closer. I was happy to have the role of the closer as long as I did, but I was one of the few relief pitchers that wanted to be a starter. I was always begging to start a game.

"I remember getting called into the manager's office the first time I got called up," Jones recalled. "The manager at that time was Pat Corrales. I thought he was just calling me in to welcome me and to give me the heads-up as to what the team was working on. But then he said, 'I don't think you are going to get anyone out in this game.' He then filled the talk with a bunch of superlatives and then he finished his talk with me with, 'Okay, you can go now and welcome to the big leagues.' But I remember I didn't go away saying to myself, 'I'm going to prove him wrong!' I was taken aback by the remarks, but I was used to it. Managers and other coaches had been saying it to me since my days in the minors. I laugh now when I think back to those words, especially when I look back at my career and the fact that I pitched until I was forty-three years old. I understand what they were thinking, especially given the fact that I never threw the ball hard. They are programmed to say it because they are too used to seeing someone going out there and throwing 90 to 100 mph."

Jones recalled a particular time when he let his head get a little too big as one of his least pleasant moments as a closer. "My most frustrating day as a closer was a blown save in Colorado at Mile High Stadium [on June 12, 1993, with Houston]," said Jones. "I remember I had been in a few All-Star Games and I was getting a little puffy about myself. I went out there with a lead and I only needed one more out in the seventh inning when I came in. I gave up a run that inning and didn't even get the final out until the pitcher came to bat. I allowed four more runs the next inning and didn't even record an out. I felt embarrassed and frustrated more than anything else. I couldn't believe it! When a guy hits a home run off of you, you say to yourself 'Well, you guessed right and you hit it,' but, like in this case, when they don't hit more than two balls out of the infield . . . that sticks with you."

With his 303 career saves, Jones obviously had far more successes than failures as a closer. But closing for teams in the bottom of the standings and for teams in the late 1980s meant more innings and less saves. . . . He experienced, first hand, the evolution of the closer's role.

"I remember when I first came up with the Indians in 1986; I was pitching a lot of two- and three-inning saves. I remember the manager would often say to the pitching coach, when we had a lead after five innings, 'Time to get Jones up?' But that was the mind-set and the role of the closer back then.

"The closer role changed a lot during my career. It was probably the mid-nineties when many of these changes occurred. But even when it began to change, some managers still went to whatever pitcher had the hot hand that day in the bullpen."

Unlike many players, Jones actually believes he had a complete professional career, with maybe one exception. "Like most players who didn't get there, I would have loved to play in a World Series," Jones confessed.

Jones seemed to have been preparing for his current job, as pitching coach at San Diego Christian College, since his playing days. "Most of my career I was the guy who used to sit with the young kid who just got called up and help him along," said Jones. "That is how I approached the game as the closer at times. I tried to be a good example for the others on the team. Over the years, I worked with a lot of young pitchers as they were coming up through the organization. I worked with Todd Jones, Ricky Bottalico, Rudy Seanez, and Armando Benitez. It was a privilege for me to be able to do that. It even extended my career. I remember I was about to retire, and then Oakland asked me to return to the game to, again, work with some of the younger guys and provide a veteran presence in the clubhouse. I'm glad I did stay around. It was in Oakland that I got my three hundredth save, and that was fun to do."

Jones said it was the mentoring of a pitching coach that gave him the confidence to succeed when he was young. "We had this coach in the Milwaukee organization named Don Rowe, who made the greatest impact on my career," reflected Jones. "He was the first coach I ever had that broke down the mechanics of delivering the baseball . . . in practical, understandable terms, instead of just baseball lingo, and he made it easy for me to coach myself in that sense."

Jones credits his mind, more than his body, for his success. "There was never anything very physical about what I did," he stated. "It varies from pitcher to pitcher, some are 100 percent physical, meaning they throw every pitch as hard as they can to feel they are being effective. It wouldn't matter if I threw the ball as hard as I could; it wouldn't be very hard. I had to rely on my control, my change of speeds, and having the same delivery every pitch so that every pitch looked the same and they couldn't tell what was coming. And because they didn't know what pitch was coming, they couldn't decipher what speed the ball was coming at them. My job was to throw strikes and make the hitter swing the bat and hopefully cause them not to hit the ball very hard or at least in the general direction of our defensive players."

Despite Jones' success, and perhaps because of his unassuming nature, he was never courted by the media, so when he was sought out by the media for a story, it was a big event for the right-hander. "I remember a reporter for *ESPN Magazine* was going to do this story on me. I was very excited," Jones shared. "I had all of these grand ideas about the article and how it was going to be. Low and behold, it turned out to be this quarter-page story on me. But here is what I do remember the most about the story: the reporter asked a few of my teammates about me, and one of the best comments came from one of my teammates when he said, 'I'll tell you one thing about Doug Jones, if his career goes to hell in a hand basket, he's gonna turn out just fine!' That was something that always stuck with me. I think that was also the way I played the game and I hope others thought the same about me," Jones said.

"I loved to win and I hated to lose. One of my tools I used as a pitcher was to never let the opposing team see me scared or nervous. I needed every advantage I could muster up, especially when I throw the ball at 80 mph. Therefore, I could never intimidate anyone else; but then again I would never let them intimidate me."

ROGER MCDOWELL
1985–1996

Roger McDowell, like many pitchers in his era, began his professional career as a starter.

The Ohio native was selected out of Bowling Green State University by the New York Mets in the third round of the June 1982 draft. He quickly started his professional career playing for two single-A teams in the Mets organization in 1982, compiling an 8-4 record, with a 2.95 ERA in sixteen games, fifteen of them starts. Of McDowell's forty-six games over three years in the minor leagues, forty-three were starts. He made his major league debut on April 11, 1985, in relief against the Cardinals.

Once he appeared in the major leagues, he never returned to the minors. The six-foot-one right-hander played for twelve years in the majors for the Mets, Phillies, Dodgers, Rangers, and Orioles. He made two starts early in his MLB career, but spent the rest of his career in the bullpen. At the age of twenty-five, he became part of the 1986 world champion Mets.

"That 1986 season was special," McDowell recalled. "We won 106 games that year. We had the right combination of rookies, young players, and veterans. It all worked so well that year. I remember they tried everything that year. I remember Kevin Mitchell was our team's fifth infielder and our fourth outfielder. Rick Aguilera was our swing guy. We had three positions (second base, third base, and centerfield) that were platoon spots. They had three platoon spots based on who was pitching. That was unheard of, especially today. And then they had Jesse Orosco and myself as co-closers. It wasn't egotistical at all, even though there were some egotistical guys on the team. Yet that never played a part in how we won ballgames. Whether it was myself or Jesse who got the save, we were both happy for each other, and the same went for the platoon guys. We kept winning and everyone was happy!"

McDowell's career was unique in that he began closing in his first major league season . . . although, as he stated, he shared his closing role throughout his tenure with the Mets—first with lefty Jesse Orosco, then with lefty Randy Myers.

He finished his career with a 70-70 record, a 3.30 ERA and 159 saves in 723 games.

McDowell credits much of his success to his first pitching coach and manager in the big leagues, Mel Stottlemyre and Davey Johnson. "Mel, from the standpoint because he was my major league pitching coach my first years up during my initiation into the big leagues. Davey Johnson was also important for me because he helped me understand the patience I needed once I got here. Davey and Mel, along with the entire coaching staff, were terrific with the Mets. Probably the biggest thing I came away with from that team and its coaching staff was staying positive. Especially, from my standpoint, being a young pitcher. They were not the type that would scare or intimidate you to death."

In McDowell's mind, the role of the closer has not changed so much since his playing days, at least the mental aspects of closing. "That anticipation of going in is the same whether we are talking about the closer of today or from my days as a closer," he explained. "It is amazing you play three hours and nine innings, and it all comes down most of the time to the performance of one guy. And the trick is you have to have that one guy who is right for the role. He's got to have the ability, the talent, the physical, and the mental capabilities to handle that role. It really is a very rare combination to have.

"I think the difference nowadays," he continued, "is that the closing pitcher is groomed for the role at a very early point in their minor league career. Rather than twenty years ago when a guy worked his way up to the role because you went into the bullpen as a long guy, then you were a seventh-inning guy, then a setup guy, and then you finally worked your way into the closer role. It was an evolution years ago. Also, remember, back then, you all were starters and a lot of guys really fought hard to get back to the rotation when they were placed into the bullpen. Again, nowadays they start grooming these guys when they are in college or in the minor leagues. But when you do that you also run the risk of not being able to see these same guys in different game situations . . . or some guys just need a little more pitching experience to get them under control.

"I remember looking at the 2011 pitching statistics over the winter months; I remember looking at the numbers when it came to complete games and that it goes down every year. I think it was 2 percent in 2011. It was 10 percent just ten years ago. That is why it is so important to have a good bullpen as much as it is to have a good starting rotation."

Ironically, the closer's role is the only one in the game that demands perfection. "You are expected to be successful in this role every time you go out there . . . or at least nine out of every ten times out there on the mound," said McDowell. "If you rack up forty-plus saves, you better not have more than four-plus blown saves. Otherwise, they start saying that you didn't have a successful year."

The closer's role itself has evolved, as he witnessed firsthand throughout his career. "Obviously the role has changed since the days when I pitched, when three-inning saves were common. So, it's gone from an eight-man pitching staff during the days of Rollie Fingers and Gene Garber to a nine-, ten-, eleven-, and even twelve- and thirteen-man pitching staff. When I played it was still a ten-man pitching staff. The roles are more limited these days and so are the innings. They are limited but the game is still the same. I do believe this is the final evolution of the role; otherwise the rules would have to change," McDowell reasoned. "I think a minimum of one inning is necessary for a save situation. If you try and break it down even further, it won't work."

McDowell was a serious pitcher on the mound; however, off the mound, he was well known for being a prankster throughout his career, and is most famously known for his "hot foot." The hot foot was a prank in which he would take a wad of gum and stick a lit cigarette in it and attach it to a teammate's cleat. Eventually the shoe would get hot and cause a lot of irritation to the victim.

He also has his share of amusing stories, one standout occurred at Candlestick Park in San Francisco. "I remember I was working on a cutter when I was with the Dodgers," McDowell recalled. "It was probably my seventh or eighth year in the big leagues. I was working on the pitch with Ron Perranoski, my pitching coach at the time. I remember facing Will Clark, who just came off the bench to bat. I didn't always fair well against Clark, but there were two outs. Clark stepped up to the plate and the crowd was going nuts, and here comes Ron out of the dugout and to the mound. He said, 'Tommy [Lasorda] wants me to remind you to keep Clark in the park!' I said, 'No problem . . . no problem.' I was a sinker-ball pitcher so I thought to myself that I've got a pretty good chance at doing just that. So, for whatever reason, I said to myself, 'Hey, I'm going to work on that cutter!' I threw him one a little up and away, and he swung and missed it. 'Okay,' I said to myself. 'Let's try that one again.' So, I threw it again and the same result, swing and a miss! Well, 'third time is the charm' as I said it to myself. But the third cutter never made it to the catcher's mitt. Clark took my 0-2 cutter and hit a home run to win the game. And if you remember back then at old Candlestick Park, everybody used to walk down the right-field foul line to get out of the park. And as I was walking I felt this presence behind me and it was Ron Perranoski, who said, 'When I said, "Keep it in the park," I meant Candlestick not Yosemite!'"

Following his playing career, McDowell moved into the coaching ranks, first in the minor leagues with the Dodgers, and then in the majors with the Braves, where, since 2006, he has been a successor to pitching guru Leo Mazzone.

"This is still the best office in the world for me," McDowell admitted, regarding his role as pitching coach, "and to be one of just thirty other guys to have this job in this industry, and to do something you love and have so much passion for is pretty special. Every day is a different day and every year, with its different faces, makes it a real pleasure to be able to do what I do. I go to work every day and really enjoy what I do."

JEFF MONTGOMERY
1987–1999

J eff Montgomery never really did anything "by the book." A right-handed pitcher in the mid-1980s with four quality pitches, it is shocking to find that he began his pro career in the bullpen.

Montgomery grew up in Wellston, Ohio, and after graduating from high school, attended Marshall University in West Virginia. He was drafted by his "home" team, the Cincinnati Reds in the ninth round of the June draft in 1983.

He began his pro career right away and reported to Billings of the Rookie Pioneer League, where he earned five saves in twenty games. It wasn't until 1986 that the Reds organization tried to convert him into a starter. After forty-three starts over the course of two seasons, Montgomery was called up to the majors and made his debut on August 1, 1987, when he pitched two innings in relief in a 7-3 loss against the San Francisco Giants. He made just one start in fourteen appearances for the Reds that year.

"For some reason, I always will remember my first day in the big leagues, walking up the steps at Riverfront Stadium from the clubhouse to the dugout and looking out to the field. I grew up in Cincinnati and that is why it was fun for me . . . especially because it was the only major league stadium I ever saw a game in," Montgomery reminisced. "It was like playing for my hometown team. It was pretty special for me, growing up near Cincinnati and then being drafted by the Reds. After playing five years in the minors and then getting that chance to look out on that field will always be special for me. And I'm still a Reds fan. It was like coming home for me."

He added: "I do remember being somewhat naive when I got drafted, thinking that I would be in the major leagues rather soon for the organization. But it doesn't always work out that way. No one knows how long a road it can be from the last pitch you throw in high school to the first pitch you throw in the major leagues. I was pretty naive about the whole process. I made the assumption I would be in the big leagues quickly, but after many bus trips and struggles I quickly discovered the road to get there was long. Especially when you go from level to level in this game and you fight every step of the way."

After just one season with the Reds, Montgomery was traded to the Kansas City Royals on February 15, 1988. In spring training, Royals General Manager John Schuerholz told Montgomery they were putting him back in the bullpen . . . at triple-A Omaha. Montgomery worked hard that spring and made it tough to send him down, but he worked even harder at triple-A, saving thirteen games with a 1.91 ERA and thirty-six strikeouts in twenty-eight and one-third innings in twenty games.

He was recalled in early June, picking up his first major league save on June 8 versus the Oakland A's in one and two-thirds scoreless innings, but that would be his only save of the season, as Steve Farr was the closer. Two other men with a lot of experience and who had been vying for the closing role in spring training were released on July 4, 1988. They were Dan Quisenberry and Gene Garber.

"I learned a lot from some of the veterans on the Royals' staff after I came over in a trade from the Cincinnati Reds," stated Montgomery. "I learned a lot from Dan Quisenberry, as well as Mark Gubicza, Steve Farr, and Bret Saberhagen. The staff we had in Kansas City was amazing. That year alone we had Dan Quisenberry and Gene Garber both competing for the closer role. They were both competing beginning in spring training, and I don't think either one of them gave up a run during camp."

The 1989 season began much the same way 1988 ended. Montgomery was setting up for closer Steve Farr, but when Farr was disabled with a knee injury, Montgomery took over the closer's role and finished the season with a 7-3 record, eighteen saves and an impressive 1.73 ERA in sixty-three games.

The permanent closer role still evaded the five-foot-eleven Montgomery, as the Royals signed free agent Mark Davis to be the closer in 1990. But sometimes, things have a way of working out.

"At the start of the 1989 season, Tom 'Flash' Gordon and I were the setup guys for the closer role. By mid-1989, I became the closer after Steve Farr went down with an injury. I had a really good second half and I assumed that I was going to be the team's closer at the start of the 1990 [season]," Montgomery explained. "However, while home in Cincinnati in the off-season I see a story on ESPN, and then I see Mark Davis wearing this Royals cap and jersey. And then the story went on to announce that Mark Davis, the National League Cy Young Award winner with the Padres the previous year, was now a Kansas City Royal. My expectations about being the closer changed dramatically after that point. I went from the setup guy at the beginning of 1989, to the closer, and now back to the setup guy for the start of the 1990 season."

"But wouldn't you know it," he continued, "Mark Davis had some injuries in 1990, and there I was again the team's closer for the rest of the season. Fortunately, the roller coaster stopped for me by 1991, and then to the end of my career in 1999, I was the team's full-time closer. I was still nervous something else might happen, so it took me a while to really settle back into the role again."

According to Montgomery, adrenaline is the key to pitching effectively. "It didn't matter whether it was March 16 during spring training in Baseball City, Florida, where the Royals played, or if it was a game in late September, there was always adrenaline. And it also didn't matter if there were 5,000 fans or 50,000 fans in the stands. Once you get the adrenaline, then your focus takes over."

The mental aspect is also more challenging than the physical demands, according to Montgomery. "I think it is considerably more mental," he said. "The closer role allowed me to elevate my game to a higher level. Meaning, in a close-game situation, my five-foot-eleven frame became a six-foot-five frame. The role allowed me to bring out the most of my physical abilities. Being the pressure cooker that it is with little room for any mistakes, it helped me to execute and focus and then lock into the situation Again, it allowed me to feel like a giant."

Helping him get through those pressure cooker moments was his favorite pitching coach with the Royals, Bruce Kison. "I remember one time he came out to the mound and said to me, 'I want you to walk out behind the mound and have a mental cigarette!' Meaning, give yourself a moment to catch a breather and forget about everything else and just regroup," said Montgomery. "And every time he said that, it worked and it helped me to get the break I needed. It helped me to slow down the situation and focus better on just closing it out.

"Sometimes you do have to stop and regroup before you can move forward. Sometimes the best way to do something is to start over and begin it with a break. I would usually take that mental cigarette to get me through a tough situation."

One of his more disappointing moments came in 1993. "We were in a big series against the White Sox," Montgomery recalled. "It was a must-win game and I gave up a three-run homer to Frank Thomas to lose the game and blow the save [August 13 in Chicago] Again, we were at a pivotal time in the season for us to win, and I didn't get the job done. I remember I threw a 3-2 pitch that I thought was a strike, but I didn't get the call. That put runners on first and second and Thomas stepped up to the plate and hit a home run. I thought I had the game put away and the next thing I know everything changed with one swing of the bat."

But Montgomery also has some great memories he cherishes. "In 1996, Ken Griffey Jr. was chasing the single-season record for home runs and I was with my son, Connor, at the ball park. He must have been only about eight years old and he used to love coming with me to the ball park. We were ready to go into the clubhouse and we ran into Ken Griffey, Jr., who was in a Seattle uniform at the time. Griffey was going on the field to take batting practice. He walked up to me and my son and said, 'Hey, who do we have here?' I said, 'This is my son, Connor.' Then I said, 'Connor, this is Ken Griffey.' Griffey was really friendly, asking how he's doing and all that. My son replied, 'Mr. Griffey, if you break the record, can you not do it off of my dad?'" Montgomery recalled with a good laugh.

In his thirteen-year major league career, Montgomery saved 304 games, which ranks him twentieth on baseball's all-time list (as of September 2012).

"I felt like I left on my own terms so . . . yes, I do feel like I had a complete career," said Montgomery. "I played seventeen seasons, and sixteen of those seasons I was productive, but that last season I had hip-related injuries and by the end of that year I wanted no more baseball. My tank was empty. I felt like I had poured every ounce of my ability into the game and I could give no more. I was ready to move on—and that was to help raise my children and that was going to be the next chapter in my life."

The right-hander played twelve years for the Royals, and holds the club record with 686 relief appearances, 543 games finished, 304 saves, and 378 save opportunities. He was elected to the Royals Hall of Fame in 2003, his first year of eligibility.

"It was really special for me when I got elected to the Kansas City Royals Hall of Fame in 2003. Fortunately, it was the last winning season the Royals had, so it was nice to see the ball park filled with 40,000 fans. It was overwhelming to see that type of crowd."

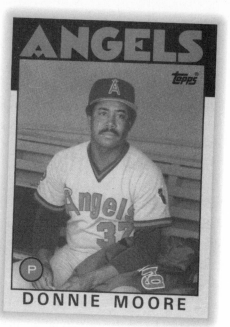

DONNIE MOORE
1975–1988

DONNIE MOORE

D onnie Moore lived life on the edge.

The right-handed pitcher was the only black student at Monterey High School in Lubbock, Texas. But his athleticism and sense of humor helped him to be named the fourth-most popular student in the school.

The Boston Red Sox selected him in the twelfth round of the June 1972 draft as an outfielder. But Moore wanted to pitch and opted instead to attend Ranger College, where he led the school to the National Junior College Championship in 1973. In the meantime, the Chicago Cubs selected him in the first round (third overall) of the January secondary draft in 1973; he signed on June 3.

That year, he also married his childhood sweetheart, Tonya Martin.

He made his major league debut a little over two years later, on September 14, 1975, in a 13-7 loss against the Philadelphia Phillies. Moore threw two and two-thirds scoreless innings in relief.

In his thirteen years in the majors, he pitched for the Cubs, St. Louis Cardinals, Milwaukee Brewers, Atlanta Braves, and California Angels.

Moore had the best season of his career in 1985; compiling a 1.92 ERA in sixty-five games, with a career-best thirty-one saves for the Angels. He was also surprised to be selected to his first and only All-Star Game, although teammates (and future Hall of Famers) Rod Carew and Reggie Jackson were not selected.

His success came at the right time, garnering him a lucrative three-year, $3 million contract with the Angels.

Despite suffering an injured shoulder at the start of the 1986 season that caused him to miss five weeks, Moore finished the regular season with a 2.97 ERA and twenty-one saves in forty-nine games.

Then came the 1986 postseason and the moment Donnie Moore is most remembered for. The Angels were leading the American League Championship Series 3-1 over the Boston Red Sox. Game five was on October 12 in Anaheim, and the Angels were one strike away from earning the first World Series berth in club history. With two outs and a 2-2 count, Dave Henderson hit a two-run home run off Moore to give the Red Sox a 6-4 lead.

The Angels had been leading the game 5-2 entering the ninth inning. Starter Mike Witt allowed a two-run home to Don Baylor to cut the lead to 5-4. One out later, Gary Lucas was brought in the game and he immediately hit Rich Gedman with a pitch. It was then that Moore was brought into the game.

Moore finished the inning and the Angels tied the game in the bottom of the inning. Despite suffering from an undiagnosed back injury, Moore stayed in to pitch not only the tenth, but also the eleventh inning. The Angels had several offensive chances to win the game, but Henderson's sacrifice fly off Moore ended the game, and eventually the Red Sox won the Series.

Fans would not forgive him . . . and thanks in part to numerous injuries, his career never rebounded.

"Donnie was the closer for the Angels the first year I got called up to the major leagues," said Bryan Harvey, who moved into the closing role for the Angels after Moore. "Donnie was there and then I became the closer by the end of the 1989 season. Given the situation, Donnie was a very good guy and a good teammate. He treated me very well. He was always there talking to me and ready to give advice to a new pitcher. I liked Donnie Moore a lot."

Harvey continued: "Unfortunately, everybody remembered that game five of the ALCS and the home run he gave up, and there are so many that didn't want to let it go. Everybody remembers the bad stuff. I remember the days when I would be down in the bullpen with Donnie and you would hear the shouting and the cursing at him. The way they talked to him after that game, you couldn't but feel sorry for him. That home run is what they remember. They don't remember how the Angels got the bases loaded in the bottom half of that inning and could have won the game. They also had some chances in the next two games, but all they remember is that home run that Donnie Moore gave up to Dave Henderson. There is something about when things happen late in a game that people don't forget. I guess it is because so many people got so excited and you are on the verge of winning and then one pitch turns it all around. You go from the highest high you can be and ready to celebrate, to 'Holy cow, what just happened and what do we do now?'"

Moore was released from the Angels in 1988, and he tried to latch on with another team. The Kansas City Royals gave the thirty-five-year old an opportunity to pitch in the minors, but he was released again a short time later. Moore's career ended with a 3.67 ERA and eighty-nine saves in 416 games.

In the meantime, he was having marital issues, his money was running out, and he wanted to move his family from their expensive house in Anaheim back to Texas.

Tragedy occurred on July 18, 1989, when, during an argument with his wife, Moore shot her three times. Their daughter, Demetria, rushed her to the hospital and she survived, but in the meantime, Moore turned the gun on himself, killing himself in front of one of his sons.

His daughter was quoted on what she believed drove her father to commit such drastic acts of desperation, "When he was cut by Kansas City, he'd really been depressed about that. I mean, here he is, the high-life career . . . then all of a sudden, it's gone. He comes back home . . . and the marriage, the family, is all destroyed. I mean, what else does he have left?"

JESSE OROSCO
1979–2003

J esse Orosco, a left-handed specialist, had an exceptional career, pitching in the major leagues for twenty-four years and appearing in 1,252 games—the most by any pitcher in history. He retired at the age of forty-seven with 144 saves.

"I still hold the record for appearances and I am very proud of that accomplishment," stated Orosco. "I appeared in 1,252 games over four decades. I was blessed with a rubber arm and I always knew when I wasn't able to go in. There is no need to be a hero if you aren't going to be effective because it will always bite you later. I learned very quickly my limitations. And when I was ready to pitch my manager was always the first to know. But there were other factors that helped me attain the record. I always had the right manager and the right combination of guys in the bullpen to support me."

Orosco's career began when he was selected by the Minnesota Twins in the second round of the January draft in 1978. He was traded to the New York Mets on February 7, 1979, and made his major league debut less than two months later, on April 5 at Wrigley Field in Chicago. He pitched to the final batter in the ninth inning in the Mets' 10-6 win.

Orosco ended up pitching for nine different major league teams in his career—the Mets, Dodgers, Indians, Brewers, Orioles, Cardinals, Padres, Yankees, and Twins.

"There were a few managers that made a great impact on my career," said Orosco. "I remember George Bamberger, who was my manager in 1982 and 1983 [with the Mets]. He taught me how to throw the slider and what I needed to know to keep it effective. He was also the one who put me in the closer role. Then there was Davey Johnson [Mets manager 1984–90], who really believed in me. He kept putting me in the right situations and allowed me to excel in the role. Those two guys probably had the greatest impact on my career."

But his career didn't start out so easily. He started the 1979 season in the major leagues, making his debut, but his final two appearances that year were as a starter—on June 6 and June 11. After those starts, he was optioned to triple-A Tidewater to gain some experience as a starter. He didn't fare so well, and was demoted in 1980 to double-A Jackson, where he returned to relieving. He had a mixed season in 1981 at Tidewater, making ten starts in his forty-seven games, until a September recall to the majors.

Orosco returned to the majors for good in 1982, making two spot starts in his fifty-four appearances, and picking up four saves.

"The 1986 baseball season was pretty special. Yet, I can't forget 1982, when I was made the left-handed setup guy for the first time and 1983, when I was made the closer," recalled Orosco. "I thought that was a great accomplishment given the struggles I went through a few years before that. What made 1983 so special for me was that everything clicked for me on all cylinders that year. I made the all-star team and I was up for the Cy Young Award in 1983.

They were all great years for me."

Orosco was on the mound for the final out in the Mets' 1986 World Series Championship. "Interestingly, everything seemed to happen so fast for us during that seven-game series. During the season you feel like you have all kinds of time. You get together as a team during spring training and then you take the year to come together as a team. Then before you know it, it's the playoffs and the World Series and everything goes by so quickly. I remember being so fired up during the whole playoffs and World Series. I remember being so tired in game six against the Astros, but there was no time to relax and you just have to give everything."

The lefty pitched out of the bullpen for nearly his entire career, which spanned four decades; however, he was only the closer for a few years, 1983–87.

"I remember at some point during my career the closer role changed. I went from throwing a hundred-plus innings a year at the start of my career to thirty innings a year by the end of my career. I remember we used to average three to four guys appearing in each game, and occasionally just one or two. Today, there might be five or six pitchers a game on average. I remember on several occasions the manager would call me in during the fifth inning and say to me, 'It's your ballgame now!' But that was the way it was back then. You just don't see that any more. I was very fortunate to play the number of years that I did. I started pitching in the 1970s, and then I pitched in the 1980s, '90s, and 2000s. I've seen so many changes, and many of those were big changes, and I was very fortunate to be a part of it."

Orosco, however, does not necessarily believe he could be a closer today. "I would say about 98 percent of the closers you see today are fireballers," he said. "I saw some great closers in my day that were never considered fireballers. I was Doug Jones' setup guy at one point and I learned so much from him. I think our group helped pave the way for the closers of today."

As a closer, the worst experience one could have is blowing a save. "We have one job as a reliever and closer, and we always hope it doesn't end in reverse," said Orosco. "Being a ninth-inning guy out of the bullpen, if you start blowing saves, it can change the whole complexion of a game and the season."

Hitters can go three for ten and have a Hall of Fame career, but that does not hold true for closers. "If you go three for ten as a closer, you would be considered a failure. Even if you go eight for ten, then there are always people out there that will doubt your ability. Going ten for ten keeps you in the role, and an occasional blown save is all they will ever give you."

Orosco truly enjoyed his job. He told *Sports Illustrated* in 2002 that, "I feel the same way I did when I was in Little League... the games are thrilling." However, following the 2003 season, in which he pitched for three different teams and his ERA ballooned to 7.68, he no longer felt "that excitement in me to get going" and opted to retire.

He summarized his career, "I played professional ball for twenty-six years, and I never imagined myself playing three or even five years, and never did I believe I could have played the number of years I did. I am so truly grateful for the time I had in this game."

DAN PLESAC
1986–2003

D an Plesac had an eighteen-year major league career. It began in 1986 as the closer role was solidifying its place in baseball history.

The left-hander grew up in Indiana and attended North Carolina State University before becoming the Milwaukee Brewers' first selection in the June 1983 draft. Less than three years later, he made the Brewers club out of spring training, making his debut on April 11.

"I made the team in 1986 in spring training as the team's fifth starter," Plesac explained. "We had several days off that April, so Manager George Bamberger decided to go with a four-man rotation and he put me in the bullpen for the first three weeks of the season to get me acclimated to pitching in the big leagues. This way the four starters before me would always pitch on their normal pitch day. I would provide long relief and then when May came around I would move into the rotation as the fifth starter. I pitched really well out of the bullpen those first three weeks and I remember George Bamberger calling me into his office and telling me there was a change of plans. I said 'Okay.' I was a rookie and I was just happy to be there in the big leagues. He went on to say, 'We think there is a chance that you could be the Brewers' version of Dave Righetti.' I took it as a great compliment. So they kept me in the bullpen. It was the best thing that ever happened to me. I would have never played eighteen seasons as a starter."

Just two weeks after his debut, Plesac had to face a player he idolized growing up—Carlton Fisk. "I grew up a White Sox fan and I remember the first time I faced Carlton Fisk when he was in a White Sox uniform [on April 23, 1986, in Milwaukee]. I remember how he stepped into that batter's box and all I could think about was that 1975 World Series home run against the Reds. And I kept saying to myself 'Hey, Dan, get a hold of yourself. You've got to get this guy out and get your job done here. I can't admire you anymore. I gotta get you out.' And I did. Fisk grounded out to the shortstop."

Plesac was selected to the All-Star Game in three straight seasons, 1987–89, very early in his storied career.

"I think my greatest moment of my career came at the 1988 All-Star Game. I struck out Darryl Strawberry with two outs in the ninth in a one-run game. It was my third season and I started to feel good in my role."

He explained further, "During my second year in the big leagues I made the All-Star Game, too, but I felt out of place, I was in Oakland and my locker was next to Dave Righetti, Nolan Ryan, and Bret Saberhagen. Two years before that I was pitching in the minors in El Paso, Texas. I was like a fish out of water that first All-Star Game. I remember saying to myself, 'What the hell am I doing here being amongst all of these other guys?'

"But by my second go-around, at the 1988 All-Star Game, I felt a little more comfortable. I was pitching pretty well, having gotten off to a good start that season, and I had finished strong in

1987. I really started to believe that I belonged there, and then when I struck out Strawberry, I thought to myself, 'My stuff plays and I have arrived!'"

Plesac pitched in 1,064 games in the majors. He accrued 158 career saves, 124 in his first five seasons, when he was the closer for the Brewers. Later in his career, the lanky six-foot-five pitcher's primary role was as a left-handed specialist.

"The most difficult part of the closer job is that the great ones—like Dennis Eckersley, Trevor Hoffman, Mariano Rivera, Goose Gossage, and Bruce Sutter—make those twenty-fifth, twenty-sixth, and twenty-seventh outs look easy," said Plesac. "And it's not that easy, especially after you sit around all day hoping the circumstances are right for you to pitch—your team has to be three or fewer runs ahead. And everybody in the entire stadium is expecting you to come in and for the game to be over."

Reflecting back on his career, he analyzed how he met with the success he had. "Early on, your stuff gets you by. You might have that big fastball, but as times goes on, and sometimes when your velocity goes down, you begin to disguise your fastball by mixing in other pitches. And then you learn to pitch players a little differently each time in an effort to throw off their timing.

"I remember I had this conversation once with Pete Vuckovich in 1988," he shared. "We were working out and he said to me, 'Have you ever thrown a 2-2 fastball for a ball purposely, just so you can throw a 3-2 slider for a strike?' I looked at him and said, 'Are you from Mars? Who the hell does that?' I thought to myself. 'I don't want to put any more pressure on myself than I have to in order to throw a slider with a full count.' But, wouldn't you know, six years later I pitched against this left-handed batter and I threw a 2-2 fastball off the plate and then I followed it up with a 3-2 slider for a strike. And I remember saying to myself that first time I did it, 'Wow! That Pete Vuckovich was right!' That is what experience gives you and that is confidence in your pitching. You can never do that early on because the game is moving so fast for you."

He elaborated: "You have to have the physical skills first and foremost. I think it is . . . 70 percent physical skills and 30 percent mental. And if you can will yourself into believing that your stuff is better than everyone else's stuff, then you can be an indispensable member for this role as closer.

"Incidentally," he went on, "no matter who you are or at what level you put on that big league uniform, you are going to get hit every now and then, and you are going to get hit hard . . . it's just going to happen! If you are a reliever and you end up pitching in an average sixty-five games a year, you are normally going to have five games you'll want to forget that you were even a part of. You can't stop it, it's a bloop, and then a blast, it's a close pitch, it's a bad call you thought should have gone your way, and then all of a sudden that three-run lead is gone and everything changes. It's those five games or so that you will want to forget but you can't, and they will haunt you."

Plesac, a gifted orator, shared a story. "I gave up a home run to Mickey Tettleton in old Memorial Stadium in September 1988. To this day, that game and that home run still haunts me because we were closing in on first place and we were just three games out with two weeks to go in the season. I'm not saying if we won that game we would have gone on to win the American League East pennant, but it was a big game and we knew it. That two-out home run to Mickey Tettleton and that loss is still something I think about today," recalled Plesac.

"Everybody that does this role just better have short-term memory," said Plesac. "The guys that are successful in this role are the ones that can take the bad games. You can ask all of the greats about the bad outings, and they were able to move on. Anyone who has to go out and get those last three outs over the course of time is consequently going to have a bad one. It's just the nature of the beast."

Plesac believes the transformation of the closer role is complete. "I think teams have come to the realization that if they want to be successful, have a caliber team and earn championships, then they better have a good closer.

"Let me sum it up this way: If the team you root for has a bad bullpen, it sticks out like a sore thumb. If the team you root for has a good bullpen, then you don't worry about the bullpen. But you better have a good bullpen in the month of September if you want to compete."

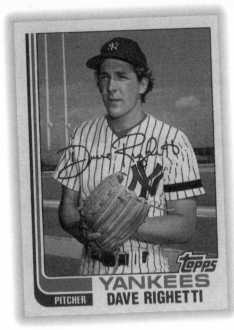

DAVE RIGHETTI
1979–1995

Dave Righetti was another closer who pitched towards the end of the transitional years of the position.

He was the first-round selection of the Texas Rangers in the January 1977 draft and began his professional career as a starter. Following his second season in the minors, he was traded to the New York Yankees, and made his major league debut in a start for them in just his third professional season, on September 16, 1979. The left-hander lost his debut, 8-4, against the Detroit Tigers.

"I remember the first day I came up to the big leagues [Yankees Manager] Billy Martin turned to me and said, 'Go talk to [Ron] Guidry and have him teach you his slider,'" Righetti recalled. "And that was a pitch that Sparky Lyle taught him, and then I went on to teach it a few years later to Al Leiter when he came up. Guidry showed me a different grip that would allow the ball to go down a little farther than what I was throwing. When Billy said that to me,

I said to myself, 'What the hell! Why not learn the pitch from the reigning Cy Young Award winner!'"

Righetti made three major league starts in 1979, but was not recalled in 1980. He returned to the majors in May 1981 and ended up with an 8-4 record and a league-leading 2.05 ERA while earning American League Rookie of the Year honors.

Righetti remained in the starting role through the 1983 season. He even threw a no-hitter—on July 4, 1983, against the Boston Red Sox—the first one by a Yankee in twenty-seven years. Despite his success, Righetti was moved to the closing role the following season to fill the void left by the departure of Goose Gossage.

"I always thought I'd start again," said Righetti. "I kind of had this feeling that I was just going to go into the bullpen until we found somebody to do the closer's job and I'd go back."

During his time with the Yankees, Righetti experienced one of the more interesting mound visits. "It's amazing what you're likely to hear behind the scenes, but I do remember our pitching coach with the Yankees, Art Fowler, came out to visit me once," Righetti began. "It was just after I had signed my first big contract after the 1983 season. I remember I was getting a little wild and here comes Art. He said, in that classic North Carolina accent, 'Hey buddy! With all that money you are now making, you ought to buy yourself a strike zone!' And then he turned around and walked back in the dugout. That was it and the extent of his advice. I think that was also the last time he ever paid a visit to me."

Righetti remained with the Yankees for the majority of his career (1979–1990). He signed with San Francisco following the 1990 season and pitched three years there, before bouncing between Oakland, Toronto, and the Chicago White Sox for the final two seasons of his career.

"Just when you think you've made it in this game, you didn't, and then you did and then you didn't . . . but that is how you felt when you played for the New York Yankees during the 1980s. You never felt like you were on solid ground," Righetti said.

Righetti cited playing for the Yankees in their 1981 playoff series against the Athletics as one of his career's fondest memories. "We beat them three straight and I got the victory in that deciding game. My whole family was also there for the first time. Also, in 1981, I won the Rookie of the Year Award and that was pretty special."

Unfortunately, the worst moment of his career followed shortly after the playoff triumph. "It actually happened a few days later, after I got the victory in the playoffs against the Athletics," Righetti shared. "I didn't pitch that well during the World Series and I came out after three innings. I always thought I was going to get another chance to pitch during the Series, but I didn't. And we certainly didn't know it, or would have guessed it at the time, but we didn't see any further postseason play for the rest of the 1980s. But that division we played in was a powerhouse. You could win ninety ballgames and still finish in third place. That was a big disappointment for me and it still stays with me to this day."

Even with all the success he had early in his career, Righetti was not named to an all-star team until 1986. "I remember I always had bad luck when it came to All-Star Games," he said. "I remember I was going to be selected in 1983, but I threw a no-hitter the day before and they didn't select me because I wouldn't have been able to pitch in the game and I was no good for them. Back then they didn't pick you just so you could call yourself an all-star, and then go and select someone else. They didn't pick you even though you might have deserved it. So bottom line I didn't get selected for the 1983 All-Star Game, and then in 1984 I sliced my finger open a week before the big game and I wasn't picked then. In 1985, I broke my little toe just before the All-Star Game, so I wasn't selected then either. I was so frustrated by then, and finally in 1986, I was selected.

"But then a week before the game I read a story in the Toronto newspaper about the team and how George Steinbrenner was not happy at all with the team's play and he basically blamed the bad play on me! I felt like I could never do anything good. He said in the article, 'How could one guy (meaning me) mess up a team more?' And here I am, I just got selected for the 1986 All-Star Game and I felt like I was really helping my team up to that point. All I could think about was, 'Why is this guy always on my ass?' I am usually pretty thick-skinned and I can take it, but there comes a point when you just can't. So, I guess that was my defining moment: I get picked for the All-Star Game and my owner doesn't think I should be there and says so publicly. All I'm thinking is, 'Nothing was ever good enough,' but then I said, 'Screw it!' It was a very emotional time for me and I had no place to hide."

Righetti pitched two-thirds of an inning in the 1986 All-Star Game, earning a hold in the American League win. He also earned another all-star berth in 1987.

The six-foot-four Californian earned 252 saves over his sixteen-year career. He currently ranks sixteenth on the all-time list.

"In my day, it wasn't about the save," Righetti explained. "It was doing what you had to do to get the victory for your team. I would often go in during the seventh inning and in many cases help to get the victory or keep them from scoring even more. Today, that is unheard of, not necessarily from a player's perspective, but from the media's point of view. There are those that will criticize you the next day for throwing your closer out there for more than an inning . . . that's a load of crap. That is why so many closers back then were involved in so many decisions. I went 12-7 one year [1985] as a closer. A manager would get fired in five minutes if they used their closer like that nowadays."

Righetti is currently the pitching coach for the San Francisco Giants. "Today, the closer is groomed in the minors at a very young age," he said. "But I always ask the question, 'What happens when they can't pitch in that spot when they reach the big leagues? What if they fail?' A lot of these guys might not be able to recover. In San Francisco, we want our pitchers to experience pitching at all the levels."

Righetti was never sure how long he would remain a closer. "I honestly didn't think George had any patience for young pitchers and that is probably why I stayed in the role. And I didn't think they thought they were going to lose Goose and that he was going to sign again. These were all reasons why I stayed in the role for as long as I did."

Although he accomplished a lot, he still does not believe he had a complete career. "I grew up in the 1950s and I had a different mind-set for this game," he said. "I should have done more for myself conditioning-wise. I should have fixed my arm when I had the chance. Hell, I was twenty-nine years old and my arm was shot. I didn't do anything and I should have, but you always felt like you were under contract. You never sat out a whole year like some pitchers do today. Surgery and those types of procedures always seemed so drastic. They just seemed like miracles, unlike today when they do it routinely. And the philosophy back then was that you didn't have any surgeries on you until you stopped growing. I remember I was nineteen years old and a skinny kid when I came up with the Yankees and I still was growing. There is just so much more conditioning nowadays."

JOHN ROCKER
1998–2003

C losers are a unique breed. The role has provided sports fans with the some vivid and memorable personalities. It is a position that demands perfection in an imperfect sport. But of all the unique closer personalities, the most controversial, or misunderstood, is likely to belong to John Rocker.

Rocker grew up in Macon, Georgia, playing baseball like many other kids. "I remember playing Little League and only being able to play a certain number of positions because I was a lefty. I played a lot of first base. I even remember getting my first first-baseman glove; it was from Wilson Sporting Goods. It was my first big league glove. I thought that mitt was the best thing ever."

He began pitching when he was about fourteen years old. He attended First Presbyterian Day School, where the lefty played centerfield and pitched—throwing three no-hitters. The well-rounded athlete was an all-region player in football and an all-star in baseball, and caught the eye of the Atlanta Braves, who selected him in the eighteenth round of the 1993 June draft.

"It was out of necessity that I made it to the bullpen with Atlanta," admitted Rocker. "Because the word from the club was that they were in need of some left-handed arms out of the bullpen. At first they wanted me to get my feet wet in the role until I could fully make the transition from the starting role. But I immediately liked it because it allowed me to enter the game with a specific purpose. Once I started in the bullpen, the light for me came on immediately.

"I admit the change was tough for me. I had the mind-set of a starter my entire high school and pro career. But what the new role did allow me to be was a consistent major leaguer, which was something that I was striving for. After about five relief outings I knew I had found my calling. I was much more comfortable after five appearances in the bullpen than I was with the same number as a starter," Rocker recalled.

"I was a beat starter, with a .500 record and an ERA in the fours all through the minor leagues. What helped me with the transition more than anything was that I had a football mentality. I was extremely aggressive, but that type of mentality doesn't always translate well in the starter role. You are in the constant attack mode as the closer, which doesn't work well over several hours of play as a starter, where strategy and a game plan are more significant. Meaning, starters say to themselves, 'I want to pitch this guy this way in the first, so I can pitch them this way when I see him again in the fourth.' The closer role does not involve that kind of strategy. A closer will say, 'I want to get this guy out right now and I don't care if I'm going to face him again tomorrow.'"

Although he did not become a reliever until 1997, Rocker still credits Jerry Nyman, his first pitching coach (when he was at Danville, Virginia, in 1994) as the man who had the greatest impact on his career. "Jerry was a great pitching coach and he was perfect for someone like me. Jerry taught me a lot. He taught me about the proper delivery, and then on the mental side he'd say, 'Forget about everything that is going on around you, like the 50,000 screaming fans and stay focused on the game. I remember how he'd come to the mound and he wouldn't get all technical, like you're not doing this or doing that right, he'd say, 'John, take the ball out of your glove and go downhill from there,' and then he'd walk away.

"I remembered what he said four years later. It was at Yankees Stadium and I was facing Derek Jeter and Tino Martinez was in the on-deck circle with two outs in the ninth. I remember saying to myself, 'John, take the ball out of your glove and go downhill from there.' It was a simple solution to a complex problem."

The six-foot-four lefty was fortunate enough to play for the Braves during their heyday, when they won an unprecedented fourteen straight division titles (1991–2005) and made five World Series appearances. "There was some added pressure playing for a contender," admitted Rocker, "but overall it really doesn't matter what team you are on. I played for other teams who were not that successful, but you still approach your role the same way each time. There is a sense and expectation to win no matter what team you play for and with it comes the pressure to perform, no matter what."

Rocker certainly did perform on October 8, 1999, in game three of the National League Division Series against the Houston Astros. "The series was tied, 1-1, and it was the tenth inning. I remember Russ Springer had loaded the bases with no outs in the tenth. There were 55,000 screaming fans in the Astrodome. They were all cheering, knowing that the winning run was only ninety feet away, said Rocker. "I remember I came in, and I immediately reframed the situation. I said to myself, 'Screw it! It's not my run out there, and I won't get the loss if I lose this one. There will still be another tomorrow. This isn't such a big deal. I've done this before.' These were all things I said to myself in an effort to downplay the situation. I knew full well that it was an extremely big deal and it was going to be tough for us to come back.

"I remember getting the first out on a slowly hit ground ball and there was a throw to home plate for the force out. Out two came on a rocket to Walt Weiss, who made a snow cone catch, recovered, and threw home to record the second out. Then I struck out the final batter to end the inning. We ended up winning the game in the twelfth inning. I got the victory because we went ahead in the eleventh and Kevin Millwood saved the game. We then went on to win the next game, and then beat the Mets to go to the World Series. But for me, it all came down to that game three in Houston and getting it done for my team and that was my greatest moment. I know things could have been completely different if we lost that game, because we played the next day back in Houston and they would have had the momentum going into that game. That game three in Houston was a very important turning point for the Braves organization. It is amazing how those last three outs can be so important."

Following that season, things began to fall apart for Rocker after he did an unfortunate interview with *Sports Illustrated* in December. The story portrayed Rocker as a racist after he allegedly made several off-color remarks about New Yorkers and Mets fans. "That one article and the angle used gave the media all the ammo they needed to go after me," said Rocker. "I've done so many interviews since then and the media person would often say how he was going to let me clear the air on this, and when I got the article back or read it I'd say to myself, 'This isn't what we talked about!'"

The controversy swirling around him may have played a part in limiting Rocker to only six major league seasons, but the biggest reason his career wasn't longer was because his dedication to the game led to irreparable damage to his left shoulder.

"I would have liked to have played for another four to five more years. I always wanted to get to my ten years. As a player you strive for that, but my injuries changed my plans. And I know I pitched probably when I shouldn't have. I'd say to myself, 'I gotta win this one for the team. I need to be out there,'" recalled Rocker. "I still remember when my shoulder was so bad that I'd come out to take my warm-up pitches, and the first few wouldn't even reach home plate and they would bounce up there."

Looking back, one of Rocker's fondest memories of the game was a conversation with a Hall of Fame pitcher. "I remember meeting with pitching great Bob Feller years ago while I was in Cleveland [2001]. It was during spring training and we talked and talked after one of the games. I remember about fifty people had gathered around us while we talked. He was an amazing man. I really enjoyed the fifteen to twenty minutes we shared together. He gave me a lot of grandfatherly advice I will always remember."

JEFF RUSSELL
1983–1996

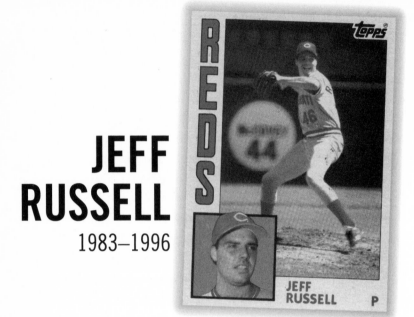

J eff Russell pitched for fourteen years with the Cincinnati Reds, Texas Rangers, Oakland A's, Boston Red Sox, and Cleveland Indians. Not unlike Dennis Eckersley, Russell spent the first half of his career as a starter before moving into a closing role.

A hometown selection for the Cincinnati Reds in the fifth round of the June draft in 1979, Russell was a starter in the minor leagues for less than four seasons before making his major league debut on August 13, 1983 . . . and what a debut it was. Russell pitched a complete game, defeating the San Diego Padres, 3-1, while allowing just five hits and one unearned run.

"My debut was probably the biggest moment for me," said Russell. "I never got to a World Series and some of the seasons were too long to get really excited. But my major league debut will always be special to me. And on April 10, 2010, when my son [James] made his major league debut, that was pretty special for me, too!"

Russell continued starting, but had some tough times. He led the National League with eighteen losses in 1984. He began the 1985 season in the minor leagues with triple-A Denver, and was traded to the Texas Rangers on July 23.

"My first opportunity to be with the Rangers came after I went 6-18 as a starter in Cincinnati," Russell recalled. "I was in my early twenties when I went to Texas, but I was happy to get a fresh start somewhere else."

Russell spent ten of his fourteen years in the majors (1985–92; 1995–96) with the Rangers. He moved into the closing role in 1989 and had some of his best seasons as a closer. The two-time all-star (1988, 1989), led the American League in saves (thirty-eight) and games finished (sixty-six) in 1989, while posting a 1.98 ERA and seventy-seven strikeouts in seventy-one and two-thirds innings. He reached the thirty-save mark again in 1991 and 1992 for the Rangers, and then again with Boston in 1993.

"[Ranger's pitching coach] Tom House was probably the coach that had the greatest impact or was the most instrumental person in my career, primarily because Tom helped me straighten myself out as a pitcher," stated Russell.

"One of the best things I remember I learned from Tom House," he continued, "was that the warm-up was just a warm-up period to give your arm the opportunity to warm up and get loose. Meaning, so many young pitchers get all upset if their slider or curveball aren't working as well in the bullpen warming up. Tom taught me not to worry about that because you were not between those two white lines yet and that adrenaline is not yet there. Yes, Tom House was definitely the coach that had the greatest impact on my career. He taught me and sculpted me. And it wasn't just about the chemistry a player has with his coach, it was above that. Tom was there with us in the weight room and would oversee our nutritional needs. He was like a father figure to us all."

Russell enjoyed his role as the closer and did not have any secret desires to return to the starting role. "The closer role really allowed me to be who I wanted to be," Russell said. "Once I got to the closer role, I loved it! I loved the closer role because I was able to get into sixty to seventy-five games each year. If I was a starter, I would have only been in thirty to thirty-five games a year."

Russell tried to downplay the importance of the closer role in order to help himself prepare for it. "The way I approached and got my mind set for the role was that I would tell myself, 'How hard can it be to pitch just one inning?' That is how I approached it," he revealed.

"I think the move towards the one-inning save came about because so many guys get so hyped up, that it is tough to do it again for another inning," Russell analyzed: "You rev yourself up so much and you've got all of that adrenaline going. That is why I think they went to the one inning save. It's tough to repeat it for a second inning. I really never thought about it before though, and it never bothered me to go into the game for that extra inning."

"We all knew who was going in the game during a certain situation. We all knew our place and I knew I went in during the ninth inning. And once I got into that ninth inning I really did feel invincible, but it is a feeling that so many closers get."

That invincible feeling would leave once a save was blown. "The worst thing for me as the stopper was the blown save," said Russell. "That starter could go out there for seven or eight innings and bust his ass, and then I'd come in for one inning and make one mistake, and it would be all over. It's a terrible feeling!"

Russell finished his career with a 3.75 ERA over 589 games, with seventy-nine starts, eleven complete games, and 186 saves.

"It would have been nice to get to a World Series," said Russell. "I got to the playoffs later in my career with Oakland, but getting to the World Series would have been nice . . . but don't get me wrong I'll never be bitter for what I was able to do in this game."

LEE SMITH
1980–1997

O ne of the best quotes concerning Lee Arthur Smith came from fellow closer Kent Tekulve, who said, "Everything that Lee Smith did in his entire career was in slow motion, except what he did on the pitcher's mound. That is where he scared the s--- out of the hitters. It was never fun to face Lee Smith!"

Lee Smith was a classic example of a pitcher whose career spanned the transitional period of the closing role.

When Smith began his major league career with the Chicago Cubs and he became a closer, 55 percent of his appearances were more than an inning. It dropped to 42 percent when he went to the Boston Red Sox (1988–90), and by the time he went to the St. Louis Cardinals (1990–93), just 17 percent of his appearances went more than an inning. It dropped further over his final four seasons, when just 5 percent of his 163 appearances lasted more than an inning.

When Smith retired in 1997, he was the all-time MLB leader

in saves, with 478. He is continually considered for the Hall of Fame, but has yet to garner enough votes to get in.

Smith grew up in Jamestown, a small town in Louisiana, where he attended Caster High School. "My first love was actually basketball, and I loved the Philadelphia 76ers with Bobby Jones, Dr. J, Moses Malone, and Maurice Cheeks. Those guys were unbelievable."

Not surprisingly, he played basketball in high school; and showed no interest in baseball. "I was forced into playing baseball," admitted Smith. "I went to a very small high school growing up, and we didn't have enough guys to field the team and that is why I had to play, so this way we had enough. With basketball you didn't need many things and because my family didn't have much money, I grew up playing basketball. That is why I didn't get the chance to really know the game of baseball until I made it to the big leagues. I never played Little League and I only played one year of baseball in high school."

The six-foot-five right-hander was selected by the Chicago Cubs in the second round of the June draft in 1975. "When I got drafted, it was Buck O'Neil [the Negro Leagues star who became the first black coach in the major leagues, for the Cubs in 1962] who really provided me with the insight of what the game was all about and what it had to offer."

"I remember me and my brother used to throw little plum peaches that grew on our property at our mailbox. My brother used to try and hit the mailbox, and I tried to hit the flag on the mailbox. I guess that is why I have always had pretty good control," Smith explained.

"For some reason my mom never knew nor understood why we went through so many mailboxes when we were younger," he continued with a grin. "Yet this was still not baseball; it was two boys just playing around. I still remember the mailboxes we had to get. They used to have wheels on them and we would have to drag it into our property each day because some people in our community would look to damage it, because there was still a lot of a racial tension in my small Louisiana town."

After four and a half years of starting in the minor leagues, Smith moved into the bullpen in 1979 for double-A Midland. He made his major league debut the following year, on September 1, 1980, pitching a scoreless fifth inning in the Cubs' 5-2 loss against the Atlanta Braves.

"There were lots of players and managers that helped me in my career," said Smith. "I remember Randy Hundley, who was my manager in double-A; he was really the one that talked the Cubs into bringing me up as a relief pitcher. And when I got to the Cubs, I had Lee Elia as my manager and he always went to bat for me. I remember coming into my first game in Houston with the Cubs, I pitched four innings and only gave up one earned run and they didn't give me the save. Lee Elia asked why I didn't get the save and they told him that I wasn't effective."

One of his shining moments when he got to the big leagues was meeting his idol. "When I got to the major leagues, I actually got to play with my baseball idol, Ferguson Jenkins," Smith raved. "Interestingly, we had similar styles and we looked very similar. In fact, in one of the Chicago Cubs books they published, the caption read 'Ferguson Jenkins captures his 3,000th strikeout' but the photo was actually of me. You can see my face and a portion of my number on my back, and Fergie was No. 31."

Smith made five starts for the Cubs in 1982, from June 19 to July 5. After that brief, but largely unsuccessful stint (0-4, 4.94 ERA in thirty-one innings), he moved back to the bullpen. From mid-July through the remainder of the season, Smith became the Cubs' closer, picking up fifteen of the seventeen saves he earned in the final two-plus months.

"When I came up, I didn't want to be a relief pitcher," Smith admitted, "I wanted to be a starter. But I was very fortunate to be in a Cubs bullpen that had Jay Howell and Bruce Sutter in it. I do remember quitting for a year when I was in the minors because I wasn't getting called up. It took a visit by Billy Williams [the soon-to-be Hall of Famer who played outfield and coached for the Cubs] to my small town to convince me to give it another try. I went home to play basketball, and Billy told me to give it one more chance. I told him that I went 9-5 this past year [1979] and I didn't get called up and I told him I didn't want to play anymore. Billy said back to me, 'Boy, you ain't done s---!' They were his exact words. I came back, and in six weeks I was in the big leagues and I never got sent back again."

He continued: "I used to spend a lot of time with Billy Williams when I did make it to the big leagues, because I wanted to learn as much as I could about what hitters were thinking. I loved playing in St. Louis because it was there that I got to play for my favorite manager, Joe Torre. You always knew what he expected from you. He also gave me one of my greatest compliments, 'Lee Smith is only one of two relievers that I never had to worry about, and the other is Mariano Rivera.' For me that was awesome!"

Smith talked about the differences in pitching in the 1980s as opposed to closers of today. "In our day, we didn't just pitch one inning," he declared. "When I started, a relief pitcher was someone who came in when the game was on the line and not just the ninth inning. I remember when Trevor Hoffman broke my record for saves. He had pitched in so many less games than I did. In my day, you came in during the seventh inning with the tying run on second or bases loaded and no one out. We didn't come in during the ninth inning with a three-run lead. Things were different back then.

"But on the flip side," he continued, "today's closers may only pitch one inning and it puts more emphasis on the blown save. I remember when Atlanta was interested in trading for me, but they were concerned I had already pitched too many innings, and yet I only had 180 saves at that point. I still had 300 saves left in me. And yet in my mind, I didn't think I had thrown enough."

Despite the physical demands of the closer role in his day, Smith still believes the role is more mentally challenging. "So many guys let the blown save wear on them," he said. "I always tried to make it a positive. I would always say to myself: I threw the best pitch I could and the batter got the best of me. And maybe I'll see that same batter again tomorrow and then I'll see how good he really is. I would never hide from the media if I did blow a save, because if you did give up the blown save you have to be a man about it. There was a saying back in our day that if you were a closer, you never wanted to be on *This Week in Baseball* or *SportsCenter* because they would never show the closer when he did something well."

Smith pitched for the Cubs (1980–87), Red Sox, Cardinals, New York Yankees (1993), Baltimore Orioles (1994), California Angles (1995–96), Cincinnati Reds (1996), and Montreal Expos (1997) in his eighteen-year MLB career.

"Billy Connors was probably the craziest pitching coach I ever had," Smith said of his Cubs coach. "Billy was one of George Steinbrenner's gurus of pitching for years. I remember one day I had bases loaded and here comes Billy out of the dugout. I thought he was going to take me out the game, but he said, 'Smithy, look over my shoulder at that blond sitting behind home plate.' I said 'Billy, you're as crazy as a loon.' And then he said 'Can you get this s--- over because she's waiting for me?' Billy had this ability to get you to calm down and not let the pressure get to you. He wanted you to relax and focus on getting the job done, because the game and the closing role come with enough pressure."

Smith was named to seven all-star teams (1983, 1987, 1991–95). "The best story I can remember was in 1987," Smith recalled. "It was the All-Star Game and I was the next-to-last pitcher in the bullpen. I ended up pitching three innings and became the game-winning pitcher that day. I even struck out Mark McGwire twice. It was at that point in my career that a lot of people that were in the media were referring to me as one of the best closers in the game. It was a turning point in my career."

Smith's trademark walk to the mound was slow and deliberate, but when the big right-hander got to the mound, he was dominating and intimidating. He led the league in saves four times, temporarily setting the single-season saves record at forty-seven in 1991, when he was the runner-up to Tom Glavine in the National League Cy Young Award balloting.

If Smith was fortunate enough to finally be selected by the Hall of Fame, he would have to decide which hat would be worn on his plaque. "That is a tough decision; it would be tough to choose between the Cubs and the Cardinals," said Smith. "I have so many great feelings for both of these teams. Even though my heart goes out to St. Louis, my plaque would probably be with the Cubs."

Smith has no regrets concerning his career. "I came from a small town known as Jamestown, Louisiana, and they still don't even have a traffic light," he began. "There were twenty-six people in my graduating class. Never did I ever imagine playing in 400 games, let alone dreaming of saving over 400 games. My greatest dream would be for the Hall of Fame to recognize my career. It would mean so much to me given my background."

BRUCE SUTTER
1980–1997

The fact that Bruce Sutter not only had a major league career, but a Hall of Fame career is somewhat miraculous.

Sutter went to Donegal High School in Mount Joy, Pennsylvania. In his senior year, he was drafted by the Washington Senators in the twenty-first round, but opted not to sign. Three months later, on September 9, 1971, the Chicago Cubs signed him as an amateur free agent.

He began his professional career with the Bradenton Cubs in the Gulf Coast League, however, after two games, he injured his arm. The six-foot-two right-hander needed an operation on a pinched nerve in his right elbow. He had the surgery and paid for it himself, but lost his fastball.

"I didn't think an injured pitcher would get any chance at all," explained Sutter, "and I was afraid they would release me if they knew I was hurt. I chose not to tell them because why would they pay for an untried pitcher and someone would say 'There goes another sore-armed pitcher.'"

Without a fastball, Sutter's career would have been over; however, in 1973 at Quincy (single-A), he met his career savior—pitching coach Fred Martin. "He taught me how to throw the split-finger," said Sutter. "Fred, without a doubt, had the greatest impact on my career. Unfortunately, Fred passed away in 1979 [from cancer at age of 63]."

Sutter's new pitch suited him well and he quickly rose through the ranks, making his major league debut on May 9, 1976, in a 14-2 loss to the Cincinnati Reds in which he pitched the final scoreless inning. And he never looked back.

Sutter pitched for the Cubs for five seasons. He was traded to the St. Louis Cardinals on December 9, 1980, where he remained for four seasons before signing with the Atlanta Braves as a free agent on December 7, 1984. In his twelve years in the majors, he compiled 300 saves in 1,042 innings over 661 games.

The bearded pitcher moved into the closer's role very quickly. "When I first came up I was with Chicago. Darold Knowles was the team's closer. I didn't pitch the eighth and ninth innings, Darold did that. I pitched normally the sixth and seventh innings. But I remember the time we played the Big Red Machine [Cincinnati Reds] and Joe Morgan came up. Both Darold and I were warming up in the bullpen and the manager brought me in, in the ninth inning, to face Joe Morgan. Morgan was a left-handed batter and Darold was a left-handed pitcher, I was naturally a right-handed pitcher, but they brought me in to face Joe. Darold turned to me at that time and said to me, 'I know my job is over!' Meaning, he knew I was the team's closer from that point on. And that was it."

The six-time all-star earned the National League Cy Young Award in 1979, when he went 6-6 for the Cubs, with a league-leading thirty-seven saves. He had a 2.22 ERA in sixty-two games and struck out 110 in 101$\frac{1}{3}$ innings. He became just the third reliever in history to win the prestigious award (joining Mike Marshall and Sparky Lyle).

Still, Sutter felt his best season came three years later, when he won the World Series with the St. Louis Cardinals. "The best year for me was 1982, by far," stated Sutter. "Whenever you can do what you set out to do, and do that with your whole team, and win the World Series that makes it special.

"My best moment was in 1976, when I got called up to the major leagues . . . that was really special being able to walk out on a major league field my first day. My induction ceremony, when was I was elected to the National Baseball Hall of Fame, was also really special for me. Giving that speech during my induction was probably the most nervous thing I ever did in my life." He continued, "And then there are games that stand out and that are special. There was this one in 1982 against the Phillies with about two weeks left in the season. We were fighting them and they were fighting us. Steve Carlton was on the mound for them and John Stuper was on the hill for us. The game finally got to the eighth inning and we were up 2-1. Mike Schmidt came to the plate with one out and the bases loaded. Whitey [Herzog] came to the mound and made the move to bring me into in to pitch to Schmidt. I eventually got Schmidt to ground the ball back to the pitcher's mound. I got it, threw home for the force and then back to first for the double play. I then finished up the ninth inning and that was a big, big save and victory for us . . . beating the Phillies and Steve Carlton that night. And with the victory that was what the Cardinals needed to propel us into the playoffs and eventually the World Series. That was a big night!"

In his day, it was not uncommon for a pitcher to throw multiple innings to earn a save; whether he was called a reliever or closer did not matter to him. "We weren't tied to names back then," said Sutter. "But everyone knew if we had a slim lead, I was probably going to be the pitcher and the game was all set up and designed to get the ball to me. But I said probably, because if the starting pitcher was doing well, he'd stay in. Starting pitchers finished games back then. Back then, those starting pitchers were getting paid, in most cases, on the number of complete games they racked up. And, in those cases, they didn't want to be taken out.

"The closer role is ultimately a role that you have to know that it's you. When you wake up in the morning and go about your day, you ultimately have to know that you're the guy who is going to throw that final pitch tonight that will either win the game or lose the game for your team. You have to live with that."

Dealing with the blown save takes a little more effort. "You just had to learn how to forget it . . . you just had to," said Sutter. "For me, it might have been a little easier than for others, because I was a one-pitch pitcher. I never had to second-guess myself, meaning I didn't have to say to myself, 'Should I have thrown this pitch or that pitch?' I didn't have to think about it. If my split-finger hung, then it was a pretty good pitch for a hitter to hit, and then I was probably going to get beat."

Continuing on that line of thought, Sutter believes the closing role is more mentally challenging. "You've got to learn to be able to shake that stuff off. When you pitched well after a game, you didn't think much about it. You weren't worried, nor did you care, about the media waiting for you after the game to talk about a blown save, like they are today. It was when you pitched bad, that you felt like you let down the whole team. The whole game is managed to give you the ball. It's in your hands and when you didn't do the job, you felt like you let everyone down.

"The physical part of it is what it is. I remember I hurt my shoulder in 1985 and prior to that, I could pitch a lot. I never went up to my manager and said, 'Hey, I need a day off!' You just didn't do that back then."

Sutter reached baseball's pinnacle in 2006, when he became just the fourth relief pitcher inducted into the National Baseball Hall of Fame, and the first inducted who never made a start in the major leagues. At his induction speech, he spoke of the honor.

"On January 10, I got the call from Jack O'Connell and Jane Clark informing me that I'd just been elected to the Baseball Hall of Fame. After hanging up the phone, my emotions got the best of me and I didn't quite know why, but in the six months since I've had the time to reflect on how important that call was; it brought closure to a baseball career that did not end how and when I had always hoped it would. The call answered a question that had been ongoing for thirteen years, a question, quite frankly, I would ask myself every year at election time: do you belong?

"I would like to thank the baseball writers for answering that question and bestowing on me the highest honor that a player can receive. The thought of having a plaque with my name on it beside the greatest players who have ever played the game is truly an honor and humbling experience."

—Bruce Sutter Hall of Fame induction speech, July 30, 2006

BOBBY THIGPEN

1986–1994

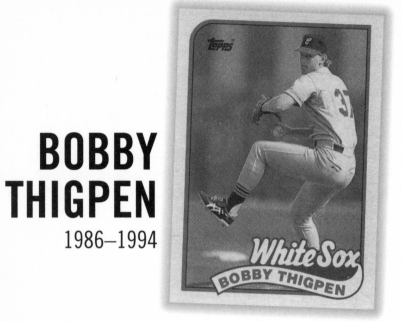

B obby Thigpen's major league career lasted nine seasons, but he is most remembered for one — 1990.

In 1990, Thigpen became the first major league reliever to break the fifty-save mark, with fifty-seven saves, a record that held for eighteen years. He also led the AL in games (seventy-seven) and games finished (seventy-three). His ERA was a miniscule 1.83, and he walked just thirty-two with seventy strikeouts in eighty-eight and two-thirds innings. He also made his first and only all-star appearance in that memorable season.

"The 1990 baseball season flew by," Thigpen recalled. "It seemed like it was over before it got started because of the amount of work I was able to do and the success of the team that year. The four previous seasons we really weren't that good. Then all of a sudden things took off for the team and the White Sox have been consistent as an organization ever since. That year was a turning point for the White Sox."

Thigpen's professional career began in 1985, when he was selected out of Mississippi State University in the fourth round of the June draft by the Chicago White Sox. Fourteen months later, he made his major league debut—on August 6, 1986—pitching the final three innings in a 9-0 White Sox loss in Boston.

"I would say Jim Fregosi [White Sox manager, 1986–88] was the manager that had the greatest impact on my career, because he was the one who put me in the closer role for the first time," said Thigpen. "I also remember Art Kusnyer; he, too, had a great impact on my career. He was my bullpen coach in Chicago."

Thigpen remained with the White Sox and as their closer until 1993, when he lost the closer's role and was traded to the Philadelphia Phillies on August 10. Thigpen aided the Phillies through the playoffs and into the World Series in 1993—his only taste of the postseason.

He signed with the Seattle Mariners in 1994 as a free agent, but his career ended when he was released on April 29 of that year. He went to Japan and pitched well for the Fukuoka Daiei Hawks for two seasons, but a comeback in 1996 was hampered by back ailments.

"During my first three years of pitching in the closer role, I was going two-plus innings to get the save, but by 1990 my role was pretty well-defined," said Thigpen. "I became at that point a one-inning saver and a lot had to do with the success we had as a team and how everything clicked that year."

Reflecting upon his experience, he believes that the closer role has finished evolving. "The closer role, I believe, will continue to be that one-inning specialist," said Thigpen. "I also believe Tony La Russa and Dennis Eckersley should be given credit for perfecting the closer role in helping to mold what that closer role is today."

Thigpen's biggest disappointment in his career was his inability to finish it as he wished. "Later in my career when my back went out, I thought I could have played a few more seasons.

Then I eventually had back surgery in 1996 and that was pretty much it for me, and yet I was still only thirty-two years old. I wish I knew about steroids back then!" he added with a laugh.

"I felt like I wanted to play for a few more years," Thigpen said, "and as a player you always want to get to that ten-year mark in the game. But for the past six years I've been into coaching, and I really enjoy it and I am so happy watching these kids and feeling like I'm having some part in their success. It is very, very satisfying and it really is a special treat," said Thigpen, who has been coaching in the White Sox minor league system since 2007.

The six-foot-three right-hander finished his nine-year career with 201 saves, including four seasons with thirty-plus saves. Unlike some closers of today, Thigpen did not like to waste any time on the field. "I preferred to get out there on the field as quickly as possible, get those final outs, and then get off the field. I hated to waste time!" he confessed. "I needed to get the job done. But sometimes I ended up walking the first batter. I think it was a concentration thing and it used to drive my manager crazy. But then it used to help with my focus and get the adrenaline going, knowing I had someone on."

One of Thigpen's craziest experiences on the mound came when a pitching coach visited him there. "I remember one pitching coach who came out to the mound and he *never* said a word," he recalled. "He looked at me and never said anything. All he did was kick dirt around!"

Like many other relievers, Thigpen also believes the role is more of a mental challenge than a physical one. "We are all physically capable of going out there and, hopefully, pitching every day," he said. "It's the mental side that you will always have to deal with. The more I pitched, the better I got. If I was off for a few days, then I wasn't as sharp."

As he implied, routine and repetition is the key; but the game is unpredictable. "It's funny, sometimes you warm up in the bullpen and you say to yourself, 'I really got electric stuff today' and you feel invincible," said Thigpen. "And then you go out there and you can't get a single out. And then sometimes you are in the bullpen and say the opposite to yourself, thinking you don't have what it takes, and then you go out there and do great. It's a crazy game, baseball. For me that is why I was always ready to pitch."

Thigpen concluded: "What was special for me over the years was some of the opportunities I had as a ballplayer. I got to play with George Foster, I got the save for Steve Carlton's first American League victory, and I got the save when Charlie Hough got his two hundredth win. In fact, it took me two tries to get that save, and Charlie has never let me forget it. There were so many of those things that helped make my career special for me. And that is what made it special—being a part of those moments of the game. Every day was different. I enjoyed every minute of this game I played."

In 2012, Thigpen became another former closer to secure the job of a major league pitching coach for the Chicago White Sox.

MITCH WILLIAMS
1986–1997

M itch "the Wild Thing" Williams was not unique among closers in that he began as a starter in the minors; what was unique about Williams was his major league success, despite his apparent lack of control.

He was selected by the San Diego Padres in the eighth round of the June 1982 draft out of West Linn High School in Oregon, where he was the winningest pitcher in state history his senior year, going 17-0 with 191 strikeouts.

At seventeen years of age, he began his professional career in Walla Walla, Washington. The six-foot-four lefty walked seventy-two and struck out sixty-six in fifty-eight and one-third innings that season. In 1983, he pitched for Spokane (fifty-five walks and eighty-seven strikeouts in ninety-two and one-third innings with fourteen wild pitches) and Reno (sixty walks and forty-four strikeouts in fifty-eight innings). He pitched for Reno again in 1984 (127 walks and 165 strikeouts in 164 innings, with nineteen wild pitches).

Williams was selected by the Texas Rangers in the Rule Five draft in December 1984. The Rangers were unable to keep him on their double-A roster, so they returned him, but immediately made a trade in order to keep the lefty.

It was with the Rangers that Williams made his major league debut—on April 6, 1986, against the Toronto Blue Jays. And it was there that he met Pitching Coach Tom House. "Tom mechanically had the greatest impact on my career," said Williams. "He helped me to be just a little more consistent with my mechanics."

He continued: "I remember Tom House said something to me that stuck with me my entire career. He said once during a bases-loaded situation, 'Even though this may seem like your worst jam in baseball, bases loaded and nobody out, you're still just one pitch from being out of it.' I have always lived by that statement. Now, granted, it's got to be a triple play to get you out of the inning, but we've all seen triple plays turned and I've always lived by that. I didn't care how many guys ever stood on that square base in a game; I only cared about how many guys crossed that five-sided base.

"Tom did a lot of inventive things in this sport. I think he was the first to have his staff throw with a football to warm up. It's a great exercise. It gives you instant results. It's a strengthening exercise because the ball is naturally heavier and it's instant feedback because if you can't throw a spiral, then your mechanics are all off. So it's pretty simple stuff."

Williams was traded to the Chicago Cubs following the 1988 season. "The best story I can remember was my first game in the National League," recalled Williams. "It was opening day in Chicago in 1989. I was brought into the game in the eighth with two outs in a 5-4 game. It was my first game with the Cubs and Rick Sutcliffe started the game, having pitched seven and two-thirds of the game. I think there were one or two guys on base and I was able to get the last out in the eighth. I then went out in the ninth and the first three batters got broken-bat singles off me. I'm standing on the mound and I said to myself, 'This league isn't very fun!' I then was able to strike out the side, finishing the game and getting the save. It was one of my fondest memories — that could have broken me that day being my first game, but I was able to come out on top. It was a great initiation."

It was also in Chicago where Williams picked up his nickname, Wild Thing, an acknowledgement of his favorite character from the movie *Major League*. "I can't say for sure if I inspired the character or not, but the movie did come out before I got the nickname." Fans and media could not get enough of the "wild" man. His teammate Mark Grace said, "Mitch pitches like his hair is on fire."

"I wasn't crafty, that's for sure," admitted Williams. "But I think I was a lot smarter than people gave me credit for. I never went out to the bullpen at the start of the game. You can't see locations of pitches and what the hitters were looking at. I stayed in the clubhouse for the first five or so innings so I could see the pitches from that location on the television. I could see the hitter's weaknesses so much better. All hitters have strengths and all hitters have weaknesses, and all hitters can hit a fastball, but they can't hit a fastball in all four zones. I also watched hitters in batting practice to pick up weaknesses. When I came up, I was twenty-one years old and I didn't talk to pitchers. I really didn't care what they had to say; I talked to hitters. I don't care what is going through a pitcher's mind; I only care about the hitter's mind.

"Being a closer is absolutely mental. It's mental on your part and it's perception on your opponent's part because hitters perceive weaknesses like a shark smells blood. If you walk up to that mound and they notice any question mark on your face as to whether you can get them out or not, then you're gonna get hit and hit hard."

Prior to the 1991 season, Williams was traded to the Philadelphia Phillies. "I'm glad to be here," said Williams at the time, "I'm excited I'm going somewhere where I know they want me."

Williams reminisced about the beginning of his time in

Philadelphia: "When I got over to the Phillies, [Pitching Coach] Johnny Podres was the best I ever dealt with who didn't concern himself with mechanics," said Williams. "He helped me to deal with my head. I remember I walked the bases loaded one time, and he came out of the dugout to talk with me. He said to me, 'You're throwing the ball great.' Then I said to him, 'Dude, are you watching the same game I am?' But he was one of those guys who was great at taking your mind off the game and the situation and all of that negative stuff that was going on around you."

The 1993 season with the Phillies provided the greatest and worst moments of his major league career. "My greatest moment on the mound was game six of the 1993 National League Championship Series against the Braves." The game was played on October 13 at Veterans Stadium in Philadelphia, and Williams was on the mound for the final out in the pennant-clinching game. Ten days later, came his career's biggest disappointment. "I gave up the home run to Joe Carter in the World Series against the Blue Jays," recalled Williams, of Carter's World Series-ending blast.

After such a dramatic season with a bunch of misfits outperforming their opponents, that infamous home run was tough to get over. "The pain went away for me a long time ago," said Williams, "and I explain to fans all of the time: they can either accept my explanation or they won't. There was never a game I went into that wasn't less important than the next game or the last game. Whether it was spring training, the regular season, the playoffs, or the World Series, they all meant the same to me. My job was the same for me no matter what the game. My job was to go out there and get people out and if I didn't do that, I was pissed about it."

He went on: "I loved Philadelphia fans. I got booed all of the time. The problem players have in Philadelphia is honesty. If you want to get cheered all of the time, then don't go and play in Philadelphia. Mike Schmidt hit 548 home runs for that town and he got booed regularly. I've always said Philly fans are not booing the player, they are booing the performance, and they have every right to do just that. They love their blue-collar players and that is what I thought of myself as a player.

"In Philadelphia, we had the perfect storm in 1993. There are still people today who claim they loved that squad equally or more so than the 1980 [world champion] team. Philly fans could relate to us better because [we] were more like the fans who followed us. There was one pretty boy on the team and that was Dutch [Darren Dalton]. When the playoffs began in 1993 against the Braves, a reporter asked me about the series and I said, 'It's America's team against America's most-wanted team' and that is how we all looked at it. We weren't a bunch of guys who you'd invite to dinner, but if you wanted to play baseball against the 1993 Phillies, you'd better be ready to play all twenty-seven outs, and we played twenty-seven outs every night."

Williams was traded following the 1993 season, but he was never the same pitcher. "When I left Philadelphia in 1993, I was pretty much done with the game," Williams honestly stated. "And the reason why, I just went out and had the best year of my career, made it to the World Series, and then I got traded and that took all of the fun out of the game for me. I knew I couldn't go anywhere else and be a part of a team who had twenty-five guys who were all going in the same direction. I knew this wasn't going to happen again for me. So, I played about two more seasons, but I can honestly say that I was not into it like I was before."

Williams looked back and analyzed his years as a closer. "There is no safety net, there is no one behind you, and there is no one who can help out. If you are in the bullpen as a setup guy, there is someone who can come into the game if you get in trouble. The closer, it's you against them, and that is why I liked it. I hated it when I was sent to the mound as the closer early in my career and they would bring me in, but then they would have someone throwing behind me. It didn't happen until I got to Chicago for the Cubs and Don Zimmer gave me the ball and would say, 'The game is yours.'

That is the kind of pressure I liked. I wanted to know that this game was mine to win it or lose it. It may not be pretty, but more times than not I was going to get the job done."

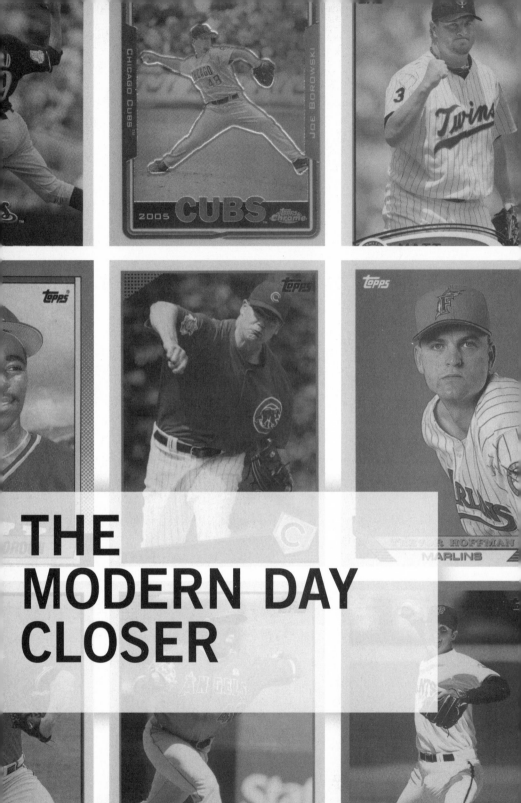

THE
MODERN DAY
CLOSER

JOHN AXFORD

2009–PRESENT

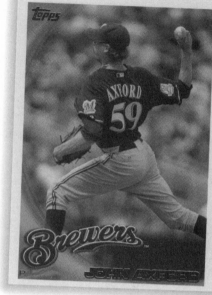

J ohn Axford is a newcomer to the closing scene. Unlike many players of this era, the start of this Canadian-born right-hander's career was like a roller coaster.

It started with a lot of promise, when the Seattle Mariners drafted him out of Assumption College School in 2001, but he opted to attend the University of Notre Dame and ended up pitching for the Fighting Irish in the 2002 College World Series as a freshman.

In 2004, the right-hander underwent Tommy John surgery, returning to Notre Dame in 2005 to pitch just three innings.

Again the scouts liked him, as he was selected by the Cincinnati Reds in 2005; however, this time he chose to attend Canisius College (Buffalo, New York) for the 2006 season.

Finally, on August 11, 2006, he signed with the New York Yankees as an amateur free agent. Axford spent the 2007 season pitching for four teams in the Yankees organization, compiling a

1-4 record with a 3.29 ERA in twenty-seven games, with five starts, eleven games finished, four saves, and sixty-seven strikeouts in sixty-three innings.

The Yankees released the six-foot-five pitcher on December 4, 2007. Axford was just twenty-four years old and struggling to get by. Recalling those days, he said: "There were a lot of times where I couldn't get money out of the ATM because I didn't have enough."

He took a job as a bartender, earning $8.25 an hour at an establishment called East Side Mario's in his native province of Ontario, Canada. During that same time, Axford also worked for $8 an hour selling cell phones for a Canadian telecommunications company at local Wal-Marts and Best Buys. Axford's journey from Best Buy to the Brewers is a remarkable story of perseverance and determination. Always wanting to keep his dream alive, Axford continued to train and work out and hosted a session on his own for scouts to watch him pitch. A snowstorm hit the area, and just one scout showed up. That scout saw him pitch and convinced the Milwaukee Brewers to sign Axford on March 4, 2008.

After striking out 178 in 163$\frac{1}{3}$ innings in seventy-one games over two seasons, he was called up to the majors. A mere eighteen months after signing with the Brewers, Axford made his major league debut on September 15, 2009, at Wrigley Field. He earned his first major league save on October 4, 2009, in relief of Trevor Hoffman in the tenth inning of a 9-7 win at St. Louis.

The strikeout pitcher made an immediate impact. He became the closer in 2010. His twenty-four saves that year tied the record for most by a Brewers rookie.

He recalled his first save that season—on May 23 at Minnesota. "My first save in 2010 was one of my more memorable," noted Axford. "I loaded the bases and allowed a run to score. But I wiggled my way out of it, and at that moment, I felt like, 'I can do this.'"

His 2011 season was even better. He made the opening day roster and finally spent his first full season in the majors. His forty-six saves (in forty-eight opportunities) tied for the best in the National League and he earned the 2011 NL Rolaids Relief Man Award. Hall of Famer Rollie Fingers was the only other Brewer to earn that award, which goes to each league's top relief pitcher.

There is still one thing Axford strives to achieve. "Consistency. As a closer, one of the toughest things is that many variables are out of your hands, so the best thing to do is stay as consistent as possible."

Axford had a lot of positive influences on his career to get him where he is today. "On the physical side, two coaches in the Brewers minor league system were very influential: Fred Dabney, one of my minor league pitching coaches, and Lee Tunnell, the pitching coordinator. They've helped me establish where I am now, solidifying my mechanics," he said.

"From a mental standpoint, it has to be Trevor [Hoffman]. Just watching him day in and day out, how he prepares, regardless of what role he had." Hoffman pitched the final two years of his stellar career (2009–10) as a teammate of Axford with the Milwaukee Brewers.

The Axeman recalled his fondest memories on the mound to date. "One that comes to mind was when I actually had a blown save, game five of the 2011 National League Division Series against the Diamondbacks. I would have preferred to do my job in the ninth, but I came back out in the tenth and kept us in the game, and Nyjer Morgan had a walk-off hit to send us to the National League Championship Series."

His other fondest memory occurred verses St. Louis on September 7, 2010, when he set up Trevor Hoffman's 600th career save. "I pitched the eighth and watched him get the save and everybody couldn't have been happier for him."

RAFAEL BETANCOURT
2003–PRESENT

R afael Betancourt is new to the closing scene, but he is certainly no stranger to the relieving role, although it did not start out that way.

The six-foot-two Venezuela native was signed as a middle infielder by the Boston Red Sox as an amateur free agent on September 13, 1993, out of his hometown of Cumana, Sucre. After three years toiling in the Red Sox minor league system, he was converted into a relief pitcher in 1997, but it would still take another six years before he would pitch in the major leagues.

Betancourt compiled thirty saves in three minor league seasons before he was sold to Japan's Yokohama Baystars in 2000. He returned to the Red Sox in 2001, pitching in relief at double-A when his elbow troubles began. On July 23, he underwent surgery on his right elbow to transpose the ulnar nerve and had a metal rod placed in his forearm. His recovery lasted through the 2002 season.

His roundabout road to the majors continued through Cleveland when he was signed by the Indians on January 20, 2003. Finally healthy, he pitched well at double-A, triple-A, and in three stints in the majors, including his major league debut that same year, on July 13, against the Chicago White Sox.

He finally had his first full major league season in 2004, and actually had a short stint as the Indians' closer in late April/early May, accruing two of his four saves of the season. He suffered from right bicep tendinitis and arm fatigue midway through the season, but finished with a team-leading twelve holds while allowing just one run in his final dozen games.

Betancourt was a solid reliever for the Indians in 2006 and 2007. In 2008, he got another brief opportunity to close at the end of April when Joe Borowski landed on the disabled list. However, he soon lost the position due to his inconsistency.

The 2009 season was pivotal for the right-hander. The year began much like the previous three seasons—with him working as a reliever in the Indians' bullpen. But on July 23, he was traded to the Colorado Rockies and almost immediately became the setup man for closer Huston Street. He picked up his first save for the Rockies on September 16 in San Francisco.

He met with continued success in the setup role in 2010, finishing second in the majors with an 11.3 strikeout/walk ratio (eighty-nine strikeouts/eight walks) and twenty-three holds. But it was the second half of the 2011 season, beginning on August 8, when Street was sidelined with an injury, that Betancourt was finally presented the long-awaited opportunity to close . . . and he did an admirable job, converting eight of nine save opportunities and finishing thirteen games.

The Rockies had enough confidence in him that they traded Street to the San Diego Padres in the off-season and handed the closing job to Betancourt. "It feels good to be the team's closer," said the Venezuelan. "It is an opportunity I've been working towards for a long time. It has always been one of my goals as a relief pitcher, but I am more excited at the opportunity to help my team."

His adjustment to the new role has been smooth sailing. "I think I have always been ready for the next step. No matter what inning I used to come in . . . I always treated it as important," said Betancourt. "Maybe I've had the mind-set of a closer and that has helped me. Having confidence in the closer role is so important. If your confidence level goes down, that could affect your pitching and keep you from pitching well."

At the age of 37, Betancourt is finally a major league closer. His determination helped get him to this point in his life, but he also benefitted from observing others. "I've always had good teammates around me," he admitted. "But I also always look at those who have done the role and I admire them and the work ethic they bring to the game, like Mariano Rivera, Trevor Hoffman, and Joe Nathan. I like to look to those guys for inspiration. I have also been blessed with some really great coaches and managers throughout my career."

Although still hoping for an even greater moment on the field with a World Series Championship, Betancourt admits he's still had many great moments, like "when we as a team clinched the American League title in 2007 when I was with Cleveland will always be very special for me. I wasn't the closer back then; we had Joe Borowski on the team. But, I had a chance to pitch in the later innings of the game we clinched against Oakland. And Joe Borowski was one of those great guys that I played with and learned from because he gave everything he had every night to the game."

As for the not so great moments, he laughed as he said, "I've had a lot of those, too. I just don't like to think about those too much."

JOE BOROWSKI
1995–2008

J oe Borowski pitched in the major leagues for twelve years, from 1995 through 2008, except for two years, 1999 and 2000, when he struggled not only to return to the majors, but to stay in professional baseball. His up-and-down ride showcased the importance of patience and perseverance to succeed in baseball.

Born on May 4, 1971, in Bayonne, New Jersey, the right-hander was an All-American at Marist High School in both baseball and football. He was also selected as All-State in both sports in his junior and senior years. In 1989, his senior year, the Chicago White Sox selected him in the thirty-second round of the June draft, and two months later he signed with them.

After one year with the White Sox organization, he was traded to the Baltimore Orioles. He spent five years in the minors, pitching in relief, before getting the call to the majors. His debut on July 9, 1995, was in Chicago against the White Sox, where he pitched a perfect ninth inning in the Orioles' 11-2 win. He made three visits to the majors that season, pitching in six games while posting a 1.23 ERA.

In December 1995, Borowski was traded to the Atlanta Braves. He pitched most of two seasons with the big club, combining for a 4-6 record in forty-two games, through fifty innings. The New York Yankees selected him off waivers on September 13, 1997, to shore up their bullpen for their playoff run, but he was only used in one game. He did not fare much better in the 1998 season, as he pitched primarily in the minors, appearing in just eight games for the Yankees.

The Cubs signed him in 2001, and he pitched in thirty-nine games for triple-A Iowa. He also made one appearance for the Cubs—his only major league start—on August 11 verses the San Francisco Giants. He lost, 9-4, pitching one and two-third innings, but it was his first MLB appearance since September 22, 1998.

Borowski's time with the Cubs got progressively better. He picked up his first two major league saves in 2002 and ranked third among relievers with ninety-five and two-thirds innings. He struck out ninety-seven and walked just twenty-nine that year. He became the Cubs' closer in 2003, earning thirty-three saves in thirty-seven chances. In 2004, he was again the team's closer, earning the save on opening day.

Bad luck found Borowski when a line drive fractured a bone in his right forearm in spring training in 2005. He did not pitch again until May 20 and was released after eleven games. The Tampa Bay Rays picked him up on July 11 for the remainder of the season and he rebounded by pitching in thirty-two of the Rays seventy-three remaining games, keeping opponents scoreless in his first twenty games and twenty-one innings.

He signed with the Florida Marlins as a free agent for 2006, and ranked third in the National League with thirty-six saves. He moved on to Cleveland, where he led the American League with a career-best forty-five saves in 2007 and helped the Indians past the Yankees in the American League Division Series (ALDS).

With his career peaking, Borowski returned to the Indians in 2008, but a nagging right tricep injury inhibited his play and he managed just six saves in ten chances, with a whopping 7.56 ERA. He was released on July 4. Boston gave him a try, but he was still not 100 percent. He tried one more comeback in 2009, but no teams would commit to him, so he announced his retirement in February.

"I think my greatest challenge in this game was not being able to mentally understand what I needed to know early in my career and what it meant to be a complete player," said Borowski. "Unfortunately, it took me almost my whole career to figure it all out. Anybody can go out there and pitch when everything is going well. The real challenge is pitching well when things are not going as well."

David Justice was one player who gave Borowski sound advice that eventually helped him in his career. "There were a few guys I respected, not because they were pitchers, but because of the way they went about their business," Borowski began. "I remember David Justice coming up to me in the outfield one day while playing for Atlanta and asking me, 'How did I feel about failure?' What it came down to was, as he said, 'You can't be afraid of failure, but failure should be a great motivator for you.' I didn't think about what he said until later in my career and almost out of this game. It was then that what he said to me clicked, and I remember saying to myself in the mirror one day, 'Why do I struggle and worry about things that I cannot control, instead of worrying about things I can control?' My whole outlook changed and it didn't matter anymore what the coaches or GM thought about how I was playing, but rather the only thing I worried about was doing my job as well as I could and to get out major league hitters."

Borowski pitched for twelve years in the majors, and by the time he became a closer, the role was well-defined. "But today the role is even more specialized than ever before," he claimed. "Of course, then again, more and more of the roles in this game are being defined."

Borowski's greatest moment came in the 2007 ALDS in which the Indians defeated the Yankees, three games to one. Borowski earned the save in the final game of the 6-4 victory. He got Derek Jeter to pop out, Bobby Abreu hit a solo home run, Alex Rodriguez flew out, and then he got Jorge Posada to strike out swinging to end the game and series.

"My greatest moment for me happened later in my career, because I always struggled at Yankee Stadium. I got the chance to face the Yankees during the 2007 Division Series. And you have to understand, I grew up across the river in New Jersey and grew up a Yankees fan all of my life. To beat them and accomplish what I did against them, and all of that tradition that goes with it, is something that I will never forget."

Borowski sees the mental aspect of closing as vital, but mysterious. "It's funny," said Borowski, "there are guys in this game who can come in during the fifth, sixth, seventh, and eighth innings, and it's lights out whenever they come in. Nobody can touch them . . . and then they get the opportunity to close and they can't get the job done. And then there is this guy with average stuff, but he excels in the closer role. It's one of those great mysteries of the game for me."

In his twelve-year career, Borowski earned 131 saves in 423 games while pitching for seven different teams.

"I did everything I wanted to do in this game. I have no regrets," said Borowski. "I far exceeded anything that was ever expected of me. I was a thirty-second round draft pick and I got to play professionally in this game for twenty years. I sometimes say to myself, What if I didn't get hurt? Could I have pitched longer?' Who knows, and as I said before, I have no regrets and I am happy with my career. I never took anything for granted, because I always knew that this could have all gone away in a moment."

MATT CAPPS
2005–PRESENT

Matt Capps was a stellar athlete at Alexander High School in Douglasville, Georgia. He lettered in four sports: baseball, football, basketball, and cross-country. He even got a scholarship offer to Louisiana State University.

However, in his senior year, when the Pittsburgh Pirates selected him in the seventh round of the June 2002 draft, he opted to go professional. Eleven years later, Capps has pitched in the big leagues for eight seasons and is still going strong.

"I love what I do and it is something I've wanted to do since I was knee-high to a grasshopper," Capps confessed. "I will never lose that appreciation for what I do and I owe it all to my mom and dad. I remember watching my dad busting his ass so me and my brother could play Little League. Never in my wildest dreams could I have imagined being where I am and doing what I am doing, but on the other hand I couldn't believe in my wildest dreams not doing this job. I am so fortunate to do what I do, but as my dad would always say, 'Someone has to be!' I remember coming to the ball park when I was younger with my dad, and he would never put these guys on a pedestal and that is where the expression 'Someone has to be' comes from. Meaning, someone has to be out there pitching and hitting, otherwise there wouldn't be anyone in the stands watching the game, so why can't that be you?"

In the minors in 2005, Capps compiled a 2.57 ERA in fifty-two games, with twenty-one saves in twenty-nine opportunities for single-A Hickory and double-A Altoona. He was promoted to triple-A Indianapolis for their championship series against Toledo, before the Pirates called him to the majors on September 16. He made his major league debut in relief that night verses Cincinnati (one inning, one run, two strikeouts), and his career took off.

In 2006, the rookie right-hander pitched so well that he was frequently used as the setup man for closers Mike Gonzalez and Salomon Torres. He finished the season leading all major league rookies with eighty-five games pitched. He started the 2007 season as the sole setup man for Torres. On June 1, Pirates Manager Jim Tracy announced Capps would replace Torres as the team's closer.

Capps was also the Pirates' closer in 2008, converting his first fifteen save opportunities before his first blown save came on June 10. Unfortunately, a sore arm on July 2 sidelined him for two months and the Pirates granted him his free agency following the season.

The best season of Capps' career came in 2010, when he signed with the Washington Nationals. He earned twenty-three saves in the first half of the season and was selected to his first All-Star Game, where he retired the only batter he faced—David Ortiz—in the sixth inning and ended up getting the win after the National League team rallied to score three runs in the top of the seventh inning and hung on for a 3-1 win.

On July 29, Capps was traded to the Minnesota Twins and he took over the closer role from Jon Rausch. He went 2-0 with a 2.00

ERA, while earning sixteen saves in eighteen opportunities to cap off his brilliant season.

In 2011, a healthy Joe Nathan returned to the Twins and the closer's role flipped back and forth between him and Capps. After earning fifteen saves in twenty-four opportunities in 2011, Capps rebounded to have a strong start to the 2012 season, converting fourteen of fifteen save opportunities prior to the all-star break.

Capps has had so many players and coaches impact his career that he could not settle on just one. "I do remember Ray Searage, the current pitching coach for the Pittsburgh Pirates," Capps recalled. "He was my pitching coach in the minors when I was in low ball. He was there the first year I became a closer and he helped me to make the transition from starter to closer and make that change easier for me. He helped me to learn the whole dynamics when it came to pitching and I took that when I got called up.

"Then when I got called up," he continued, "I got to work with Jose Mesa with the Pirates. And it wasn't as much what Mesa said to me, but rather I watched how he went about his work. I took that away from him. Then the team signed Roberto Hernandez, another 300-plus save guy, and I spent a lot of time with him and he had a great impact on me. Then I moved over to the Twins and I got to work with Joe Nathan and observe the job he did. I've taken a little away from each closer I've worked with, and together they all had a big impact on me."

He still gets advice these days from his coaches, but he feels he actually learns more from the hitting coach as opposed to his pitching coach. "A pitching coach at this level is more of a psychologist and a mental coach," Capps explained. "And some guys are really good at that and some coaches are good at the mechanics of the game. My dad was always my mental coach before he passed away. He was my coach all through Little League and then up through high school. He passed away in 2009. I miss calling him and talking to him every day. I talked to him after every game during my pro ball career. My dad was good at motivating me all through the years. My dad would always say, 'The day you are not trying your best is the day we quit.' He would also say, 'If you don't love it enough to be your best, then it is time to give up.' My dad taught me so many life lessons that I can't wait to pass on to my own son."

Capps is a real workhorse. "I'm a believer in throwing every day. And, in all of my days as a pitcher, I've never asked for the day off. And I don't see myself ever asking, and my reasoning for that is that I am only one of thirty guys out there that does this job and I can't imagine taking the day off. There are eight guys out there with me busting their asses who want to win and who am I to say, 'I'm tired!'? This role as a closer is like a brotherhood and a fraternity and I have been blessed during my career to be around some great closers. It is something that cements us and I'll take a bullet for my team out there. I think that is the best part of the role…the camaraderie."

As for coping with blown saves, "I have the memory of a fish," said Capps with a smile. "You've seen fish. They bang into the side of a fish tank and then two seconds later they are doing it again. So if you are the closer, you better not have a good memory. If you give up a leadoff double, you better forget about him and concentrate on the next batter, because that guy on second can't do anything unless the guy that is up at bat does something."

Smart and crafty are not words the six-foot-two right-hander would use to describe himself in the closer role. He jokes, "If I were smart, then I wouldn't be doing this job. Crafty doesn't feel right, either, because I would have better control out there. The best word to describe myself in this role should be, 'stupidity,'" he said with a laugh.

Capps is a family man, with a big appreciation for all he has achieved in this game. "I fly high every day and I play a kids game and get paid very well for what I do."

He keeps sayings that he has picked up from his father and through his career on the bottom of his cap. "Two of my favorite sayings are 'Throw quality strikes' and 'It's more fun to win, so just have fun.'"

FRANCISCO CORDERO
1999–PRESENT

Francisco "CoCo" Cordero has pitched in the majors for fourteen years for the Detroit Tigers, Texas Rangers, Milwaukee Brewers, Cincinnati Reds, and Toronto Blue Jays. He has accumulated over 329 career saves and is second only to Mariano Rivera among active save leaders.

Cordero may be the most anonymous top closer in the game today. "Not being in that big market, people don't pay that much attention to you," Cordero admitted.

The big right-hander was born in Santo Domingo, Dominican Republic, in 1975. He was signed by the Detroit Tigers as an amateur free agent on June 18, 1994. Like many other closers, Cordero began his professional career as a starter.

He hurt his right elbow in 1996 and missed most of the season. Cordero was healthy when he reported to the Tigers' minor league spring training in 1997 and assumed he would resume his career as a starter with his sharp slider, but the coaches had other ideas. He was told to throw only fastballs and was forbidden to throw the slider; to help make that happen, they moved him into the bullpen.

And the result was impressive. His fastball went to a consistent 98 mph and he was so dominating in his new role that the Tigers' organization left him in the pen. He finished that 1997 season with a club-record thirty-five saves for West Michigan and was voted by *Baseball America* as the Midwest League's best reliever and as having the best fastball.

He returned to form in 1999, when he led the Southern League with twenty-seven saves and was named the Minor League Relief Pitcher of the Year by Howe Sportsdata. Cordero made his major league debut on August 2 against the Chicago White Sox, pitching the final inning of the Tigers' 6-2 loss.

Cordero was traded to the Rangers on November 2, 1999. With the Rangers, he suffered a stress fracture in his back, missing much of the 2001 season. In 2002, he earned his first major league save, on June 19 at Wrigley Field. In 2003, he was the setup man for Ugueth Urbina until mid-July when Urbina was traded and Cordero was named the closer.

The 2004 season was the first time Cordero spent an entire season as the closer. He did not disappoint, saving forty-nine games, second only to Rivera's fifty-three in the American League, and earning his first of three All-Star Game selections.

One of Cordero's priorities these days is his health. "The most important thing is to stay healthy, because you can be the best pitcher in the world, but if you're hurt, then you can't pitch and help your team," he explained.

The Tigers traded Cordero to the Brewers on July 28, 2006. In his only full season with the Brewers (2007), he was named to his second all-star team, and with forty-four saves, finished second in the National League to Jose Valverde, who had forty-seven. In 2008, he signed as a free agent with Cincinnati, where he remained through the 2011 season.

Growing up in the Dominican Republic, Cordero had several

major league players as his idols, "The player I looked up to the most was Jose Mesa because he was a closer, too. When I came up through the minors, I was a starter, but I was able to spend a lot of time with Jose Mesa when I made my break to the majors. We talked a lot and we worked out a lot in the Dominican Republic. He was the best closer I ever saw, both in work effort and ability."

He has also had many coaches impact his career, but the one he admired most was Bill Castro. "Castro was my bullpen and pitching coach from the Brewers," stated Cordero. "I played catch with him every day and I can honestly say that my career was on the rebound once I was traded to the Brewers [on July 28, 2006]. I even got my job back as the closer with them. In 2007, I had my best season. Castro would always say to me, 'CoCo, I have to tell you something.' And then he would tell me this and that, and he would always mix in some mechanics along the way. He was always so good at telling me how I should pitch. No one knew me better. What made him good was that he was always good at letting you know that you were pitching well, too."

On April 22, 2009, Cordero earned the one hundredth National League save of his career. With 117 saves in his American League career, he became just the eleventh pitcher to earn one hundred saves in each league.

He earned thirty-seven saves for the Reds in 2011, but none was as significant as the one he earned on June 1, in a 4-3 win against the Brewers. It was the three hundredth save of his career, as he became just the twenty-second pitcher in the history of Major League Baseball to reach that plateau.

On September 9, 2011, at Colorado, Cordero earned the 322nd save of his career, passing Jose Mesa as the Dominican Republic's all-time save leader.

"I can say my greatest career moment might be yet to come, because I haven't been in the World Series yet," he said with a grin. "But then again, if I were to talk about something that has happened during my career, it would have to be the 2011 baseball season when I recorded my three hundredth save. That was very special for me."

Cordero has given a lot of thought to the question of whether the closer's role is more of a challenge mentally or physically. "I sometimes think it's fifty-fifty, but as I think about it more it seems to be more mental," he said. "You've got to be ready mentally and be ready physically. Sometimes your body might be hurt, but you have to continue to concentrate and stay focused in your mind and get the job done. Once you do that, you'll forget about what's going on in your body."

KYLE FARNSWORTH

1999–PRESENT

Kyle Farnsworth is in his fourteenth year of Major League Baseball, having pitched for the Cubs, Tigers, Braves, Yankees, Royals, and Rays. The right-hander is known as a serious, intense, hard-throwing competitor, but, for him, the closing position has been an elusive one—one that patience and dedication finally helped him achieve.

In 1994, Farnsworth was selected by the Chicago Cubs out of Milton High School (Georgia) in the forty-seventh round of the June draft. Before signing his contract, he decided to attend Abraham Baldwin Agricultural College. It took nearly a year, but he finally signed with the Cubs on May 12, 1995.

That season, he made sixteen relief appearances for the Cubs in the rookie ball Gulf Coast League, but that would be it for relief appearances for a while. The six-foot-four athlete was going to be a starter, spending the next four years working on the role. He made his major league debut as a starter on April 29, 1999, at Florida. It was one of his greatest memories, "I started against the Marlins and I got the win," Farnsworth recalled. "A lot of my family were there, helping to make it more special for me."

He made twenty-one starts that first season (and six rare relief appearances), but the start on July 3, 1999, was one he would like to forget. "I was still a starter and I was facing the Phillies," he shared. "I only lasted one-third of an inning and I gave up eight runs [six earned]. That was pretty rough!"

But it was also during that first year in the majors that Farnsworth had some of his best times. "One of my best memories came shortly after I got called up to the big leagues and Terry Mulholland took me under his wing and bought me my first suit."

He began the 2000 season as a starter, but it soon became apparent that starting was not his forte. He moved into a relief role "about a year and a half into my major league career. I really didn't have a third pitch," Farnsworth explained, "and usually that third time through the order the batters were beginning to figure me out. And once I started to get hit around a little more, that was pretty much it for me being a starter and then they threw me into the bullpen. And, fortunately for me, my career took off from there."

He earned his first major league save on July 29, 2000, against the Giants, pitching three innings. But his role was not that of a closer, he became a middle reliever, then a setup man; there was more work ahead before he would earn that elusive closer position.

Farnsworth had his first real dose of closing in 2005. After an off-season trade, he began the season as the setup man for the Tigers. He had a 2.32 ERA in forty-six games, with fifty-five strikeouts in forty-two and two-thirds innings for the Tigers. But on July 31 he was involved in a bench-clearing brawl with the Royals, and two weeks later he was traded to the Braves. That is where he had some real success in the new role. He posted a 1.98 ERA in twenty-six games and went ten for ten in save opportunities.

The following season, however, he signed with the Yankees as a free agent. The Yankees had a guy named Mariano Rivera who was a decent closer, so Farnsworth returned to his setup role. Farnsworth did manage six saves for the club, which was the most by a non-Rivera Yankee pitcher since 2002.

Perhaps one of the reasons Farnsworth went to the Yankees and postponed his closer destiny was because of his mentality. "I don't want to be a loud, 'Look at me!' kind of guy," Farnsworth said during his Yankee days. "I want to get my job done and go home to my family. That's just the way my personality is. My daddy was the same way and my granddaddy was the same way."

He bounced around the majors for the next couple of years until his luck changed on January 15, 2011, when, at the age of thirty-five, he signed with the Tampa Bay Rays. The Rays handed him the closing role, and, after twelve years in the majors, Farnsworth made the most of his opportunity. The right-hander went 5-1 with a 2.18 ERA and earned a career-best twenty-five saves (in thirty-one opportunities) in his sixty-three appearances.

With his wealth of experience, Farnsworth believes the closing role is far more challenging from a mental aspect than a physical one. "You really have to prepare yourself day in and day out. Tons of guys have the physical ability, but very few guys have the mental ability to want to be in that situation as the closer," he explained. "Blown saves are tough to handle and everyone handles them differently. You might have to talk to a psychologist about the long-term effects," laughed Farnsworth, "but it really is the worst because it leaves a mark on the team in the case of a loss. You say to yourself, 'That sucks!' and 'I don't want to do that again.' The only good thing about it, if there is a good thing, is that hopefully you can learn from a blown save by taking something away from what you did and how you don't want to repeat it again."

Through fourteen seasons in the majors with six different teams, Farnsworth certainly has evolved as a pitcher. "Over the years you continue to try and change as a pitcher and evolve as a pitcher, but all along you have to have trust in yourself to get the job done."

BRIAN FUENTES
2001–PRESENT

Left-hander Brian Fuentes has been in the major leagues for twelve years with the Seattle Mariners, Colorado Rockies, Los Angeles Angels, Minnesota Twins, Oakland Athletics, and St. Louis Cardinals.

He grew up in Merced, California, and went on to Merced Community College and was selected by Seattle in the twenty-fifth round of the 1995 draft (Fuentes earned his degree in 1996).

Although a starter in the beginning of his minor league career, Fuentes never started in the majors. In 2001, he moved into a relief role at triple-A Tacoma, going 3-1, with a 2.94 ERA in thirty-five relief appearances. He pitched well enough to earn a promotion to the majors and made his major league debut on June 2, 2001, against Tampa Bay, pitching two-thirds of an inning in relief in the Mariners' 7-4 win.

On December 16, 2001, Fuentes was traded to Colorado, where his career would take off, although he didn't realize it at first.

"I remember I was with the Rockies and I had this horrible spring training. It was just terrible," explained Fuentes. "And I remember we were playing this exhibition game against our triple-A affiliate from Memphis. After the game I got called into the office and I was told that I had a really bad spring, and then he said, 'I know you probably don't deserve this, but congratulations, you've made the team.' And I was like, 'What? But thank you!' He did follow up the comment with, 'We know you have better stuff than what you've shown us this spring and are capable of so much more . . . so, let's step it up.' It felt good because they showed me a real vote of confidence, but truly when the conversation began I didn't think it was going to end well. So as I walked out of the room, I was still saying to myself, 'I guess I made the team? I guess I'll read it in the papers tomorrow to see if I really did make the team,'" he finished with a laugh.

After bouncing back and forth between the majors and minors in 2002, Fuentes emerged as the Rockies top left-hander reliever down the stretch. He continued his dominance in the bullpen in 2003, but in 2004, a back injury sidelined him for one-third of the season. Despite the injury, Fuentes became an effective setup man for the Rockies.

In 2005, Fuentes took over the closing role when Chin-hui Tsao had season-ending surgery in mid-May. The lefty finished the season with a 2.91 ERA and earned thirty-one saves in thirty-four opportunities. He also earned his first of four trips to the All-Star Game.

The Mexican-American had the greatest experience of his career in spring training of 2006, when he was selected to play for the United Sates in the inaugural World Baseball Classic. "I never had the opportunity to play in the Olympics," said Fuentes. "And being able to play for my country was pretty special and a big deal. Going on to the field for the first time and standing there on the line wearing my USA jersey and hearing the national anthem playing made me step back for a moment and realize it was very special. I have also been in a few All Star Games and a World Series, and they, too, are special."

He met with a lot of success in the closer role, earning at least thirty saves in 2005, 2006, and 2008. In 2007, he saved just twenty games, but due to some ineffectiveness and an injury, he did not close the entire season. He reclaimed the role in April 2008.

He signed with the Angels as a free agent for the 2009 season and had one of his finest seasons, compiling a 3.93 ERA with a major league-leading forty-eight saves in fifty-five opportunities in his sixty-five games.

The six-foot-four lefty admitted, "I don't get too many visits to the mound by my pitching coach unless they are there to take me out of the game . . . and in that case, I don't want to see them anyway or even hear what they have to say to me because I'm not listening," Fuentes said with a laugh. "I did have one pitching coach who came out and said, 'The manager wanted me to pay you a visit, but I didn't want to!' because my pitching coach knew how emotional I am out there. I'm usually angry, but focused."

The sidearmer went on to describe his style of pitching. "I would say that I am more crafty as a pitcher. I've never been the smartest guy out there. I have also been around some exceptional catchers over my career that I've built up so much trust with. I throw the fastball and then I have this quirky delivery and it seems to work and get the hitters out. I try and move my pitches around a lot and I have pretty good control. I also think my mental approach to the game helps, knowing that I have to get three outs before the other team puts any runs on the board."

He believes the role is significantly more of a mental challenge than a physical one. "It's funny, I've been around a lot of guys that have had better stuff than I'll ever have, but there is something about working the ninth inning that makes them unable to perform in that role," said Fuentes.

"You are expected to do the job every time and the one that you drop is the day the fans and the press are all over you. Everyone comes down pretty hard on you when you do get the blown save, but I know that is just them doing their job. If I closed out the game and got the save and the media did talk to me it was probably because I came close to doing something to possibly lose the game.

"Mariano is really the oddity in this game. He's blown a few saves and he still makes it hard on the rest of us guys," he said kiddingly. "I remember hearing stories about Trevor Hoffman. When he'd get the save you'd rarely see him. He would be in the trainer's room getting a treatment or something. But he knew he could do that because the media didn't want to talk to him because he did what he needed to do and got the save. Yet, when he did blow the save on those rare occasions, he was the first guy to sit in the front of his lockers and wait for the questions by the press. He knew they wanted to talk to him and he handled it so professionally. He's the kind of guy I want to be like in this role as the closer . . . I want to be like him. As a closer, as a person, he is the epitome of someone in this game you strive to be like."

ERIC GAGNE
1999–2008

Eric Gagne was torn between two loves—ice hockey and baseball. Fortunately, the Los Angeles Dodgers convinced him that baseball was the way to go when they signed him as an amateur free agent on July 26, 1995.

Not many people recall that Gagne began his professional career as a starter in 1996, striking out 131 in 115 innings for Savannah (single-A).

Unfortunately, he missed the entire 1997 season after having Tommy John surgery on his right elbow in April.

Gagne returned to baseball in 1998, still as a starter, striking out 144 in 139^2/$_3$ innings for Vero Beach (single-A). He had a strong season in 1999 at double-A, going 12-2, with a 2.63 ERA in twenty-six starts, striking out 185 in 167^2/$_3$ innings, and earning a September recall to Los Angeles. He made his major league debut on September 7, 1999, in a start in Florida. He had a no-decision in the Dodgers' 2-1 loss, pitching six innings, allowing two hits, one walk, and striking out eight.

Gagne continued to start over the next two seasons, bouncing between the major and minor leagues. Midway through the 2001 season, he finally stuck in the majors, and down the stretch he was moved into the bullpen.

Things came together for the French-Canadian born pitcher in 2002. He lost out on a spot in the rotation in spring training, but was given a spot in the bullpen. He earned his first major league save on April 7 against the Colorado Rockies, and after earning a second save on April 11 at San Francisco, Manager Jim Tracy named Gagne his closer.

Gagne excelled in the closer role. Over the next three seasons, the right-hander accumulated 152 saves for the Dodgers, blowing only six opportunities in that time. He earned fifty-two, fifty-five, and forty-five saves respectively for the 2002, 2003, and 2004 seasons, while also earning all-star bids each season.

In 2003, Gagne had a near-perfect season. He went 2-3 with a 1.20 ERA, struck out 137, and walked just twenty in eighty-two and one-third innings; but more importantly, he was fifty-five for fifty-five in save opportunities, leading the majors in saves and tying the National League single-season record. He earned the National League Cy Young Award for best pitcher in the league, NL Pitcher of the Year by *USA Today Sports Weekly*, and Pitcher of the Year and Reliever of the Year by the *Sporting News*.

Even more impressive was the streak. Gagne had eighty-four straight appearances without blowing a save opportunity. The streak began on August 28, 2002, and lasted through the entire 2003 season, not ending until he blew a save on July 5, 2004, against the Arizona Diamondbacks.

"In addition to the streak, the greatest moment for me was when my manager, Jim Tracy, gave me the job as the closer," said Gagne. "I remember it was in San Diego. It was the first time I ever had a defined role. Prior to that, I struggled trying to find my place for those first few years on the team. Plus, when I got called up to the major leagues in 1999; that was pretty special. They were my biggest moments."

Not surprisingly, another moment that stands out in his memory was the blown save that halted his eighty-four consecutive saves streak. "It was in Los Angeles and I got a standing ovation," Gagne recalled. "And it's not very often you get a standing ovation after a blown save! That was very cool and very touching, because failure is not often celebrated. I never realized at the time how special the streak was, but looking back now, it was a pretty special time in my life.

"The funniest thing about the streak, though," he continued, "was that I did have a blown save during the eighty-four consecutive saves. It came during the All-Star Game that year. I gave up a home run to Hank Blalock in Chicago to win the game. So I did have a blown save, but thank goodness it really didn't count!" (Statistics are not counted during All-Star Games.)

Most baseball fans believe his streak of eighty-four straight saves is one that will never be broken. Gagne isn't sure. "I don't know . . . there are so many factors that have to be just right, and not to mention there is a certain amount of luck associated with even a single save. Everything has to be just right, it has to be perfectly aligned, and the stars have to be just right.

The injury bug struck Gagne again, as he managed to pitch in just fourteen games in 2005 and two in 2006. He had surgery on his right elbow on June 24, 2005, and surgery to repair a herniated disc on July 8, 2006. He finished his Dodgers career with 162 saves in 167 opportunities, signing with the Texas Rangers as a free agent following the 2006 season.

Gagne looked like the closer of old, converting sixteen of seventeen save opportunities with the Rangers, prior to being dealt to the Boston Red Sox at the trading deadline, July 31, 2007. He did not pitch well after the trade, carrying a 6.75 ERA over twenty appearances and blowing each of his three save opportunities.

"The worst moment for me was in Boston when I got booed off the field at Fenway," admitted Gagne. "I felt so bad, because I tried so hard. I wanted to go to Boston, but my role changed, and mentally everything for me was going in reverse. I couldn't even get my old No. 38, but I certainly understand why. It belonged to Curt Schilling at the time. But in my head everything seemed to be traveling in reverse and everything seemed to go wrong."

Gagne's biggest challenge over his ten-year career was staying healthy. "Most people don't realize how demanding the closer role is," he said. "You warm up a lot during the season. You warm up before the game. You throw long toss. I remember counting one season how many times I got up and threw during a game; I wasn't in every game, but I got up 107 times during a season one time. The closer role is so much wear and tear on your body. You are always sore and you always seem to have some injury going on. But on the flip side, closers don't want the day off, because you feel like you are letting the team down if you don't pitch. It's your job to go there. You almost have this guilt complex all of the time."

That being said, the role is mentally challenging as well. "It is more mental," said Gagne, "but only when you are healthy. We are all creatures of habit in some way. I used to get dressed the same way before each game. I would take my shower at the same time before each game, and I would eat the same time before each game, too. I would even get the massage I needed on my shoulder before each game at the same time. But that is what it is like to be a major league closer. And, as all this is going on, you know in the back of your mind that your failure can cost your team so much.

"I always wanted to pitch. I wanted to pitch all of the time," he continued. "It's almost like telling an infielder not to catch a ground ball; you can't. We never knew when we were going in, but we had to be ready all of the time. When I pitched, I didn't want the day off. My manager tried to give me a day off now and then, but I didn't want it. And, when he did sit me to give me a rest, I actually got mad and I would say 'I can pitch through my soreness!' Looking back, I wish I would have taken a little more time off and maybe it would have extended my career, but I have no regrets. I took so much pride in the job I did."

Gagne's MLB career was anything but a failure, though he does have one regret. "I'm very proud of the years I had, but I wish I could have played longer," admitted Gagne. "I wished for longevity, but I didn't get it. I did get my World Series ring though, and not everyone can say that."

TOM GORDON
1988–2009

Tom "Flash" Gordon pitched for twenty-one years in the majors for eight teams including, among others, the Kansas City Royals (1988–95), Boston Red Sox (1996–99), New York Yankees (2004–05), and Philadelphia Phillies (2006–08). His career began in the late 1980s, when the closer role was becoming more clearly defined.

His professional career began in 1986 when he was selected by the Royals in the sixth round of the June draft out of Avon Park High School in Florida. He made his major league debut just over two years later, on September 8, 1988, pitching two innings in relief of Bret Saberhagen in a 5-1 loss against the Oakland A's.

Gordon's biggest obstacle to the big leagues wasn't necessarily whether he would be a starter or reliever, but for the five-foot-nine right-hander, it was whether he would even be a pitcher.

"It all started with me in Kansas City with my pitching coach by the name of Jerry Cram," Gordon recalled. "He was a small guy too and he made it up to the majors and played mainly for the Mets for a few years. The two of us really connected and he was always there to talk about pitching. Yet, the Royals were still thinking about making me a position player. I would still pitch when the other pitchers were out there, but when they went in I was taking batting practice, fielding ground balls, and learning how to steal bases. I had to do all of this extra work and still pitch. Eventually, I found out what they were doing and it was Jerry Cram who went to bat for me and he was on my side for me to be a pitcher.

"After I left Kansas City I had some other great coaches too, like Rich Dubee and Joe Kerrigan; the two of them were always encouraging me to follow my dream," Gordon continued. "And then there was Mel Stottlemyre who really put the icing on the cake for me. Mel helped me to find fundamental flaws in my mechanics and then he helped to work them out and eventually helped me to throw strikes consistently. He helped me to become the pitcher I became! That is probably why some of my best years were in New York for the Yankees."

Although he did pitch in relief early in his career, the bulk of his appearances over his first ten seasons were in the starting role. He didn't move into the closing role until 1997. He began that season as the Opening Day starter for the Red Sox. After closer Heathcliff Slocumb departed at the trading deadline in late July, manager Jimy Williams moved Gordon into the role.

The following year, Gordon had the first of three all-star seasons as he led the league with forty-six saves and sixty-nine games finished. In his first full season as a closer, he went 7-4 with a 2.72 ERA in seventy-three games and was successful in forty-six of forty-seven save opportunities.

In 1999 Gordon was limited to twenty-one games due to a nagging elbow injury, which eventually required surgery. "I remember I just came off of Tommy John surgery and I was playing for the Cubs," Gordon shared. "I didn't know how I was going to pitch. I remember one of the first batters I faced after I came back in spring training was Sammy Sosa. I told myself, 'If I can strike out Sammy Sosa, then I'll know that I made it back into this game.' So, what happened next is that I struck Sammy out and then I whispered to myself on the mound 'I'm ready.' I did exactly what I said I was going to do and from that moment on, I knew I had the confidence to be a closer again."

Gordon moved back into a set-up role when he pitched for the Yankees in 2004 and 2005. The Yankees made it to the post-season both of those seasons, which made up two of the five post-season years for Gordon. After three years with the Phillies, he pitched his final season with the Arizona Diamondbacks in 2009.

"There were so many great moments I had in this game, but the one that probably sticks out the most to me was when I stepped out there on the pitcher's mound for the first time," Gordon said. "And again, if it wasn't for Jerry Cram being there and encouraging me to follow my dream as a pitcher, I'm not sure where I would have been. He was so positive and instrumental and even today we maintain that same relationship we had more than twenty years ago. I remember him saying to me, 'I guarantee you that even Jose Canseco and Mark Maguire won't be able to handle that drop curve ball of yours!' And sure enough, the first time I faced Jose Canseco I worked the count to 3-0 and then threw him three straight drop curveballs and struck him out."

Even Gordon's toughest moments in the game came with a silver lining. "The worst moments for me turned out to be milestones for others," he recalled. "I gave up Carlton Fisk's record-breaking homerun [Johnny Bench's record for home runs by a catcher, August 8, 1990] and I also gave up Alex Rodriguez's first homerun [June 12, 1995]. His was a major boom when he hit it. And, like Fisk's homerun, I had to sign baseballs for A-Rod's first homerun. I guess, though, I will always be remembered and I guess I am somewhere in the Hall of Fame!"

Gordon was a starter when the closer role was entering the final stages of its current evolution. By the time he was closing, the role had become the specialized one-inning job that it is today.

"I do believe the role has reached its final evolution, and it starts with the organizations that only consider these guys a one-inning pitcher. That is how they promote them," Gordon analyzed. "If I could have been a two-inning closer, I think I might have worked a little harder. It's a psychological thing how you approach the game nowadays.

"I always knew I wanted to help my team along the way, so role didn't always matter to me. I loved to get thrown into the fire as a pitcher. I believe it made me stronger, but that has been the case for me my entire career and life. I always had to work hard for everything I got. I never was born with a silver spoon in my mouth. I always enjoyed being in the role of the fighter.

"I remember the two years I spent as Mariano Rivera's set-up guy. I learned so much from Mariano. [He] would often come up to me in the locker room and say, 'thank you.' Sometimes he would say, 'you deserve the ball; it was your save. . . . If it wasn't for Flashy, I wouldn't be getting the saves I got.' That is what makes the closer role so special. Every day is so different, but as long as you have that ice in your veins and the confidence to be the guy then you will always know you will be the guy."

KEVIN GREGG

2003–PRESENT

K evin Gregg was born on June 20, 1978, in Corvallis, Oregon. The six-foot-six right-hander was selected by the Oakland Athletics in the fifteenth round of the June 1996 draft out of Corvallis High School. And from that point on, his career has been about as predictable as the weather.

He began his career, like many closers of his generation, as a starter. It wasn't until 2001, when he was with the double-A team in Midland, Texas, that he mainly pitched as a reliever, but that did not last either. In 2002, he returned to starting with a few relief appearances sprinkled in, and following the season, he was granted free agency.

After being signed by the Angels, Gregg's career seemed to be on an upswing. He was a starter at double-A and triple-A before getting called up and making his major league debut on August 9, 2003, at Cleveland, in game one of a doubleheader.

Gregg's roller-coaster career continued, as he had to fight for, earn, and sometimes lose his closing roles. The Florida Marlins slotted him as a middle reliever in 2007, as they tried out different closers. Finally, he took over the role in mid-May and earned thirty-two saves in thirty-six chances, ranking him eighth in the National League that season. He retained his closer position in 2008, but a nagging knee injury put him back in a middle relief role in September.

With the Cubs in 2009, he earned the closing role only to lose it and move into the setup role again in late August.

He had his finest season in 2010 with the Toronto Blue Jays, earning a career-high thirty-seven saves, which ranked fourth in the American League.

"I spent seven years in the minor leagues," Gregg shared. "It was *Bull Durham* all of the time. I remember everyone telling me all of the time I didn't have the right stuff to make it as a big leaguer. They'd say my slider wasn't good enough or I didn't throw hard enough! And now, I have eight years of major league experience behind me . . . go figure. I guess all of that negative talk helped me over the years, feeding my desire to prove them wrong. But for the most part I've had good coaches who were there for me and that is why I am here today."

Gregg has also had a few interesting experiences with coaches in his career. "I had one coach ask me on occasion if I could go through my delivery with my eyes shut! It was explained to me that pitching with your eyes shut . . . would increase your body awareness. It helps you focus on every aspect of your body and the way it moves," he explained. "Also, my high school pitching coach had me throw as hard as I could and focus on control, as opposed to the other way around for many others, which focuses on control and then velocity. He put velocity in front of control."

Gregg has played for five different major league teams (Angels, Marlins, Cubs, Blue Jays, and Orioles), and accumulated 144 saves in his ten years in the major leagues. "I get excited each time I go into a game as the closer. I want the chance to go in and get involved," he said, "I personally don't think you can prepare for the closer role. Every situation is different and every game is different. The only preparation you have is being able to know yourself and trust in yourself. To me, it is all about the mental preparation of the game more than anything. All the physical confidence comes from staying strong. And I do believe by staying physically strong this then helps the mental side of the game for you."

He continued: "The closer role is kind of a thankless position. A lot of us guys refer to ourselves as the offensive line in football. I guess it runs in the family for me; my brother played college football and he was an offensive lineman. We don't get in trouble unless we mess up."

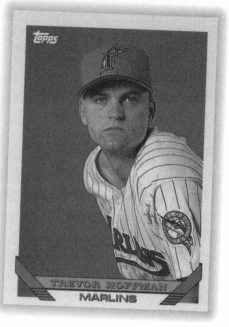

TREVOR HOFFMAN
1993–2010

One of the most respected and popular players in the game, Trevor Hoffman is a sure bet to make it into the Hall of Fame. But if he had been able to hit a little better, we may have never seen one of the game's best closers in the major leagues.

Hoffman grew up in California, the youngest of three brothers and the son of an ex-marine and professional singer. He had a strong arm, but played shortstop, like his older brother, Glenn, in high school. "My dad wanted to protect our arms, so we weren't allowed to pitch after we were twelve," said Hoffman. "He had pretty good vision."

Scouts didn't take much notice of him out of high school, so he went to Cypress College, then the University of Arizona, where he again played shortstop in 1988 and 1989. He led his team with a .371 average in 1988, batting thirty-seven points higher than teammate and future major league first baseman, J. T. Snow.

The Cincinnati Reds selected him in the eleventh round of the

June draft in 1989. He played shortstop and third base for the Billings Mustangs of the rookie Pioneer League in his professional debut, and again for single-A Charleston in 1990. Hoffman hit just .212 in that second pro season. "I couldn't hit with a wood bat," Hoffman said with a laugh. His manager, Jim Lett, recognized his strong arm, thanks in part to his constant overthrowing of first base, and suggested he convert to pitching.

Hoffman began his pitching career in 1991. He was left unprotected for the expansion draft on November 12, 1992, and was selected by the Florida Marlins with the eighth pick. That season, Hoffman made his major league debut with the young Marlins team, on April 6, 1993, striking out the final batter in a 4-2 loss against the Los Angeles Dodgers, just two years after converting to pitching.

"I was very fortunate to have an older brother. His name was Glenn and he was nine years older than me. And he was drafted right out of high school by the Boston Red Sox," said Hoffman. "When he hit the big leagues, I was only ten or eleven years old. And it can't get much better for a young kid [than] to have your older brother in the big leagues, playing for the Red Sox alongside players like Carlton Fisk, Jim Rice, Marty Barrett, Dennis Eckersley, and Carl Yastrzemski. My brother Glenn became larger than life. I so much appreciated what he did when I eventually made my major league debut. So, over time, I got to appreciate guys like my brother and those guys he used to play with.

"From a closer standpoint, I was a huge Goose Gossage fan. I respected his entire body of work. He was one of those guys that helped define the role of the closer for all of us. The role was so different back then and I could never compare myself to him."

Hoffman was among a group traded to the San Diego Padres on June 24, 1993, for Gary Sheffield and Rich Rodriguez. Padres fans were not happy that the organization was trading its stars for young, inexpensive talent, and so Hoffman was booed in his first couple of outings. It wouldn't be long before the fans realized they had a special player on their team.

Hoffman's best pitch, the change-up, developed over time, partially because he hurt his shoulder playing Nerf football and volleyball in 1994 and lost some speed on his fastball. Former Padres teammate Phil Nevin caught Hoffman when he first joined the Padres in 1999 and was impressed by how quickly Hoffman mastered the pitch.

Hoffman pitched for eighteen years in the majors, fifteen and a half of those seasons with the Padres. The seven-time all-star finished his career with 601 saves in 677 opportunities, and a 2.87 ERA in 1,089$^{1}/_{3}$ innings over 1,035 games.

He shared his secret to success and longevity. "You have to keep doing your best and hope that you continue to bring value to your team. I think I was motivated by the expectation of success that I created," analyzed Hoffman. "That was part of the question I had to ask myself each year I went out there. 'Was I able to match the expectation I created for myself on a day-to-day basis?' The answer for eighteen years was 'Yes.' And when I was not able to answer the question with a 'Yes,' I then knew it was time for me to retire."

He retired following the 2010 season with a major league record 601 saves. Mariano Rivera passed that record on September 19, 2011. No one else has even come close.

"Some people ask me what was my greatest moment and I say to them, 'I've had 601 saves over my career, but they are sometimes just a blur' . . . but I am still haunted by my blown saves."

One of the elite closers of the game, Hoffman felt obligated to teach those who followed, like he was helped on his way up. "When I first came up, I was certainly a sponge, trying to learn from everyone. For example, when I first came up I had an average change-up and it wasn't until a pitcher by the name of Donnie Elliott joined the team, in the Fred McGriff trade with Atlanta, that I was able to perfect the change-up and achieve the proper grip," said Hoffman. "What I learned quickly was to take a little bit from this guy and from that guy, and then sprinkle it with what I knew and then polish it all up to become a young and confident pitcher. When I became older and more successful, I always felt very comfortable helping some of the younger guys."

Hoffman had a complete career, but one of his greatest moments in baseball came after his career had ended. "On August 21, 2011, the San Diego Padres retired my No. 51 and the video of the national anthem was that of my father singing the anthem during a Red Sox game thirty years earlier!

"Here's what happened," Hoffman explained. "Carlton Fisk left the Red Sox and became a free agent with the White Sox. On his first trip back to Fenway, they filmed everything involving that game, including the pregame show and the national anthem. And the reason why my father was there was because when my brother signed his first contract with the Red Sox right out of high school he asked that if he would ever make it to the majors could they fly our dad out there to sing the national anthem. Now, it wasn't that big a stretch or that unusual a request because for years my dad was a professional singer," said Hoffman.

"So, here I am at the ceremony, alongside some of my former teammates and widows of former teammates I had played with. There was also the other players who had their numbers retired over the years: Randy Jones, Steve Garvey, Dave Winfield, and Tony Gwynn. They presented me with a black 1958 Cadillac Convertible with an "SD 51" plate. My two older brothers were there reminiscing while looking at old family pictures that were both funny and heartwarming. Then the Marine Corps color guard marched onto the field and lined up behind second base. Then the PA announcer said, 'Can you please rise for the national anthem.' And then the big surprise happened, it was the video of my father, Ed Hoffman, singing the national anthem. I didn't know it was coming. The whole day was filled with so much emotion and I didn't have anything left by that time and I lost it emotionally. It was a pretty awesome day!"

JASON ISRINGHAUSEN

1995–2012

D espite beginning his career as a starter and having an injury-riddled career, Jason Isringhausen beat the odds and reached the three hundred–save plateau.

His professional career began when he was selected by the New York Mets in the forty-fourth round of the June 1991 draft, out of Southwestern High School in Brighton, Illinois. He signed a year later, on May 24, 1992.

On July 17, 1995, the right-hander made his major league debut, with a no-decision start in the Mets' 7-5 win over the Cubs at Wrigley Field. Isringhausen pitched seven innings, allowing two runs on two hits, with two walks and six strikeouts. He remained in the majors the rest of the season and ended up going 7-0 in his last eight starts.

The following season, he made the first of several visits to the disabled list. On September 27, 1996, he had a labral tear in his right shoulder repaired and bone chips from his right elbow removed. That surgery caused him to miss the beginning of the 1997 season, and then a broken wrist and a diagnosis of tuberculosis sidelined him until August 27.

His bad luck continued. On January 13, 1998, he had reconstructive surgery on his right elbow, causing him to miss the entire 1998 season. He returned to the majors on May 24, 1999, and made five starts, before going to the minors to learn how to be a reliever. Isringhausen had made fifty-two consecutive starts before his first major league relief appearance came on July 6, 1999. Ironically, he earned his first major league save in that first appearance, pitching three innings in the Mets' 10-0 win against the Montreal Expos.

The Mets sent Isringhausen to the Oakland A's at the trade deadline, July 31, 1999. And from that point on, he never again started a major league game. After a few relief appearances, he eventually took on the closer's role, earning his first A's save on August 27 in Chicago. He finished the season going nine for nine in save opportunities.

"[Oakland General Manager] Billy Beane had the greatest impact on my career," stated Isringhausen, "because he was the one that traded for me and put me in the closer role. I thank him a lot for what he did for me. There was also Art Howe, my manager, for trusting in me in the closer role. Then there was Tony La Russa and all of those years in St. Louis and the trust he had in me in that role. Even after I was hurt and when some questioned whether I should be in the closer role. Tony stuck by my side and believed in me, and that meant a lot to me."

Isringhausen remained with the A's through 2001, earning his first all-star bid in 2000 and pitching in the American League Division Series in both in 2000 and 2001. On December 11, 2001, he signed with the St. Louis Cardinals as a free agent and had some of the best seasons of his career.

His first season with the Cardinals (2002) saw him earn thirty-plus saves for the third straight season and gain his third straight postseason appearance.

His stellar 2004 season had him finishing tied for the National League lead with a career-high forty-seven saves. He also led the league with sixty-six games finished and returned to the postseason, where the Cardinals earned a World Series berth, but lost to the Boston Red Sox. Unfortunately, in the off-season he once again went under the knife, this time for surgery on his left hip.

He had another great season for the Cardinals in 2005, earning his second all-star berth and posting a 2.14 ERA in sixty-three games with thirty-nine saves. And he was fortunate enough to appear in the postseason for the fifth time in six years.

He was having another strong season for the Cardinals in

2006 when another hip issue forced him to miss the final month of the season and the postseason. It was that postseason that Isringhausen recalls as his most disappointing time.

"We played the Nationals in DC. I blew the save and then I went up to Tony La Russa and told him that I couldn't pitch anymore because of my injury," Isringhausen admitted. "We then went on to the playoffs and won the World Series and I didn't get to pitch. That was probably my biggest disappointment. And to this very day I have never put on that World Series ring. It's in my safe and I'll never put it on because I don't believe I earned it. I had thirty-three saves up to the point I got hurt at that game in Washington. I remember standing on crutches in the dugout during the Series. Believe me, it was fun to watch and I worked a lot with the young guys in the bullpen, like Adam Wainwright who was the rookie closer after I went down. I talked to Wainwright every day, helping him to understand what to expect and what it will be like to have your team mob you on the mound after you get the final save and win the World Series. I would try and tell him that the game is in his hands and that he controls the pace of the game, the playoffs, and the crowd and that should make it easier to stay focused and to be prepared."

He rebounded from his hip injury to have a stellar 2007 season, finishing first in the NL (and second in the majors) with a 94.1 save percentage (thirty-two saves in thirty-four opportunities). His picked up his two hundredth save as a Cardinal on August 26 versus Atlanta, becoming just the fifteenth player in major league history to post two hundred saves or more with one team.

Isringhausen signed with the Tampa Bay Rays as a free agent in 2009. Unfortunately, after just nine appearances, he returned to the DL and underwent Tommy John (ligament transplant) surgery.

In 2011, he returned to the Mets, just seven saves shy of reaching the three hundred–save plateau. He began the season as the setup man, but by July, he was closing some games again. On August 15, 2011, in San Diego, he pitched the tenth inning in the

Mets' 5-4 win and earned his seventh and final save of the season as he reached that elusive save No. 300.

"Recording my three hundredth save was certainly one of my greatest moments," Isringhausen shared. "Especially, after I sat out for a year and a half with an elbow injury, and that is why I worked so hard to get back to the game and get those final seven saves. I remember in 2008, I was just nineteen saves away, and then I got hurt. It took two years to eventually get back on the mound to achieve my three hundredth save. That was very gratifying to me and to go through all of that adversity to get back. And then there were all of those years with the Cardinals and pitching in the playoffs. That was also very special and gratifying to me, because I grew up near St. Louis and that was the team I always followed when I was younger, and it was the team my parents followed, and my grandparents."

After all his visits to the disabled list, one would think Isringhausen's greatest challenge is to stay healthy, but it is not. "For me, I'm a lot like Dennis Eckersley, which the two of us have talked to each other about, which is that fear of failure said Isringhausen. "I never wanted to lose the trust my teammates had in me, rather I wanted them to feel comfortable with me whenever I came in."

Part of the comfort level of his teammates comes with knowing that Isringhausen was always ready to pitch. "I always had a routine," he revealed. "I would start the game in the dugout and by the fifth inning I would be down in the bullpen. Then I'd get down there and there would be all of the goofing around, but by the seventh inning, it was time to buckle down and to start thinking about the pitches I needed to throw to this batter or that batter and to accomplish my game plan and get the save and the victory for my team."

JIM JOHNSON

2006–PRESENT

Very new to the closing role is the Baltimore Orioles' big right-hander, Jim Johnson.

"J. J."—as he is called—is in his seventh season in the major leagues, but his first full season as the closer.

He was born in upper New York in Johnson City. "My idols were mostly pitchers," Johnson recalled. "Interestingly, when I turned around twelve years old I started to follow players more so than teams. I liked watching Nolan Ryan especially, and there were some players I was drawn to a little more."

The six-foot-six pitcher was a member of the 2001 New York State Championship baseball team at Union-Endicott High School. He was drafted in June that same year by the Orioles in the fifth round.

In 2004, he finally made some progress, advancing to Delmarva (low-A), then Frederick (high-A). "My back was pretty much against the wall," Johnson said. "I went into camp and actually didn't make a team out of camp that year, which was shocking. After a month of waiting it out, I started seeing a return, which made it a little easier."

He finally made his major league debut on July 29, 2006, in a start against the Chicago White Sox. He lost the game, 13-11, lasting just three innings. It would be not only his only major league appearance of the season, but his only career major league start.

In 2007, he again appeared in just one game in the majors—on April 25 against the Boston Red Sox—pitching two innings in relief.

"When you spend seven years in the minor leagues, for the most part, without really getting a foothold in the major leagues, you're going to be thinking, maybe this isn't going to work out," Johnson said. "I wasn't a first-round pick who was fast-tracked to the big leagues. I had to grind it out every step of the way."

In 2008, Johnson began to establish himself. He began the season at triple-A, but was recalled on April 11 after one game. Johnson posted a 2.23 ERA in fifty-four games and briefly held the closer role after George Sherrill went on the disabled list in mid-August. His season ended prematurely on September 1, when he suffered a right shoulder impingement.

Johnson's 2009 season was his first full one in the majors. He appeared in sixty-four games and, again, moved into the closer's role when Sherrill was traded to the Los Angeles Dodgers at the trade deadline.

He had his first real dose of closing late in 2011, when he took over the closing role and finished the year by successfully saving each of his final seven opportunities. Johnson had his first all-star season in 2012 in his first full season as the Orioles closer.

"There were a few players that have been my teammates over the years that have had a big impact on my career," said Johnson. "But, it has also been the guys that I work with in the bullpen that have helped me so much. They've helped teach me to prepare day in and day out, and what it means to be a closer. To be honest, they have helped me more than any coach, primarily because they've been there and some have been where I am now in the closer role."

In his brief experience in the role, Johnson has come to recognize what is needed to succeed. "You still have to reach your energy or adrenaline level while keeping them under control," he said, "because if you don't, it lends itself to reckless aggressiveness. If you don't control your emotions, those emotions can eventually control you, and it's like driving a car without a steering wheel."

With such a limited time in the role, Johnson shared that he does get a little nervous before pitching. "There is still anxiety and butterflies I get during each game and every appearance, and they start building up during the sixth and seventh innings. But once I start to warm up, it goes away."

The young Oriole believes his biggest challenge in the game is always trying to get better. "You have to in this game. Yet it's still fairly new to me, so I'm learning every day."

The role is still so new to him that he won't identify a greatest career moment yet. "I think my greatest moment hasn't been written yet," said Johnson with a grin.

TODD JONES

1993–2008

T odd Jones is a perfect example of patience and diligence paying off, as well as proof that good guys really do win (and save).

Jones pitched sixteen years in the majors, compiling 319 saves, which currently ranks him fifteenth on the all-time list. However, 42 percent of those saves (133) came in his last four major league seasons, all after he turned thirty-seven.

Jones grew up in Marietta, Georgia. He was selected by the New York Mets in the forty-first round of the June draft in 1986, his senior year at Osborne High School, but the right-hander opted instead to go to Jacksonville State University.

Three years later, Jones was selected by the Houston Astros in the first round of the June draft, and was the twenty-seventh player selected overall. It wasn't until 1992 that he moved into a relieving role. He picked up his first professional save on April 16, 1992, at Shreveport and finished that season with twenty-five saves.

With twelve saves at triple-A Tucson, Jones was called up and made his major league debut on July 7, 1993. He never looked back, finishing the season in the majors and consistently pitching in the eighth and ninth inning by season's end.

Jones pitched for three seasons with the Astros. He was traded to the Detroit Tigers on December 10, 1996. In the middle of his fifth season with the Tigers, he was traded to the Minnesota Twins. Jones went on to play for the Colorado Rockies, Boston Red Sox, Tampa Bay Rays, Cincinnati Reds, Philadelphia Phillies, and the Florida Marlins. Finally, as a free agent, Jones returned to the Tigers for three years (2006–08) to end his career.

A closer with a great sense of humor, Jones had his finest season in 2000 with the Tigers. He led the American League with a (then) club record forty-two saves and was named to his first and only All-Star Game. He also pitched in the postseason for the Red Sox in 2003 and for the Tigers in 2006.

On September 16, 2007, at Minnesota, Jones earned career save No. 300, becoming just the twenty-first pitcher in major league history to reach that plateau.

"I was very fortunate to have a few great moments in my career," Jones said. "I was the last pitcher to take the mound at Tigers Stadium (September 27, 1999) and I had the privilege to pitch for my country in the first World Baseball Classic (2006). They were both very special for me. I also got a chance to play in the 2000 All-Star Game in Atlanta. I grew up near Atlanta, so it felt so surreal and it was a lot of fun, especially meeting Dale Murphy, who was one of the base coaches for the National League."

Of course, with the good times, come the bad times. "I had several of those, too . . . just look at my career statistics and you'll see that I had several rocky points during my career," Jones said with a grin. "I think every ballplayer can say the same thing, but with all of those ups and downs, it eventually made me the pitcher that I was."

Jones admitted that he had more trouble with the mental side of the game, "because physically I was able to bounce back night after night. I could always throw, but mentally getting through the anxiousness of the game and dealing with the ups and downs and the possible failure after the game was always a big part of the game for me."

Every major leaguer has a fellow player or coach who helped him get through the tough times, and Jones is no exception. "I had several that helped me along the way," he said. "Buddy Bell comes to mind. Buddy really believed in me, and that means a lot to a ballplayer at times. As for a player who had the greatest impact on my career, that would have to be the current pitching coach of the Houston Astros, Doug Brocail. We were together in Houston. We were a good combo together."

Being prepared is the key to being successful as a pitcher, according to Jones. "That is the luxury of being a closer today," he said. "I knew when I was going in, depending on the game situation. So I was always ready. And I don't say that boastingly. That was my job because you know who the seventh-inning guy is and you know who the eighth-inning guy is. And you know exactly who you are going to face because you've just watched the eighth-inning guy and knew who he faced. I remember the phone would ring and I was always ready and all of that anxiety went away."

In his eight combined years with the Tigers, Jones earned a club-record 235 saves. He earned his two hundreth Tigers' save on July 4, 2007, versus Cleveland, and became just the fourteenth major leaguer to earn 200 saves with a single team.

During his hot streaks as a closer, Jones had four straight seasons with twenty-eight-plus saves (1997–2000) and three straight with thirty-seven-plus saves (2005–07). Between those streaks, he endured some tough times, so Jones saw it all.

"I was so blessed in my career," Jones stated sincerely. "You have to understand, I was a starter and then I lost my job and then I got my job back, and, eventually, when I became the closer I was truly able to appreciate what I had. With that said, I wouldn't change anything in my career. I am grateful for everything I had. I ended my career with 319 career saves (currently fifteenth on the all-time list) and over one hundred holds and nobody is going to take that away from me. I'm good with everything I have. I'm not a Hall of Famer, nor do I deserve to be one. I'm okay with that and it's more than anything I thought I'd have."

CRAIG KIMBREL
2010–PRESENT

C raig Kimbrel is not only a young closer (twenty-four), but a member of the generation who began closing from the very start of their careers. Kimbrel is also a favorite of many old-time relief pitchers and closers. Dennis Eckersley summed it up best when he said, "I like that kid in Atlanta [Kimbrel] because he is no-nonsense out there. He doesn't waste your time. You know he's going to throw you heat and he does with confidence."

The Huntsville, Alabama, native played baseball and football at Lee High School. After graduating in 2006, he was headed to Wallace State Community College, where he was to pitch on the baseball team; however, before he got to school, he broke his foot in an accident in which slabs of sheetrock fell on him. Strangely enough, that broken foot helped Kimbrel to become the impressive pitcher he is today.

He was unable to put much weight on his foot after the accident, so he long-tossed from his knees, and soon was able to throw the length of the field. It was during his first season at Wallace that he also realized the importance of weight training throughout the year. "It's kind of weird to say that breaking your foot is the best thing that could happen to you, but it seems like it ended up working out that way," said Kimbrel. "It helped me understand how I move my upper body. Once I started using my lower body, it all came together."

The five-foot-eleven right-hander was selected by the Atlanta Braves in the thirty-third round of the 2007 June draft, but opted to continue with school. They selected him again in 2008, this time in the third round, and this time he did not hesitate to sign.

"I grew up a big Braves fan, being from Alabama," said Kimbrel. "I watched the Braves since I was little. I remember watching Smoltz, Glavine, and Maddux. But my idol was really Chipper Jones. I was a big Chipper Jones fan. It's kind of weird to say it now. I guess I'll tell him at the end of the season when he retires. But I can't do it now . . . and admit to him I was his biggest fan."

Kimbrel pitched for three minor league teams after he signed in 2008. In 2009, he continued his way up the ladder, pitching for four teams, and in 2010 he pitched solely for triple-A Gwinnett. In those three seasons, he compiled an 8-7 record, with a 1.85 ERA in 121 games, with fifty-one saves. In 151 innings, he walked ninety-five and struck out 242.

He made his major league debut in 2010, on May 7 against the Phillies. That season, Kimbrel was recalled and optioned back to triple-A four times, but somehow managed to compile a 4-0 record with a 0.44 ERA in twenty-one games, with his first major league save on September 19 against the New York Mets.

By pitching in the majors in 2010, he also got the opportunity to pitch for the Braves longtime manager, Bobby Cox, who retired following the season. "When I got drafted, my goal was to play for Bobby Cox," said Kimbrel. "I grew up a Braves fan. Bobby Cox was everything a manager could be and he is everything anyone has ever said about him. He was the perfect manager. He understood the situation; I guess that's why he's been around the game forever. And to be able to play for a manager like Bobby Cox was awesome!"

Kimbrel's 2011 season was one for the record books, literally. He broke the major league rookie record with a National League-leading forty-six saves, also led the NL with sixty-four games finished and was second with seventy-nine games pitched. In addition, the rookie was named to the NL all-star team. His year culminated with him being named NL Rookie of the Year.

"Winning the Rookie of the Year Award was pretty special for me," Kimbrel recalled. "I was on vacation when I heard the news. I got the call and I knew it was either going to be me or Freddie [Freeman]. But when they said it was unanimous and I won, it really blew my mind. I never thought it would have happened the way it did. And to win it, being in the role of a closer, I considered it a win and a victory for the entire team. Because without my team making the unbelievable plays they do in the field, this award never would have been possible for me to achieve."

Kimbrel knows he has to keep improving to keep achieving. "I'm learning everyday . . . I keep a journal that lists my workouts and the pitches I throw," he said. "After I pitch, I'll go in and target the pitches I threw, their velocity and locations. And I'll also record things I pick up from the hitters on those days; it might be a certain pitch or where I threw it in a particular count. This way I can go back and look at my workouts and say to myself, 'I like what I did that day and this is how I achieved it.' This way if I was successful I can look to repeat it the next time I go out to the mound. So, I can constantly try and improve my pitching based on my previous outings."

Kimbrel's pitching coach with the Braves is former reliever and closer Roger McDowell. "Roger is good at sitting back and letting me pitch, and yet he is able to pick up on the smallest of details when something is not right," said Kimbrel. "He has this great balance of knowing when to joke with you and when to be serious. When the game starts, he is all business."

Kimbrel tries to be all business as well when he takes the mound. "Physically, I will always be ready to pitch, but mentally every day is different," he said. "The more you pitch, the more tired you are going to be, but that is why you have to separate yourself from how you feel mentally. That is why you have to be mentally ready every day. Because if you are not mentally ready when you get on the mound you are going to get beat."

With his constant observing of hitters and note-taking, it can be tough for Kimbrel to rebound after a game, especially after the difficult outings. "In the closer role, there are always a bunch of disappointments, but you have to survive and to be able to pitch the next day in this role," he revealed. "The one thing I try to do in each of my outings is to get the leadoff guy out. If he does get a hit, then I need to work that much harder. If you can get that first guy out, then the next two guys can almost play into your hands. So my philosophy is to attack and get the first guy out."

The thoughtful right-hander had a taste of the playoffs in 2010, when he faced the San Francisco Giants in the NL Division Series, and it just whet his appetite for more. "I feel like every day is a new challenge, and as a team our goal is to get to the playoffs and eventually the World Series. For me, I was fortunate to get called up at the end of 2010 and therefore got to pitch in the playoffs. It is just a completely different experience being in the playoffs."

BRANDON LEAGUE
2004–PRESENT

New to the closing scene is Los Angeles Dodgers Brandon League. Although he has been relieving since he made it to the majors in 2004, he did not become a closer until he was the beneficiary of an unfortunate hip injury to then-closer David Aardsma when he was in Seattle in September 2010.

League always showed potential. He was a three-time All-State selection in baseball at St. Louis High School in Honolulu and was the 2001 Gatorade Hawaii Player of the Year. The six-foot-two right-hander was selected by the Toronto Blue Jays in the second round of the June draft upon graduation in 2001.

He was strictly a starter in his first couple of professional seasons. However, going into the 2004 season, *Baseball America* selected him as the one of the top ten prospects in the Blue Jays organization and that was also the season he began testing the reliever role.

With New Hampshire of the Eastern League, he had a great 2004 season, starting just ten of his forty-one games, and earning his first two saves. *Baseball America* kept him on its radar, naming him the seventeenth best prospect in the league, and the Blue Jays did as well, bringing him up in September to make his major league debut.

"The best advice I ever got," confessed League, "was to keep it simple and throw strikes. This game is complicated enough. Just keep it simple!"

His first full season in the majors was 2009, after which he was traded to the Seattle Mariners in one of the biggest breaks of his career.

The right-hander, of Japanese, not Hawaiian, descent, led

The Modern Day Closer

All-American League relievers in wins (nine), was second in innings (seventy-nine), and tied for tenth in appearances (seventy) in 2010, and he was the go-to guy when Aardsma went down in mid-September.

He proved himself enough in that short time to be handed Seattle's closer role in 2011, at the age of twenty-eight . . . and he made the best of it, being named to his first all-star team and finishing third in the American League with thirty-seven saves.

In 2012 he was traded to the Los Angeles Dodgers. "You can never prepare totally for the role," admitted the right-hander. "The only way you can fully prepare is through experience. If it's the eighth inning and our team is up by a lot of runs, you kind of know that it's probably not your night. And vice versa, if it's a close game and the game is moving along, then you are probably going to see some action. But of course in your mind, you hope you are going to get that call. I'd rather pitch than sit."

League has "lost" his closer role a couple of times, but quickly earned the role back. "For me the role is definitely mental," he said, "but as the season drags on it becomes more physical. By the end of the season you are so worn out that it can become a physical toll on your body. Six months is a long time to pitch. But if you make it into the postseason, it's back to being mental again."

RYAN MADSON
2003–PRESENT

R yan Madson has done it all in eight major league seasons—working as a starter, middle reliever, setup man, and closer. When the Philadelphia Phillies selected him in the ninth round of the June 1998 draft, the six-foot-six right-hander was projected as a starter. He pitched almost exclusively in that role from the day he signed in 1998 through the 2003 season, with one exception.

On September 27, 2003, he pitched in relief (two scoreless, hitless innings) for the Phillies in his major league debut against the Atlanta Braves. It was his only major league appearance that season, but to Madson, it was one of his greatest moments. "It was a long time coming," he said, "but it felt good and it meant a lot to me. The other great moment for me was pitching in the World Series [with the Phillies in 2008]."

In 2004, he won a bullpen spot out of spring training. He wasn't starting, or closing, but he was on the major league roster and remained there the entire season. Madson earned his first major league save on May 13 at San Francisco, and made his first major league start on June 8 versus the Chicago White Sox. He pitched when and where he was needed.

But it took a roller coaster of a season in 2006 for him to finally land where his destiny intended him to be—in the bullpen. The Phillies needed a fifth starter and, because of Madson's experience in the minors, he was called upon. So after six mostly average starts, Madson returned to the bullpen, when the team promoted their No. 1 starter prospect, lefty Cole Hamels.

Mad Dog, as he came to be known, became a very effective setup man over the next few years. He was the "bridge to Lidge" for the 2008 world champion Phillies, with his 3.05 ERA in seventy-six games.

When Lidge was placed on the disabled list in September 2009, Madson was handed the closing role. When a closer was needed again in 2011, Madson stepped up and earned a career-best thirty-two saves in thirty-four opportunities.

"Taking steps and building up to the closing role has helped me," admitted Madson, "but there are some advantages to stepping into the role right away, like you see in the case of some closers around the league, because sometimes it's good to get thrown in the fire. It's kind of what happened to me to a degree. I began as a starter, and then I got thrown into the bullpen, and then it was a matter of survival and sometimes that is when you are at your best—when your back is against the wall."

One downside of Madson's career is the number of visits he has had to the disabled list—four in seven years. So his main objective as a closer is "staying healthy and proving that I can do the job; and also getting comfortable with the grind, which is not an easy thing to do," stated Madson.

In 2012 Madson signed with the Los Angeles Angels of Anaheim. He has found that each role in the bullpen is a little more challenging than the last. "When I started the setup role, I said to myself, 'Well, there is a little difference with this job than pitching the sixth and seventh innings.' So like everything else in life, you have to progress and move up, like taking steps and making adjustments along the way. When I progressed up to the closer role, I treated it the same way. The only difference is a big mental change in the closer role. When you pitch the ninth inning there is always so much more pressure, but you just have to get used to it or you won't survive. Once you become more accustomed to the role and get used to it, then you can get through the inning much easier," Madson said.

"The closer role does demand perfection, but more importantly it demands real knowledge of the game. Once you get to that level, you almost have to learn all over how to pitch. It's more about learning—learning your opponents and what works and what doesn't work. You can't just say, 'I'm going to throw strikes now.' That might work for some guys, but that is why I was always talking with Brad Lidge, when I was his setup guy, as to what to look for with this guy or what do you think he is going to look for."

Through it all, there was one person in particular who helped prepare Madson for the road to success—his minor league pitching coach, Rod Nichols. "The words he used really worked for me," explained Madson. "There was a lot of mechanical and mental stuff he taught me. But his overall approach to pitching really helped me to get over the hump and then get me to the next level. He would often say, 'Let the hitters have the pressure on them' or 'Don't own all of the pressure, put it back on them because they are the ones who have to score the runs.' So as simple as that sounds, they were the words I needed to hear and I still think back to those words from my minor league days."

JASON MOTTE
2008–PRESENT

I t isn't often that one of the best defensive catchers in the minor leagues becomes a major league closer, and gets on the mound for the final out in a World Series game seven . . . but that is what happened with Jason Motte.

Motte went to Iona College in New York, where he was a catcher with a rifle of an arm, frequently throwing out base runners at second base from his knees.

Scouts wanted to see him pitch when he was in college, but Motte wanted to catch, and his coach didn't want him blowing out his arm.

Still, the St. Louis Cardinals selected him in the nineteenth round of the June 2003 draft. In his professional debut, he caught nine games at Johnson City in rookie ball, then was promoted to Peoria (low-A), where he caught forty-eight games.

In 2004, he led Florida State League catchers with sixty-two assists and was rated the league's Best Defensive Catcher by *Baseball America* and as having the Best Tools in the FSL. His fate began to change when he fractured his right thumb on June 29, 2005, causing him to miss the remainder of the season.

He had been catching well, but not hitting so well. So in 2006, after ten games behind the plate, he began his conversion to pitching.

In 2008, just two years after he made the switch, he was named the eighth-best prospect in the Cardinals organization by *Baseball America*. Additionally, he earned a September call-up.

He made his major league debut on September 3, 2008, pitching one and one-third innings in a 4-3 loss in Arizona. He earned his first major league save on September 18 at Cincinnati, in a 5-4 win in which he pitched the final third of an inning.

In 2009, Motte blew his first save opportunity in his first game of the season, on April 6 against the Pittsburgh Pirates, by allowing four runs in one inning. However, he did appear in sixty-nine games that season, and was ranked fifth among National League rookies.

"It was one of those crazy things," said Motte. "I came up as a catcher. I didn't start pitching until 2006. I think shortly after that they decided to make me a closer. I was just hoping to get a hitter out. I remember when I came up in 2009 I blew my first save. I blew a three-run lead and that was it for my closer chance. But then I got another go at it in 2011. From that point on I pitched and tried not to worry about things too much. So I took one game at a time and that seemed to work and [Manager] Tony [La Russa] gave me another chance. In 2011, there were nine other guys who tried to give it a go in that role and it didn't seem to work out for them. So I said to myself, 'Well, why not just give it a go, and, again, take one day at a time and one pitch at a time.'"

Being in the right place at the right time, Motte was given the job as closer the last month of the season. He earned nine saves during that time, blowing just one opportunity. Motte was also the Cardinals closer during their postseason run in 2011, ultimately making it to the World Series.

Despite having just five seasons in the majors, Motte experienced one of the greatest moments a baseball player could imagine—being on the mound and pitching the final out in game seven of the World Series. "The greatest moment for me was game seven of the 2011 World Series," Motte revealed. "However, in game six when I gave up the home run to Josh Hamilton, that was what I thought was going to be my worst moment in the game, I remember thinking to myself, 'I just lost the World Series!'"

Motte said a teammate helped him bounce back. "I remember after I gave up the home run to Josh Hamilton in game six, and then we scored to tie up the game, Adam Wainwright [the Cardinals starting pitcher who was on the disabled list in 2011] came up and said to me, 'Do you know what this means? It means that you are going to be out there for game seven and will win it for us! So forget about what just happened. Get your rest and be ready to win it for us tomorrow.' He said this all to reassure me that things will work out. It was something else, and I still get goose bumps thinking about it," Motte revealed.

"Also during game one of the World Series, Bruce Sutter, Bob Gibson, and Adam Wainwright got to throw out the first pitch. Bruce Sutter asked that I catch him," Motte recalled. "I remember Bruce Sutter turning to me before we walked out of the tunnel and he said to me, 'Hey, keep doing what you are doing. You don't have to do anything different. Do what got you here, and next year there will be four of us out there throwing out that first pitch, not just three of us!' I remember someone asked me shortly after that game seven and the Cardinals victory what I was thinking about before I came into that last game. I remember I took my time before coming in and I tried to take it all in, and all I remembered were those words of Bruce Sutter and Adam Wainwright."

Motte also credits his manager, Tony La Russa, with helping him become a better pitcher. "Every time Tony came out to visit me when I came into the game he would say, 'Just breathe!' The first time he said that to me, I said to myself, 'What are you talking about?' What he meant was just relax, get focused, and calm down if you get in trouble. And think about what you are doing because the game happens so quickly; so that is why you just have to breathe."

JOE NATHAN
1999–PRESENT

The majority of closers have unique personalities, and Joe Nathan is no exception.

Nathan actually began his career as a shortstop. He was selected by the San Francisco Giants in the sixth round of the June draft in 1995 out of SUNY Stony Brook University. He began his professional career as a shortstop in rookie ball with Bellingham.

In 1996, he did something very few players have done in the history of professional baseball: he took a year off to work on finishing college. He earned a degree in business management from SUNY Stony Brook in 1997, after which he returned to baseball, not as a shortstop, but to begin his transition to pitching.

Again, he did not follow the standard script, as he began as a reliever and finished his 1997 season as a starter.

He made rapid progress as a pitcher and just two years after he began pitching professionally, he made his major league debut. He won his debut, a start against the Florida Marlins on April 21,

1999, when he threw seven shutout innings in the 4-0 win.

His 2000 season was interrupted by two stints on the disabled list with shoulder ailments. He eventually underwent surgery on his shoulder in the off-season, causing him to spend the entire 2001 and 2002 seasons in the minors. He returned to the majors as a September recall in 2002, making four relief appearances.

He missed one more season due to injury in 2010, this time with an elbow injury. Upon his return, he moved immediately into the closer role.

Nathan has already spent over twelve seasons in the majors with the Giants, Twins, and Rangers. The right-hander has pitched solely in relief since 2002, specifically as the closer over the last eight seasons, compiling nearly three hundred saves.

"For me, I think success starts with your parents and then your family," said the introspective Nathan. "But from the baseball side, I have had the opportunity to meet some great people along the way. When I came up to the big leagues I was with San Francisco and I had Robb Nen to learn from. I wasn't closing at the time; I was a starter, but there was this sense at the time that I would make a good closer. So having Nen around was pretty cool. He taught me to keep it simple. And he helped me realize rather quickly that these guys [closers] do have a pulse and are human and you didn't have to be a superhero to be in this role."

Nathan hopes his greatest moment in the game has not come yet. "Hopefully, that story is still waiting to be written," said Nathan. "But to this date it would have to be game 163 in October 2009 against the Tigers when I was with the Twins," in which the Twins won the game 6-5 in twelve innings to make it to the postseason.

For the five-time all-star, the closing role is demanding both mentally and physically. "The physical part is preparing yourself every day to pitch and get out there to pitch. And maybe it's not even the physical aspects of getting it done, but the process of just getting ready each day can be physically taxing at times.

Then obviously the mental side and keeping yourself focused is very challenging to any closer. Keeping yourself focused by watching the game and determining the situation and all of that is, again, very taxing."

The key to success is being able to handle the disappointments. "There is always going to be some down moments," said Nathan. "That is how the game works, but putting the bad experiences behind you is also important, too. It's like any blown save—you have to allow yourself to get pissed off, blow some steam, get disappointed, but once you leave this place, you have to be able to leave it all behind you."

ROBB
NEN
1993–2002

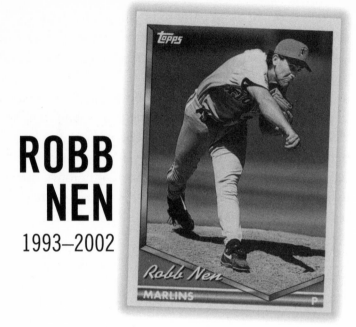

R obb Nen is of the newer generation. When he began his pitching career, closers were already believed to be the key to a team's success.

At six foot four, Nen is typical of what the current generation of closers are expected to be—big and strong. But he didn't start out as a closer, or even a pitcher for that matter. Nen was primarily a third baseman at Los Alamitos High School in California, only pitching occasionally. The Texas Rangers changed his life when, in 1987, his senior year, they drafted him in the thirty-second round as a pitcher.

As the son of former major league first baseman Dick Nen, Robb knew he did not want to go to college, but wanted to begin his professional career right away, even if it was at another position, so he signed with the Rangers.

"When I first came up, I was a starter," recalled Nen, "and when I ended up making the team in Florida, I thought they wanted me to be a starter, but I began pitching in relief to 'save' my arm, and I began to like it. I really liked the closer role and all that it involved, and I was good at it. I enjoyed pitching every day and my arm could handle it. And as soon as I got into the closing mode I absolutely loved it . . . it was what I loved to do. I think most pitchers in my day began as starters and figured they might find themselves in the bullpen over the course of their careers, but they didn't think they'd be the closer right away. I don't think anyone thinks about the closer role until they reach a certain point in their career. You evolve into the role."

Many other influences—in the form of teammates—helped him evolve into the pitcher/closer he became.

"There were a ton of guys I admired," said Nen, "like Nolan Ryan, who I was able to play with in Texas. To be able to watch him and what he put back into his game always impressed me. I didn't get a chance to play alongside Nolan Ryan too long, but the time I did I was fortunate. I got to watch him in spring training and how he was the last guy to leave the ball park and how he worked his butt off. Also, there were guys like Bryan Harvey, who I was able to sit next to in Florida and pick his brain on pitching and the closer role. Now, granted, I wasn't the closer back then, but I was able to watch guys like Harvey and learn. These guys were all business and I was always so impressed how these guys went about it."

Managers also impacted his career, and Nen had two of the best. "Dusty Baker [San Francisco Giants manager, 1993–2002] was a great player's manager," said Nen. "He was a guy you'd love to play for because he never threw you under the bus. He always looked at the positive and he would say things like 'great pitch' even if it didn't go so well. If you went out there for five days in a row and he'd say, 'I'm giving you the night off,' you'd say 'No, not tonight. I need to pitch for you,' because you wanted to do everything you could for him.

"Then there was another great guy, Jim Leyland [Florida Marlins manager, 1997–98]. He was really a smart manager. I called him my Mister X's and O's. Leyland was a great situational manager; he knew exactly who he was always going to use in the seventh and eighth inning, and he would always call it right. He always knew what the best situation in every game we played was.

"They are by far the two managers who I learned the most from, enjoyed playing for, and had the greatest impact on me and my career," he concluded.

"My father told me, it must have been a thousand times, let everything you do show your respect for the game. Don't cheat yourself, and don't cheat your teammates." His managers and coaches treated him with the same respect.

Nen believes the closing role is both mentally and physically challenging. "The mental side of it is that a lot of guys can't do the job of closer. Coming into the ninth, the mental side of that inning is tough, and you need a lot of adrenaline to go out there and do the job every day. You always have to be ready to save a game no matter if you've pitched three or four days in a row. Adrenaline is so important to a closer. They talk about a person who is addicted to drugs and they have this adrenaline rush — it is the same adrenaline rush I needed to get out there each and every day. And that is why so many closers, including myself, struggled during spring training because the adrenaline roll wasn't there. You don't have those 40,000 fans. You can't replicate that same situation in spring training because there aren't all those fans out there and the game is not on the line like it is during the regular season."

Nen had a very successful ten-year major league career with the Rangers, Marlins, and Giants. He was a three-time all-star, finished twelfth in National League MVP voting and fourth in NL Cy Young Award voting in 2000, led the NL in saves in 2001 (forty-five), had four seasons with forty-plus saves, seven seasons with thirty-five-plus saves, and ranks seventeenth on the all-time saves list with 314. He held both the Marlins' (108) and Giants' (206) all-time record for saves when he retired. He had five seasons in which he pitched in over seventy games. He was a member of the world champion Marlins team in 1997 and the NL pennant-winning Giants in 2002.

"Hard work and paying attention to the game was always key for me," admitted Nen. "I know a lot of guys didn't take the whole experience seriously. I watched guys during batting practice and what they were trying to do. I believe the more you watch the game the more you learn every day."

Nen pitched his last major league game in game six of the 2002 World Series against the Anaheim Angels on October 26. He had already been pitching through the playoffs despite the tremendous pain in his right shoulder, despite knowing he was heading for postseason surgery and was risking further injury. He had earned seven saves in that postseason, including two in the World Series, but he was unable to hold off the Angels in that game and they went on to win the Series in seven games. A big disappointment, but fans admired his self-sacrifice. He is beloved in San Francisco and works for the Giants to this day.

JONATHAN PAPELBON

2005–PRESENT

Jonathan Papelbon is a younger generation pitcher, and although he was originally thought of as a starter, once he got his footing as a closer, he flourished.

The six-foot-four 225-pounder went to Bishop Kenny High School in Jacksonville, Florida, where he pitched, played first base and outfield, and did some catching for the baseball team. He was a three-time All-City honoree in baseball and football and committed early to Mississippi State University in his senior year.

"I played in the field and pitched beginning in high school," said Papelbon, "but then, when I went off to college at Mississippi State, someone soon realized that I would make a better pitcher."

That someone was correct. Papelbon was a fourth-round selection by the Boston Red Sox in the 2003 June draft, and just two years later was pitching in the major leagues.

He began his professional career at Lowell (single-A) pitching thirteen games with six starts. In 2004, with Sarasota (single-A), he was Boston's Minor League Pitcher of the Year, accruing a 12-7 record and 2.64 ERA in twenty-four starts.

Papelbon made four starts at triple-A, and turned enough heads that he was called up to make a start—his major league debut—on July 31 against Minnesota. He had a no-decision in an eventual Red Sox 4-3 win. Following the game, he went back to Pawtucket and made three more appearances, this time all in relief.

When Papelbon returned to the majors, he made two more starts, on August 16 and August 21. He was moved to the bullpen on August 25.

The right-hander had a strong season as the Red Sox closer in 2006, earning thirty-five saves with a 0.92 ERA in fifty-nine games, but he was shut down for the final month with shoulder soreness. To ease the daily strain on his shoulder and have him pitching on a more regular basis, the Red Sox decided to move him into the starting rotation for the 2007 season.

The experiment did not go as the Red Sox planned, but not because of a lack of success. "I hadn't been sleeping well because there was that feeling deep down in my heart that I wanted to close," Papelbon said.

He returned to the closing role and flourished, finishing with thirty-seven saves, fifty-three games finished, the lowest opponents average in the league (.146), and the highest strikeouts per nine innings ratio (12.96) in leading the Red Sox to their seventh World Series Championship. He was named the DHL Delivery Man of the Year, received the Babe Ruth World Series Hero Award, and finished second in the BBWAA Rookie of the Year voting.

"For sure, the greatest moment of my career was game four of the 2007 World Series," Papelbon recalled, "when I struck out Seth Smith to get the final out of that game and win the World Series. It was my third save [of the Series] and it will always be really special for me."

Papelbon has also had some special times in mid-seasons, when he's been selected to four straight all-star teams, beginning with his rookie season in 2006. It was that year that he met the man who would have the greatest influence on his career—Mariano Rivera.

"I was able to compete against him the first part of my career. I've always referred to him as the godfather of the modern day closer," said Papelbon of Rivera. "He is like the Babe Ruth of closers. Everybody chases him and wants to be just like him."

Papelbon holds the distinction of reaching 200 career saves in the fewest appearances (359 games), surpassing Rivera's record of 382 games, and he is the first major league pitcher to achieve thirty or more saves in each of his first six years of service.

"I don't do anything in particular, meaning I don't have a ritual that I have to do every day," says Papelbon. "I listen to my body, and when I get to the park I have a pretty good idea as to what I need to do. Whether that is spending some time in the weight room, meet with the trainer, run, any of that. But I am always prepared to go in at game time."

One of the craziest stories Papelbon recalls happened as he was preparing to enter a game. "I remember it was a night game in 2007 at Fenway Park and I was all warmed up and ready to go in. Then all of a sudden this guy in a wheelchair came down to the bullpen. He took off his prosthetic leg and chucked it over the fence and into the bullpen, and he wanted me to sign it. I didn't sign it because it wasn't the right time. It was a one-run game and I had to go in and pitch. But I will never forget it."

The key to his success is based on the advice he got from Rivera, from a Yankee to a Red Sox. "You have to have a pretty good short term memory. That is what I've always said is important to the role . . . to have a good short term memory. Good or bad you can't think about it too much. You can't worry about yesterdays and you can't worry about any tomorrows. You can only worry about the now."

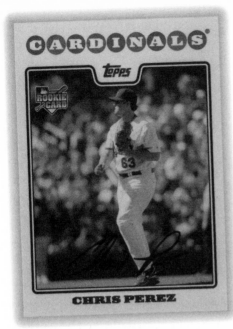

CHRIS PEREZ

2008–PRESENT

A

t six foot four, with shaggy hair, and an overly animated flare on the mound, right-hander Chris Perez was born to be a closer. In fact, he has been a closer for the majority of his career.

Perez grew up in Bradenton, Florida, and after high school he went on to the University of Miami, where he pitched for three years. He did make a few starts, but by midway through his sophomore season, he was the undisputed closer for the Hurricanes.

The St. Louis Cardinals selected him with their supplemental first-round pick in June 2006, as the forty-second player taken overall. Less than two years later, he made his major league debut against the Tampa Bay Rays, in a 3-1 loss on May 16, 2008, when he pitched one inning, facing four batters (B. J. Upton was safe on an error) and striking out one.

Perez had fifty-eight saves in sixty-three opportunities in 105 games in his two and a half seasons in the minor leagues. When he joined the major league club for the first time that May, he pitched out of the bullpen, but did not close games. However, by his second stint in the majors that year (beginning August 6), he was the closer.

On June 27, after appearing in twenty-nine games in relief for the Cardinals in 2009, Perez was traded to the Cleveland Indians. He immediately became the setup man for closer Kerry Wood, and ended up with thirty-eight strikeouts and just twelve walks over thirty-three and one-third innings in thirty-two games with the Indians.

Perez was healthy entering the 2010 season, but Wood was not, so Perez assumed the closer role. He finished the season twenty-three for twenty-seven in save opportunities, compiling an excellent 1.71 ERA in sixty-three games.

Perez got even better in his ensuing seasons. He went thirty-six for forty in save opportunities, finishing fourth in save percentage and total saves in the AL in 2011, when he was named to his first all-star team. He was again named to the all-star team in 2012, when he compiled twenty-six saves in twenty-eight opportunities with a little more than two months remaining in the season.

In just his fifth season in the majors, the twenty-seven-year-old may not have a lot of dramatic stories about the game, but he has a few that stick out for him. "I remember situations more than anything," he explained, "like the time I struck out Jose Bautista. That doesn't sound like much, but in twenty or thirty years, that might be like saying I struck out Babe Ruth or Hank Aaron. Or, having Albert Pujols as a teammate. Then again, I also remember my first time in the major leagues and the second batter I faced hit a ball down to first and Albert Pujols made an error. All I'm looking to do is impress the coaches and manager, and Albert Pujols makes an error. I'm saying to myself, 'Hey, you don't make errors . . . what are you doing it now for?' It's cool stuff like that. I also remember getting a save against the Reds. I struck out the side on eleven pitches and I never changed balls. Meaning, I threw eleven pitches with the same ball, and they never touched the ball with their bats."

He went on, "On the other hand, I didn't blow a save during a playoff or World Series game, but I remember I gave up a game-winning single in the ninth against the Twins to lose a game once. And the hit came off my old college roommate Danny Valencia. Later that night, I got a text from a buddy of ours, Jon Jay, who razzed me about it."

The discussion naturally turned to how he handles blown saves. "A blown save is like a game of poker or when you go fishing. Or any time you can say, 'What could have been?' or 'Let me tell you about the one that got away,' said Perez. "You don't have to forget about them.

"I remember in my rookie year I came into close after Jason Isringhausen went down with an injury and I blew a save. The next day, Tony La Russa came up to me in the outfield during batting practice and said, '[Dennis] Eckersley wanted me to ask if you are still thinking about that blown save?' I tried to play it off and replied, 'No, I'm not.' I knew then that La Russa knew I wasn't telling the truth, and I said, 'Yeah, I am.' That is when Tony reminded me that was why Eckersley was so good. He never forgot the blown saves and it stuck with him and that is why he worked so hard—because he never wanted to feel that way again after a game. The fear helped drive him."

Every pitcher has his own way of getting prepared and following his individual routine. Perez is no exception, although his routine is certainly exceptional. "I'm usually watching the game all of the time," he began with a grin. "Beginning in the seventh I pee pretty regularly . . . like every three outs. It's not that I have a problem with my pee, it's just nervous energy. I'm not scared to go out there, but your heart starts pumping, especially in those one-run games. So I get excited, too, and I go pee . . . it calms me. I certainly can't go once I'm out on the mound."

The Modern Day Closer

Perez likes to keep things simple. "My job is to just get those final three outs. As a closer, you don't run the bases, you don't hit the ball, you don't play defense . . . you just have to get those final three outs. You are expected to get those final three outs. That is just how it is, and that is my job."

ADDISON REED

2011–PRESENT

Very, very new to the closing role is twenty-three-year-old Addison Reed. Named closer for the Chicago White Sox in May 2012, the right-hander was selected by the White Sox in the third round of the June draft just two years before.

The six-foot-four athlete went to San Diego State University, where he led the nation with twenty saves in 2009. For his efforts, he was named Stopper of the Year by the National Collegiate Baseball Writers Association and the Preseason 2010 Consensus All-American as a relief pitcher. However, in an unusual move, when teammate and starting pitcher Stephen Strasburg was selected with the first pick in 2009 by the Washington Nationals, Reed stepped up and started for the Aztecs in 2010, going 8-2 in eleven starts, with team highs in wins, strikeouts, (ninety) and innings (seventy-nine and one-third).

Reed signed with the White Sox on June 15 and subsequently reported to rookie ball, where he went 1-0 with a 1.80 ERA in thirteen games with two starts, three games finished, and one save.

The 2011 season was quite a ride for the native Californian, who progressed through four levels, compiled a 2-1 record and a 1.26 ERA in forty-three games with five saves. It culminated with a September call-up to the majors.

He made his major league debut for the White Sox on September 4, 2011, against the Detroit Tigers, pitching one and one-third innings while giving up four hits and one earned run, and recording three strikeouts. He made five additional appearances before the season ended.

On May 23, 2012, Manager Robin Ventura officially named Reed the closer. "I hopefully will continue to be the guy in this role," said Reed. "The only thing I think about is going out there and getting the opposing team out. I don't think about everything that is going on around me. The less I think, the better off I'll be. The more I think about things and everything around me is when I seem to get into trouble."

At twenty-three years of age, Reed is low on experience, but high on learning. "I believe the closer role is more mental because of what they say, 'the last three outs are the hardest to get,'" said Reed. "For me, I love to be in those situations. The more pressure I have on me the better. I love the pressure and I love being out there in those game-winning situations."

Reed is always ready to go and wishes he could pitch every day. "I am always ready to pitch . . . always . . . every day! The more I am out there, the more fun I have in this role, and even when the team doesn't need me out there I wish I could still pitch," Reed enthusiastically said.

Like many kids growing up, Reed had baseball players as his idols. His No. 1 idol happened to be the closer for the Angels, Troy Percival. "I think it was watching so many games and seeing Troy out there that got me into wanting to close," admitted Reed. "I'm a Southern California guy and I used to go to Angels games all of the time. I also remember staying until the ninth inning each game so I could see Troy Percival. I remember watching him run out there and he used to get me excited about playing baseball and wanting to be a closer just like him. I loved watching him and hearing the music blaring and everyone standing up and cheering, especially during the World Series year of 2002."

One famous closer that Reed did not watch, but heard all about, was Goose Gossage. Gossage and the 1972 White Sox team were honored before a White Sox game in late June, and Reed had a rare opportunity to meet the Hall of Famer. "I'd never met him before," said Reed. "I know about him. I know everything he has done. It was awesome talking to him."

As for advice imparted by the man with 310 saves to the rookie who had just picked up save No. 11, Reed said it was very straightforward. "He said, 'Just go out there and don't give the other team too much credit,'" Reed said. "'Don't be friendly. Go out there and get after them.'"

"I'm still pretty new at this," he concluded. "Once it's all over, I guess I'll have my collection of stories to tell one day, but for right now I'm trying to make some good memories out there."

MARIANO RIVERA

1995–PRESENT

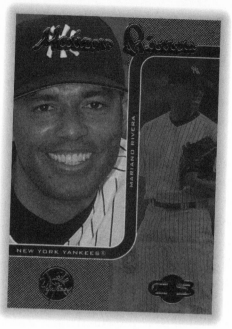

Regarded by many as one of the best closers in the history of baseball, Mariano Rivera is the epitome of a modern day closer. The majority of his saves have been earned by pitching a single, final inning, but his consistency and reliability to close a game is unmatched.

With 608 career saves, Rivera holds a tough-to-break major league record. But even more impressively, he has earned forty-two postseason saves, while compiling a 0.70 ERA in ninety-six games.

A humble Rivera set the save record on September 19, 2011, against the Minnesota Twins, surpassing Trevor Hoffman's record of 601 career saves. His teammates made sure he stayed on the mound in order to get the recognition he deserved. "It felt good," said Rivera, "but they all feel good. Let me tell you something; don't get me wrong, I never like to speak about myself. And I do get uncomfortable with questions about my accomplishments, but at the same time it did feel good. I mean, it's good knowing that I have the opportunity and the blessings to be able to do what I do."

He continued: "The reason I do what I do is because I need to get the job done for my team who is counting on me. So, that is why I can't always reflect on what I've done and say 'Look what I did!' or 'I accomplished this or that' because it is a team effort and it's about the twenty-five players that are out there and involved in a game. The closer role is very humbling and I am one of twenty-five guys. Sure, I feel blessed but it still comes back to those twenty-five players trying to accomplish something together. But that's baseball! It has and always will be a team sport. It will never be like golf or tennis or any other individual sport. Baseball is all about teamwork. Everyone is helping everyone. So, I can't sit back and say 'Look what I did!' It will never be about that for me."

The native of Panama was signed by the New York Yankees as an amateur free agent on February 17, 1990, and although he spent his first professional season as a reliever, from 1991 until midway through his first major league season in 1995, Rivera was primarily a starter.

At twenty-five years of age, Rivera made his major league debut on May 23, 1995, in a start against the California Angels in Anaheim. He made eight straight inconsistent starts, only once pitching past the sixth inning. After flipping between the starting and relieving roles, he finished the season with six appearances in relief.

His career started down the right path in 1996, when he had an outstanding season as the setup man for Yankees' closer John Wetteland. Rivera earned his first career save on May 17, 1996, against the California Angels. In all, he posted five saves that year, along with a 2.09 ERA in sixty-one appearances, while striking out a Yankee relievers' record 130 in 107²/₃ innings. Unbelievably, he finished *third* in voting for the American League Cy Young Award Award—the winner of which is usually a starter, occasionally a closer, but never a setup guy.

After that fantastic season, the Yankees felt confident enough with Rivera that they let fifty-save closer Wetteland depart via free agency and handed the closing role to the six-foot-two right-hander.

According to Rivera, two people have had the greatest impact on his career, Yankees Manager Joe Torre and Pitching Coach Mel Stottlemyre. "If you can remember my days before I was the closer, I was the setup man in the bullpen and I was always trying to strike everyone out," Rivera recalled. "I remember Mel coming out to me one day and convincing me that it isn't always about the strikeout; it was about getting players out and that the strikeouts would come naturally. He said, 'You don't have to strike out everybody out there. You've got eight other players behind you capable of making the out for you.' When I eventually realized that, I started to learn more and be fresh and be a better pitcher. Therefore, I was able to pitch longer and not be tired in October. I often say Mel helped me to bring out my strengths as a pitcher."

In his first eighteen seasons of Major League Baseball, Rivera has had no less than eight seasons with forty-plus saves. He's led the AL in saves three times: 1999 (45 saves), 2001 (50), and 2004 (career-high 53). He is a twelve-time all-star and has pitched in sixteen postseasons, including seven World Series.

After thinking very hard, Rivera shared that his greatest moment in the game was "my first World Series definitely, because it was my first World Series [1996 versus Atlanta Braves] and it will always be special. But at the same time, the 2009 World Series [versus Philadelphia Phillies] was very special for me, too, because of all of the challenges the team faced that year. Both were very beautiful and special for me because after a long drought of not winning anything, we eventually did. Maybe you sometimes take winning for granted and then when it is taken away or not shared for a while, and then you do win it, that is what is so special about it."

Rivera's philosophy towards the closer role is simple. "I'm all about business. Go out and do the job, get the job done, and let my team go home." However, he does consider the role to be more mental than physical. "Just look at me, I am not six foot seven and three hundred pounds. I am not a giant. I don't wear the Fu Manchu beard or any other crazy hair . . . I don't even have hair," he added laughing. "There is nothing I have that is about my physical body that anyone can be in fear of. But what I know and what I am comfortable with is my knowledge of the game and my conviction of who I am and who I trust."

Rivera has faced many challenges in his storied career, but he feels the challenges he faces today are greater than when he was a young pitcher. "I'm a little older now and I've got to do a little more to prepare for what I do. You always got to keep up with the younger guys and that is why it is a greater challenge for me today. I can't throw the ball at 94 mph today like I was able to do when I was twenty-four years old. You don't think about all of the preparation and conditioning when you are younger. But after you've been in this game ten or fifteen years, you have to evolve and become a different pitcher. You become a different animal out there. You start using your mental game face more than any physical attributes."

After achieving so much in the game, there doesn't seem like he has much left to achieve, but Rivera's goals are as simple as his philosophy towards the closer's role, "My challenge is the same every year . . . to be the best pitcher I can be for my team and to win the World Series. That is my challenge."

The future Hall of Famer is as recognized for his philanthropic work in the community as he is for the stellar work he does as a closer for the Yankees. "I always want to be remembered as that guy who was always there for others and one who helps bring out the best in others," Rivera revealed. "I want to be remembered as a team player, the guy who wants to talk about others and their accomplishments and not about my own. That is what I want my legacy to be."

FERNANDO RODNEY

2002–PRESENT

Fernando Rodney is from the newer generation of closers, a pitcher who was groomed for the closing role early in his professional career.

Rodney was born in the Dominican Republic on March 18, 1977. The Detroit Tigers signed him as an amateur free agent on November 1, 1997.

He began his pro career in 1998, pitching in the Dominican Summer League, making five starts in eleven appearances. In 1999, he pitched in the United States, earning eleven saves combined for the Tigers in the Gulf Coast League and Lakeland in the Florida State League.

He began the 2000 season in the bullpen, as usual, then was moved into the starting rotation on June 23. Ten of his twenty-two games were starts. The experiment continued in 2001, when he again made ten starts; but his season was marred with two visits to the disabled list, and he never made another start in his career.

Rodney made his major league debut for the Tigers on May 4, 2002, (his first of four stints with Detroit) at Minnesota. He lost the game, 3-2, pitching the final four outs, allowing an unearned run on two hits and a walk.

He had up-and-down seasons in 2003 and 2004, and some injuries in 2005. Rodney finally pitched an entire season in the majors in 2006, earning seven saves in sixty-three games. The Tigers made the World Series that year and he was able to pitch in three games in the American League Championship Series against the Oakland A's, and four games against the St. Louis Cardinals in Detroit's World Series loss.

But he was bitten by the injury bug again in 2007 and 2008. He had a strong year in 2009, earning thirty-seven saves in thirty-eight opportunities for a 97.4 percent success rate, best among American League pitchers. His sixty-five games finished also led all AL pitchers. His thirty-seven saves were four more than he had earned in his MLB career to that point.

He spent the 2010 and 2011 seasons with the Anaheim Angels. He saved fourteen games for the Angels in 2010, beginning and ending the season as the closer.

Rodney signed with the Tampa Bay Rays on January 4, 2012, where he finished with his career year, earning forty-eight saves and a record setting best .60 ERA as a reliever. (In fact Rodney's ERA was officially .6053, a tick below Dennis Eckersley's big-league-record mark for relievers of 0.61363)

"There have been so many people that have been there for me and have helped me get to each level," said Rodney. "I love all of my teammates and I have always loved the camaraderie of being with them in the bullpen."

Like a football player with an end-zone dance after a touchdown, Rodney shoots an imaginary arrow into the air following every save. "It is something I got in my mind," laughed Rodney, "and I feel comfortable with doing it . . . the shooting the arrow in the air. I don't think it offends anyone. I try and have fun with it. I think it is a great idea and everyone seems to like it."

His postgame routine is seen by all the fans, but his pregame routine and singing Latin music in the bullpen are only seen and heard by a few. "The singing is something I've always done. I feel the music in me. It gives me energy and prepares me to go in. I come from the Dominican Republic," said Rodney, "and sometimes I miss the country that I am from and I miss its music. I know a lot of songs and it reminds me of home. I sing a lot in the bullpen, and I use it as a trigger to go in and get ready."

Staying healthy and making it to another World Series are both challenges he wishes to conquer one day. But for now, the thirty-five-year-old said, "I don't try and think about any challenges. Every day you have to be ready to go out there."

The bubbly pitcher truly enjoys his job, as noted by his answer to the question of what was his greatest moment on the mound: "The greatest moment for me happens for me every game I step out on the mound and get ready to pitch. It is what I like to do and I have fun with what I do."

FRANCISCO RODRIGUEZ
2002–PRESENT

Francisco (or Freddie or K-Rod, as he is known) Rodriguez has accomplished quite a bit in his career, and he is still just thirty one years old.

The right-hander was born in Caracas, Venezuela, attended Juan Lovera High School in Caracas, and was signed as an amateur free agent by the Anaheim Angels in 1998.

"Growing up in Venezuela, my idols were all pitchers, like Ugueth Urbina and Pedro Martinez," said Rodriguez. "I used to love how Pedro went after the hitter and how Urbina had this whole mental approach to pitching the ninth inning and the game."

The young Venezuelan started his career, like many others, as a starter. It wasn't until 2002 that he moved into a relief role, and found his true potential. He went 5-6 with a 2.27 ERA in fifty games combined at the double-A and triple-A levels, saving fifteen games and striking out 120 in just over eighty-three innings. The Angels called him up in September and Rodriguez made his major league debut on September 18, in a 7-4 loss at Oakland.

In his five major league games, he did not have a decision, nor did he allow a run, and he struck out thirteen in five and two-third innings. And that is when things got interesting for the twenty-year-old.

Because of his "hot" three weeks, he was put on the Angels' postseason roster. He had not been on the roster by the August 30 postseason roster deadline, however his inclusion was permitted because the rules for postseason rosters allow for an injury replacement for any player on the forty-man roster. He was able to fill in for right-handed pitcher Steve Green, who had been on the disabled list all season.

Strangely enough, Rodriguez's first win in the majors came in the postseason—in game two of the NLDS against the Yankees. The league's youngest player went 5-1 overall in eleven postseason games. With his win in game two of the World Series against the Giants, he became the youngest pitcher ever to win a game in the World Series; the win was also his fifth of the postseason, tying Randy Johnson's 2001 mark for a single postseason.

Rodriguez struck out a record twenty-eight batters in his eighteen and two-thirds postseason innings, crushing the single postseason record of eighteen Ks.

Not surprisingly, Rodriguez recalled the 2002 season with great fondness. "I would say the '02 season, the buildup to the World Series, and then eventually getting there and going into game seven and striking out the side when I came in was the greatest moment of my career," Rodriguez said. "It was at that moment that I felt that I really belong here. And I felt the same way that following spring training. I approached that spring so differently knowing in my heart that I was part of the team and that I didn't have to worry about getting sent back to the minors. I was ready for the responsibility before me."

Still technically considered a rookie going into the 2003

season, Rodriguez had impressed the team so much that he had the more defined role as a late-inning or setup man out of the bullpen.

His 2004 season was even better, posting a 4-1 record with a 1.82 ERA in sixty-nine games with 123 strikeouts in eighty-four innings. He became the sixth pitcher in Angels' history to strikeout at least one hundred in a season without starting a game.

Prior to the 2005 season, Angels closer Troy Percival left via free agency and the closing role was handed to Rodriguez. He made the most of his opportunity, earning forty-five saves in fifty chances.

Rodriguez improved on his save total in 2006, with a major league-leading forty-seven saves in fifty-one chances. With his save on September 10 against the Blue Jays, the twenty-four-year-old became the youngest pitcher in MLB history to reach 100 saves.

The saves kept coming as Rodriguez earned another forty (in forty-six chances) in 2007, tied for second-highest in the American League; but nothing would compare to his 2008 season. On September 2 at Detroit, he earned the two hundredth save of his career. On September 11 versus the Mariners, he tied Bobby Thigpen's 1990 record with his fifty-seventh save of the season. He set the record two days later. On September 20 at Texas, Rodriguez became the first pitcher to reach sixty saves in a single season, and ended the season with sixty-two.

The six-foot right-hander emphasizes preparation, as the key to his success. "I am always prepared to pitch. You have to be," said Rodriguez. "I have a certain routine and preparation before each game. For the first three innings I am able to relax a little, but I still watch the hitters. From the fourth through the sixth innings I start my own preparation. I stretch and prepare [so] from the seventh inning on, I am ready to pitch."

He continued: "There is no room for error in the closer role. You have to be at the top of your game each and every night, especially when things aren't always going your way. You still have to get the job done. There is no break, meaning you can't say to the manager, 'Hey, I need the day off to recover from last night!' You have to be accountable every night and ready day in and day out in order to preserve that victory."

Most closers agree the closer's role is more of a mental strain but Rodriguez is able to thrive under the pressure. "I think it is a gift that God has given me," he explained. "I am more effective when the game is on the line and when it gets tougher," he explained. "It forces me to concentrate more and focus more, which then forces me to make more quality pitches. I have always loved the challenge.

"The way I handle the role, I learned from others. When I came up with the Angels, I was very young and I learned the way to pitch the ninth inning and the way to handle the pressure from Troy Percival. He was a wonderful mentor," said Rodriguez.

"At first, he was always riding me and I thought he hated me, but in the long run I realized he wanted me to do my best and that is why he helped me in every way. Hopefully, before I retire, let's say ten years down the road, I would love to be able to pass my knowledge to some young pitcher who is just starting out, and this way the tradition can continue."

JOHN SMOLTZ
1988–2009

John Smoltz pitched in the majors for twenty-one years, all but one of them with the Atlanta Braves.

He was selected by the Detroit Tigers in the twenty-second round of the June 1985 draft out of Waverly High School in Michigan, and finally signed with them on September 22. He began his professional career at Lakeland (single-A) in 1986. The following year, on August 12, 1987, he was traded to the Braves and found his future home.

Smoltz made his major league debut on July 23, 1988, in a 6-1 win at Shea Stadium against the New York Mets, starting and pitching eight innings. He never looked back.

Smoltz became a member of a dominant Braves starting rotation that led the team to the postseason eight times in the 1990s, to the World Series five times in that span, and to the World Series title in 1995.

An eight time all-star, Smoltz had double-digit win totals in ten of his first twelve seasons in the majors, including a major league-leading twenty-four wins and 276 strikeouts in 1996, the year he won the prestigious National League Cy Young Award.

In 2000, Smoltz tore the medial collateral ligament in his right elbow in spring training. After having surgery in March 23, he was placed on the disabled list and did not return to the mound until May 17, 2001. He made five starts for the Braves that season, but returned to the DL on June 10. After returning again, on July 22, he made his first regular season relief appearance that night against the Expos.

For the last two months of the 2001 season and the following three seasons, Smoltz was the closer for the Braves. He accumulated 154 saves in those three-plus seasons, including a league-leading fifty-five in 2002.

"I wanted to win a championship and that was the only reason why I entertained going to the closer role," admitted Smoltz. "If I helped make the team better and get us there, then I was willing to do it. I did the closer role for three seasons and it was a tremendous experience and it taught me a lot, even though we didn't win a championship.

"So many people like to compare my career with Dennis Eckersley's, but I kind of believe my career wasn't like anyone else's. And I don't think it parallels Dennis Eckersley's career, although we do get placed into the same category a lot. Dennis was one of the greatest closers that ever played this game. I think so many like to compare us because of the numbers the two of us have amassed."

The Braves made the postseason each of the seasons that Smoltz was a closer (2001–04), but the team failed to reach the World Series again.

Smoltz recalled that one of his first outings in his first full season as the closer didn't go so well. "In two-thirds of an inning I gave up eight runs against the Mets [on April 6, 2002]. Every goal I had going into the role as a closer seemed to be shot," he recalled.

"And then there were all of the 'naysayers' who said, 'This isn't going to work out!' I eventually went on to save fifty-five ballgames that year with a 3.25 ERA. Even though I gave up eight runs that day, I don't believe for the rest of the season I gave up a combined eight runs." (He actually gave up just twenty-one runs over the remainder of the season, in seventy-three games.)

"The next year, I went out with the goal of dominating in the role for that one inning," he continued. "I remember I had this 0.85 ERA going into the last game of the season against the Phillies and I was ready to set a record. Bobby Cox asked me that day if I wanted to sit to preserve the record. I said, 'No, I'm good.' I was also thinking that this outing would be a good tune-up for the playoffs. Unfortunately, I gave up two runs with two outs and I blew the save and my ERA shot up to over 1.00 and I felt like the biggest horse's behind! Here I was ready to have the dream of a lifetime and the season of a lifetime, and all it took was one bad outing and one bad inning. Interestingly, I do hold the Braves franchise record for saves, a record that I know will be broken soon by Craig Kimbrel."

Smoltz returned to the starting rotation in 2005, and accumulated double-digits in wins each of the next three seasons, including a league-leading sixteen wins and thirty-five starts in 2006.

"I think the closer role gets too much credit and it gets too much blame. I think it is a very difficult role to do night in and night out. It is a mental adjustment beyond any other position change," Smoltz explained. "For example, if you take a third baseman or a second baseman and you convert him over to first base, it could be a drastic change for that player, but I believe it is not as drastic a change as if you were to take a starter and place him in a closer role.

"As a closer, you've got to believe in yourself. You've got to believe you are nasty and do whatever it takes, and you better have a good short-term memory. When I went over to the closer role, I felt like I had to learn the role as quickly as I could. There was no manual I could refer to or read. I had to learn how to adjust on the fly," said Smoltz. "There is no routine to the role. You might go four days without seeing some action, and then be in the next four games. There is no set formula. You've got to trust in yourself no matter what it is.

"I know there are some people out there who say, 'What if I stayed in the closer role my entire career? What numbers could I have achieved?' I've never thought about it like that. I measure success if what I did helped our team win!

"I do recall one cool stat," Smoltz continued. "I remember pitching in seventy-three consecutive games in which our team got the victory [June 3, 2002 to May 25, 2003]. Those are the statistics I like to quote because it meant success for our team.

"Having done both roles, I quickly realized how difficult it was for a starter to actually get a victory and how equally horrible it felt to get a blown save. Interestingly, I don't think I ever blew a save then for a guy in the starting rotation, it was just guys from the bullpen."

Smoltz cites Braves Manager Bobby Cox as the man who had the greatest influence on his career. "He had this amazing ability to trust in you and still instill this sense of confidence," he reflected. "I remember in 1991 I started the first half of the season with a 2-11 record. It was Bobby who single-handedly kept me in the lineup and allowed me to pitch in three of the biggest games for us that season. I pitched the final game of the year against Houston to win the division, I pitched the seventh game of the League Championship Series, and I pitched the seventh game of the World Series. It was the pitching trifecta for me, and I could have never done it without Bobby. And who would have ever imagined that I would be in that situation given the 2-11 start I had."

Smoltz finished his career with the Boston Red Sox and St. Louis Cardinals in 2009, with a career record of 231-155 and a 3.33 ERA in 3,473 innings over 723 games.

"In my twenty-one years as a big leaguer, I felt as though I went as hard and as far as I could, and that was always my goal in this game," said Smoltz. "I am so proud and fortunate to have been a part of the Braves organization and the record-setting fifteen consecutive postseason appearances. It is hard to imagine when you spent your first three seasons on a team that lost over 300 total games in that time. How could you have ever imagined that you would be playing in that many postseasons?"

Smoltz was inducted into the Braves' Hall of Fame and had his number retired on June 8, 2012. "The ceremony was great and the day was exhausting," said Smoltz. "There were so many emotions surrounding that day."

But there should be another draining day for the right-hander in a few years, when he is eligible to be inducted into the National Baseball Hall of Fame. "Well, the great news for me was I never pitched for that," Smoltz said, "but if it did happen it would be awesome. I often say, I really did have a great career for so long and yet it should have never happened. It really should have never happened. Physically I pitched in so much pain and had so many injuries. I didn't have a body that was blessed to play sports, but it was athletic and it allowed me to do what I needed to do."

JOSE VALVERDE

2003–PRESENT

One of the more recent additions to the closing scene is Jose Valverde, who made his debut with the Arizona Diamondbacks in 2003.

Valverde grew up in the Dominican Republic, where he graduated from Escuela San Lorenzo in 1997, the same year the Diamondbacks signed him as an amateur free agent. He made his professional debut in the United States in 1999.

The six-foot-four, 255-pound Valverde—or Papa Grande as he is called—was groomed as a reliever right from the start. In fact, after making his major league debut in relief on June 1, 2003, the rookie took over as the team's closer while Matt Mantei was sidelined.

It all has come naturally for the big right-hander. "I don't really do anything special to prepare for a game," he admits. "For me, it's easy. Take the ball and throw. I do feel the pressure in this role, but it's normal for this game. And the pressure gets the adrenaline going, which then gets me focused."

Despite his success with the role, Valverde had trouble nailing down the position as his own. In 2004, he again filled in as the closer for an injured Mantei, until he injured his shoulder in mid-June. In 2005, he eventually took over the closer role and by season's end earned a team-leading fifteen saves in seventeen opportunities. Things were different in 2006, as he started the season as the club's closer. This time he lost the position to Jorge Julio, who came over from the Mets. He regained his confidence in the minors and regained his role as closer by season's end.

And since 2007, the role has been his. His trademark celebratory actions may be the one thing *not* in his control. "It is all about the victory for me during that moment and it feels so good," admitted Valverde. "Someone once asked me after one celebration and save, 'Do you see what you are doing out there after the save?' I said to him, 'What do you mean?' I don't know what I'm doing out there. . . . The body takes over and it does what it wants to do."

While Valverde inspires teammates to have fun, there had to be someone who had a great impact on him and his career. "My last pitching coach with the Diamondbacks, Bryan Price, had the greatest influence on me. He was great. He was very, very good to me. He would always tell me what was working right for me," revealed Valverde.

"But growing up my dad taught me everything about baseball," he continued. "He was a baseball guy, but he worked a lot. I think my family is very excited because they are so proud for me."

Valverde had a strong 2007, being named to the all-star team and leading the National League in saves with forty-seven, but he was traded to the Houston Astros during the off-season. He did not disappoint in Houston, as he again led the league in saves (forty-four) and games finished (seventy-one). He suffered a calf injury in 2009, shortening his season to just fifty-two games, while still accruing twenty-five saves.

He became a free agent following the 2009 season and signed with the Detroit Tigers. He has been an all-star in each of his two seasons with the Tigers, and, although his 2010 season was nothing to hang his head about, his 2011 season was one for the record books.

Papa Grande had what every pitcher strives for—a perfect season. He saved forty-nine games in forty-nine opportunities, becoming just the third pitcher in major league history to convert all his save opportunities in a single season while posting forty or more saves. He joined Eric Gagne (55 saves in 2003) and Brad Lidge (41 in 2008). "I pitched well, but I had a great team behind me," explained a modest Valverde. "Everything was great for me in 2011. I was healthy. I felt good. I was throwing great. I'd throw good pitches and the guy would swing and miss, and then I'd throw bad pitches and he'd be swinging and missing, too. It was like a book, everything fit just right."

His pitching coach with the Tigers, Jeff Jones, knew exactly how to motivate his big closer last year. "He said to me a few times last season, 'Hey, I think it's time to go home.' It was his way of saying when I pitched, let's end this game and get this last guy out. Strike him out so we can all go home."

Looking back on his career, the lighthearted Valverde laughed, "I had a couple of great moments last year. Everything about 2011 for me was perfect. I remember one game in Cleveland I got the save on just seven pitches. It was just seven pitches! I couldn't believe it. It was something I will never forget, but that is what 2011 was like for me . . . everything was going so well."

At thirty-four years of age, he has amassed nearly 280 career saves and he should have many years left to play—especially since he doesn't plan on getting old. His current manager, Jim Leyland, summed him up well, "He loves to play, loves to pitch. He has one of those personalities that makes you happy!"

THE EARLY YEARS

	W	L	W/L%	ERA	G	GS	GF	CG	SV	SO	IP
Elroy Face	104	95	.523	3.48	848	27	574	6	193	877	1375.0
Roland "Rollie" Fingers	114	118	.491	2.90	944	37	709	4	341	1299	1701.1
Gene Garber	96	113	.459	3.34	931	9	609	4	218	940	1510.0
Richard "Goose" Gossage	124	107	.537	3.01	1002	37	681	16	310	1502	1809.1
Dave Giusti	100	93	.518	3.60	668	133	380	35	145	1103	1716.2
John Hiller	87	76	.534	2.83	545	43	363	13	125	1036	1242.0
Tom House	29	23	.558	3.79	289	21	154	4	33	261	536.0
Al Hrabosky	64	35	.646	3.10	545	1	307	0	97	548	722.0

W = win | **L** = loss | **W/L%** = win-loss | **ERA** = earned run average | **G** = games played | **GS** = games started
GF = games finished | **CG** = completed games | **SV** = saves | **SO** = strikeouts | **IP** = innings pitched

	W	L	W/L%	ERA	G	GS	GF	CG	SV	SO	IP
Jim Konstanty	66	48	.579	3.46	433	36	266	14	74	268	945.2
Tug McGraw	96	92	.511	3.14	824	39	541	5	180	1109	1514.2
Joe Page	57	49	.538	3.53	285	45	182	14	76	519	790.0
Ron Perranoski	79	74	.516	2.79	737	1	458	0	179	687	1174.2
Dan Quisenberry	56	46	.549	2.76	674	0	553	0	244	379	1043.1
Kent Tekulve	94	90	.511	2.85	1050	0	638	0	184	779	1436.2
Hoyt Wilhelm	143	122	.540	2.52	1070	52	651	20	227	1610	2254.1

W = win | **L** = loss | **W/L%** = win-loss | **ERA** = earned run average | **G** = games played | **GS** = games started
GF = games finished | **CG** = completed games | **SV** = saves | **SO** = strikeouts | **IP** = innings pitched

THE TRANSITION YEARS

	W	L	W/L%	ERA	G	GS	GF	CG	SV	SO	IP
Rick Aguilera	86	81	.515	3.57	732	89	557	10	318	1030	1291.1
Jeff Brantley	43	46	.483	3.39	615	18	379	0	172	728	859.1
Dennis Eckersley	197	171	.535	3.50	1071	361	577	100	390	2401	3285.2
Steve Farr	48	45	.516	3.25	509	28	313	1	132	668	824.1
Bryan Harvey	17	25	.405	2.49	322	0	278	0	177	448	387.0
Jay Howell	58	53	.523	3.34	568	21	360	2	155	666	844.2

W = win | **L** = loss | **W/L%** = win-loss | **ERA** = earned run average | **G** = games played | **GS** = games started
GF = games finished | **CG** = completed games | **SV** = saves | **SO** = strikeouts | **IP** = innings pitched

	W	L	W/L%	ERA	G	GS	GF	CG	SV	SO	IP
Doug Jones	69	79	.466	3.30	846	4	640	0	303	909	1128.1
Roger McDowell	70	70	.500	3.30	723	2	430	0	159	524	1050.0
Jeff Montgomery	46	52	.469	3.27	700	1	549	0	304	733	868.2
Donnie Moore	43	40	.518	3.67	416	4	229	0	89	416	654.2
Jesse Orosco	87	80	.521	3.16	1252	4	501	0	144	1179	1295.1
Dan Plesac	65	71	.478	3.64	1064	14	422	0	158	1041	1072.0
Dave Righetti	82	79	.509	3.46	718	89	474	13	252	1112	1403.2

W = win | **L** = loss | **W/L%** = win-loss | **ERA** = earned run average | **G** = games played | **GS** = games started
GF = games finished | **CG** = completed games | **SV** = saves | **SO** = strikeouts | **IP** = innings pitched

	W	L	W/L%	ERA	G	GS	GF	CG	SV	SO	IP
John Rocker	13	22	.371	3.42	280	0	176	0	88	332	255.1
Jeff Russell	56	73	.434	3.75	589	79	340	11	186	693	1099.2
Lee Smith	71	92	.436	3.03	1022	6	802	0	478	1251	1289.1
Bruce Sutter	68	71	.489	2.83	661	0	512	0	300	861	1042.0
Bobby Thigpen	31	36	.463	3.43	448	0	356	0	201	376	568.2
Mitch Williams	45	58	.437	3.65	619	3	419	0	192	660	691.1

W = win | **L** = loss | **W/L%** = win-loss | **ERA** = earned run average | **G** = games played | **GS** = games started
GF = games finished | **CG** = completed games | **SV** = saves | **SO** = strikeouts | **IP** = innings pitched

THE MODERN DAY CLOSER

	W	L	W/L%	ERA	G	GS	GF	CG	SV	SO	IP
John Axford	15	12	.556	3.06	206	0	166	0	106	264	208.2
Rafael Betancourt	34	28	.548	3.15	603	0	203	0	58	657	617.2
Joe Borowski	22	34	.393	4.18	423	1	268	0	131	372	454.1
Matt Capps	29	33	.468	3.52	444	0	281	0	138	319	439.2
Francisco Cordero	47	53	.470	3.38	800	0	575	0	329	796	824.2
Kyle Farnsworth	40	62	.392	4.24	810	26	260	1	52	917	921.2

W = win | **L** = loss | **W/L%** = win-loss | **ERA** = earned run average | **G** = games played | **GS** = games started
GF = games finished | **CG** = completed games | **SV** = saves | **SO** = strikeouts | **IP** = innings pitched

	W	L	W/L%	ERA	G	GS	GF	CG	SV	SO	IP
Brian Fuentes	26	43	.377	3.62	650	0	381	0	204	639	613.1
Eric Gagne	33	26	.559	3.47	402	48	269	0	187	718	643.2
Tom Gordon	138	126	.523	3.96	890	203	347	18	158	1928	2108.0
Kevin Gregg	28	38	.424	4.13	509	8	326	0	144	585	638.2
Trevor Hoffman	61	75	.449	2.87	1035	0	856	0	601	1133	1089.1
Jason Isringhausen	51	55	.481	3.64	724	52	499	3	300	830	1007.2
Jim Johnson	15	18	.455	3.14	286	1	137	0	72	209	329.2

W = win | **L** = loss | **W/L%** = win-loss | **ERA** = earned run average | **G** = games played | **GS** = games started
GF = games finished | **CG** = completed games | **SV** = saves | **SO** = strikeouts | **IP** = innings pitched

	W	L	W/L%	ERA	G	GS	GF	CG	SV	SO	IP
Todd Jones	58	63	.479	3.97	982	1	619	0	319	868	1072.0
Craig Kimbrel	11	4	.733	1.46	163	0	127	0	89	283	160.1
Brandon League	19	28	.404	3.60	377	0	169	0	60	309	414.2
Ryan Madson	47	30	.610	3.59	491	18	150	0	52	547	630.0
Jason Motte	17	13	.567	2.87	282	0	116	0	54	273	260.0
Joe Nathan	51	28	.646	2.87	647	29	470	0	298	839	794.0
Robb Nen	45	42	.517	2.98	643	4	549	0	314	793	715.0

W = win | **L** = loss | **W/L%** = win-loss | **ERA** = earned run average | **G** = games played | **GS** = games started
GF = games finished | **CG** = completed games | **SV** = saves | **SO** = strikeouts | **IP** = innings pitched

	W	L	W/L%	ERA	G	GS	GF	CG	SV	SO	IP
Jonathan Papelbon	28	25	.528	2.34	466	3	398	0	257	601	499.1
Chris Perez	10	18	.357	3.23	290	0	186	0	107	269	279.0
Addison Reed	3	2	.600	4.62	68	0	46	0	29	66	62.1
Mariano Rivera	76	58	.567	2.21	1051	10	892	0	608	1119	1219.2
Fernando Rodney	24	0	.375	3.75	495	0	289	0	135	469	504.2
Francisco Rodriguez	38	34	.528	2.70	682	0	458	0	294	878	720.2
John Smoltz	213	155	.579	3.33	723	481	204	53	154	3084	3473.0

W = win | **L** = loss | **W/L%** = win-loss | **ERA** = earned run average | **G** = games played | **GS** = games started
GF = games finished | **CG** = completed games | **SV** = saves | **SO** = strikeouts | **IP** = innings pitched

	W	L	W/L%	ERA	G	GS	GF	CG	SV	SO	IP
Jose Valverde	26	31	.456	3.11	585	0	489	0	277	650	590.1
Brad Lidge	26	32	.448	3.54	603	1	368	0	225	799	603.1

Source: www.Baseball-Reference.com

W = win | **L** = loss | **W/L%** = win-loss | **ERA** = earned run average | **G** = games played | **GS** = games started
GF = games finished | **CG** = completed games | **SV** = saves | **SO** = strikeouts | **IP** = innings pitched